MAINSTREAMING SEX

MAINSTREAMING
SEX

The Sexualization
of Western Culture

Edited by

FEONA ATTWOOD

I.B. TAURIS

LONDON · NEW YORK

Reprinted in 2010 by I.B.Tauris & Co. Ltd
6 Salem Road, London W2 4BU
175 Fifth Avenue, New York, NY 10010
www.ibtauris.com

In the United States of America and Canada distributed by Palgrave
Macmillan, a division of St Martin's Press, 175 Fifth Avenue, New York, NY
10010

First published in 2009 by I.B.Tauris & Co. Ltd

ISBN: 978 1 84511 827 3

A full CIP record for this book is available from the British Library
A full CIP record for this book is available from the Library of Congress

Library of Congress catalog card: available

Typeset in Goudy Old Style by A. & D. Worthington, Newmarket, Suffolk
Printed and bound in India by Thomson Press India Ltd

CONTENTS

CONTRIBUTORS

Feona Attwood teaches Media and Communication Studies at Sheffield Hallam University. She has published widely on sex and the media. Her research interests include new pornographies, cybersex, women and sexualization and the study of sexual media in education. She is currently working on online pornography and women's use of online sex sites.

Petra Boynton teaches Health Services Research at University College London, specializing in research on sex and relationships. Her book *The Research Companion: A Practical Guide for the Social and Health Sciences* was published in 2005. She has published widely on sex, relationships and health and also works as an agony aunt, sex editor, radio presenter and advisor to media outlets about accurate sex information.

Sara Bragg is Academic Fellow in Child and Youth Studies at the Open University. Her research interests include young people as media audiences, media education, creative research methods and young people's participation rights in schools. Recent publications include *Young People, Sex and the Media: The Facts of Life?* with David Buckingham (2004).

David Buckingham is Professor of Education at the Institute of Education, London University, where he directs the Centre for the Study of Children, Youth and Media. He has directed many research projects on media education and on children's relationships with the media, and has acted as a consultant for the British Film Institute, the Institute for Public Policy Research, UNESCO, the United Nations, the Australian Children's Television Foundation, BBC Education and Ofcom. His previous books include *Children Talking Television* (1993), *Moving Images* (1996), *The Making of Citizens* (2000), *After the Death of Childhood* (2000) and *Media Education* (2003).

Rosalind Gill teaches Gender Studies at the London School of Economics. She is the author of *The Gender-Technology Relation* (with Keith Grint, 1995) and *Gender and the Media* (2007). Her research interests are the relationships between gender, media and new technologies. Her current research is on representations of romantic and sexual relationships in popular culture and on precarious work in the media and cultural industries. She has recently published a short book on freelancing in new media, *Technobohemians or the New Cybertariat?* (2007).

Simon Hardy is Senior Lecturer in Sociology and course leader in Media and Cultural Studies at the University of Worcester. Simon's book on pornography, men and feminism, *The Reader, The Author, His Woman and Her Lover*, was published in 1998. Since then he has written a number of articles on gender, eroticism and representation. His wider academic interests include the media coverage of war and the history of sexuality.

Samantha Holland is a Research Fellow at Leeds Metropolitan University, where she researches gender, ageing, non-mainstream leisure and subcultures. Her book *Alternative Femininities: Body, Age and Identity* was published in 2004. She is currently editing a collection on technology and relationships, *Remote Relationships in a Small World*, and is working on a study of three generations of women's leisure within families.

Brian McNair is Professor of Journalism and Communication at the University of Strathclyde. His books include *Mediated Sex: Pornography and Postmodern Culture* (1996), *Journalism and Democracy* (2000) and *Striptease Culture: Sex, Media and the Democratization of Desire* (2002).

Stephen Maddison is programme leader of Cultural Studies at the University of East London. His research is in the areas of lesbian and gay studies, gender and popular culture. His book *Fags, Hags and Queer Sisters: Gender Dissent and Heterosocial Bonds in Gay Culture* was published in 2000. He is currently working on a book on the cultural politics of the porn industry.

Rebecca Munford teaches English Literature at Cardiff University. The editor of *Re-visiting Angela Carter: Texts, Contexts, Intertexts* (2006) and co-editor of *Third Wave Feminism: A Critical Exploration* (2004), she has published on twentieth-century women's writing, the Gothic, contemporary feminist theory and popular culture. Her forthcoming work includes *Decadent Daughters and Monstrous Mothers: Angela Carter and the European Gothic* and (with Stacy Gillis) *Feminism and Popular Culture: Explorations in Post-feminism*.

Clarissa Smith teaches Media and Cultural Studies at the University of Sunderland. Her research interests are the production and consumption of pornography, sex retailing, and audiences and popular culture. Her published work has included studies of softcore pornography, readers of *For Women* magazine, and the erotic performers The Chippendales. Her book *One for the Girls! The Pleasures and Practices of Reading Women's Porn* was published in 2007.

Greg Tuck teaches Film Studies at the University of the West of England. He was awarded his PhD, *Masturbation, Sexual Logic and Capitalism: The Autoerotic in Contemporary American Cinema and Beyond*, in 2005. He has published on various aspects of the representation of sexuality and is currently co-editing a book on neo-noir.

Dana Wilson-Kovacs teaches in the Department of Sociology at the University of Exeter. Her current research interests are the dynamics between the public and the private spheres, particularly in relation to gender, work and intimacy. She has published work on consumer cultures, cultural repertoires and sexuality and was recently awarded a PhD on her research on sexual intimacy as aesthetic practice.

ACKNOWLEDGEMENTS

I would like to thank the Cultural, Communication and Computing Research Institute at Sheffield Hallam University for helping me to find time and space to develop this book. Thanks also to all the contributors who have produced such inspiring and interesting work for the collection - and for helping me learn how to edit. Thanks to I.B.Tauris for bringing the project to completion.

I would never have started this book if wasn't for the many people who have helped me to develop my interests in sex and sexualization. These include the inspirational teachers on the MA in Women's Studies all those years ago - in particular, Jill McKenna and Tessa Perkins. Thanks also to my colleagues in the Communication Group at Sheffield Hallam University and to the students on courses I've taught on gender and sexuality over the years.

Finally, thanks to Clare Harris for her support during the final stages of putting the collection together, and lots more besides.

ACKNOWLEDGEMENTS

Introduction

THE SEXUALIZATION OF CULTURE

FEONA ATTWOOD

'We are living in a pornified culture and we have no idea what this means for ourselves, our relationships, or our society' (Paul, 2005: 11).

'The whole point of a sexual politics worthy of the adjective "democratic" is that we gain and exercise the right to find, articulate and celebrate our own sexualities, while showing due respect for the tastes, desires and sensitivities of others. That is the real challenge posed by striptease culture' (McNair, 2002: 207).

MAINSTREAMING SEX

The study of sex has been an academic concern for many years. Feminist and queer theorists have challenged the taken-for-granted nature of sex, and the significance and place of sex in culture and society has been discussed in a range of disciplines. Much more recently an interest in the mainstreaming of sex - or what some writers have called a 'pornified' or 'striptease' culture - has begun to emerge. This - the sexualization of culture - is the subject of this book.

The terms 'sexualization' and 'mainstreaming' are used to describe the ways that sex is becoming more visible in contemporary Western cultures. This takes a range of forms. Pornography and other sexually explicit media representations are much more accessible than before - often only, as many commentators point out, 'a mouse click away'.

Porn stars are entering the world of mainstream celebrity, writing bestselling books, acting as sex advisors in lifestyle magazines and becoming the stars of lad mags. Porn has turned chic and become an object of fascination in art, film, television and the press. Porn *style* is also now commonplace, especially in music video and advertising, and a scantily clad, surgically enhanced 'porn look' is evident, not only in the media, but on the streets.

The expansion of pornography is not only a matter of commercial media production. Ordinary people increasingly make and circulate their own sexual images and texts, often for pleasure rather than profit. This is part of a broader tendency in contemporary Western societies in which sex and technology are stitched together so that we become sexual cyborgs. It is not particularly new in itself: most communication technologies have been adapted for sexual purposes since the invention of the printing press. However, the process now seems to be speeding up considerably and it is becoming less depend-ent on the intervention of media professionals. In addition to the representational possibilities it offers, technology has also enabled new forms of sexual encounter: phone sex, email affairs and cybersex are now part of the late modern repertoire of sexual *practices* and are becoming part of people's everyday lives.

In recent history, sex has occupied an odd cultural and social space – present everywhere as a subject for discussion and representa-tion even while its practices are often hidden away. Where sex is asso-ciated with relationships, this hidden-ness is most usually explained in terms of the privacy necessary for intimate forms of encounter, while hedonistic sexual practices are more often understood as shameful and therefore obscene – literally put 'out of sight'. In partic-ular, commercial sex has been consigned to the sleazy backstreets of culture, and sex for its own sake has been presented as meaning-less, objectifying and alienating. But today the places, products and performances associated with sex for its own sake are becoming more visible. Commercial sex is gaining a toehold in the high street and being gentrified. Strip joints have become gentlemen's clubs. The Rampant Rabbit vibrator is now almost as well known as that much older sign for sex, the Playboy bunny girl, signifying a new interest in women as sexual consumers. Porn shops have been joined by the cheap and cheerful sexual paraphernalia of the Ann Summers empire and by elegant and expensive boutiques selling lingerie, toys and erotica. Pole dancing is being repackaged as a form of keep-fit, and burlesque is undergoing a revival, producing new stars such as Dita von Teese.

All of these aspects of sexualization are connected to the ways in which the boundaries between the public and the private are changing in our culture. We are developing new forms of 'public intimacy' (McNair, 2002: 98) and what Brian McNair has called a 'striptease culture' which is preoccupied with self-revelation and exposure (2002: 81). The confessional, first described by Foucault as the modern place to discuss sex, is fast becoming mediatized. Confession no longer takes place in a church or on an analyst's couch but in talkshows and kiss-and-tell stories, and sexual exposure is getting progressively louder and more public. In the process, sex becomes the subject of a new group of sexperts - often media professionals - who are increasingly the source of our sexual knowledge, advisors on our sexual dilemmas and the architects of our sexual lifestyles. Within this lifestyling of sex, a view of sexual practice as play and pleasure - a form of recreation rather than a mechanism of reproduction or relationship - is emerging. And whether it is domesticated in intimate relationships between couples or let loose in hedonistic and uncommitted sexual episodes, sex is often now seen as central to the creation and expression of an individual's self (Giddens, 1992). Sexual relationships themselves are more 'easy to enter and to exit' (Bauman, 2003: xii) than they have ever been as the connections between people become more 'light and loose' (Bauman, 2003: xi). In the process, a new sexual sensibility is developing where sex is no longer necessarily a means of creating kinship or lasting romantic bonds, but is the source of 'transient but renewable pleasures' (Illouz, 1999: 176) and a form of self-expression.

As sex appears to become more and more important to contemporary cultures, permeating every aspect of our existence and providing a language for talking about all kinds of things, its meaning becomes more elusive and more ambiguous; politicians and their dossiers can be 'sexed up', and the term 'sexy' may simply indicate something that is noteworthy (Levy, 2005: 30). As sexiness becomes central to the way we mark what is significant, good and worthwhile about contemporary life, our ability to articulate what we mean by that becomes less certain and 'sex' becomes more slippery and more difficult to pin down. As the new uses of the term also suggest, sexiness and sexualization excite considerable suspicion – indicating superficial glamour, empty pleasures and cheap thrills. This is partly related to the development of the view of sex as play which cannot therefore be treated as real or serious. It is also a response to the commodification of sex in which sexual desire and desirability are increasingly represented by products and the vocabulary of sex is increasingly derived from commerce and the media. Public debates about sexualization tend to approach it as a social problem. Pamela Paul's book *Pornified* (2005) focuses exclusively on the ways sexualization impoverishes men and women. Ariel Levy's account of 'raunch culture' describes sexualization as 'a desperate stab at free-wheeling eroticism in a time and place characterized by intense anxiety' (Levy, 2005: 199). A report by the American Psychological Association (2007), likely to be the first of many such professional responses, recycles notions of media messages and the harm they do. While all three offer useful commentaries on sexualization to some extent, they do not make use of the frameworks for examining sexuality, the media or culture that have been developed in academic work.

PORN STUDIES

This collection is an examination of the sexualization of contemporary culture which draws on the insights of media and cultural studies. It begins with a look at the pornosphere, a thoroughly sexualized landscape where representational forms are mutating, demanding new forms of analysis and understanding. As Simon Hardy shows, new pornographies are appearing in a context where all kinds of media now blur the distinction between the real and the representational and the ordinary and the spectacular. Gonzo porn, realcore and sexblogs in particular are forms which seem to simply document the sex lives of real people, suggesting that porn is not a representation at all, but the direct presentation of actual sexual action and of authentic sexual pleasure. The foregrounding of the amateur in new sexual media seems to move them much closer to the lived reality of sex. Sexual performance is taking on new cultural significance as a source of self-definition and a means of self-expression, allowing ordinary people to put themselves into the frame of representation, circulating a greater range of expressions of sexual experience and desire than we have ever seen before.

A central concern of recent writing on pornography has been the adequacy of existing models of analysis. This is taken up in Clarissa Smith's chapter which argues that we have not yet developed a useful way of interpreting old forms of porn, never mind the newer manifestations of the pornosphere or the sexualized mainstream. Through an analysis of the erotic stories of *Forum* magazine – a genre that has existed on the margins of the media for some time – the chapter suggests that if we are to make sense of sexual media, we will have to question the accepted view that these are worthless and harmful, which has dominated most discussions of pornography. The chapter shows how sexually explicit texts can be read as fictional enactments of powerlessness which open up the possibility of sexual sensation and pleasure. Developing this kind of account, which tries to understand how pornographies work, is a priority if we are to make sense of the ways people engage with sexual media and how these articulate the 'ache of desire'. All the same, some new forms of porn have revitalized the 'old' questions about porn and power. Stephen Maddison's chapter examines current legal action in the USA inspired by extreme gonzo hardcore videoporn which features excessive violence towards women. This kind of porn is currently extremely popular and is becoming more accessible and acceptable. However, the history of highly charged and emotional political debates around porn, a reluctance to return to 'anti-porn' stances and the economic power of the porn industry itself make it difficult to build a critique. Alongside the development of a new approach to understanding how porn texts work, we need a political analysis of the role of the porn industry in the mainstreaming of sex and of the depressing emergence of a view of women as 'raw material' for men's extreme sexual performances.

The final chapter in this section looks beyond particular pornographies to examine the process of *pornographication*, tracing the development of a fascination with porn's content and style in a wide range of cultural forms – high and popular art, mainstream film and art house cinema, television and musical theatre – where porn themes and imagery are increasingly commonplace and increasingly unable to shock us. Even so, this process is far from even, and in the last few years pornographication has become the object of criticism and resistance by diverse groups including moral conservatives and some feminists. Brian McNair examines the most recent manifestations of the debate about pornographication, arguing that cultural sexualization presents us with an interesting set of challenges. How should we respond to forms of sexualization which may be profoundly contradictory in the way they mix up oppressive and emancipatory views of sex and gender, and how do we develop a critical language for the analysis of sexualization without reverting to 'pro' and 'anti' positions on pornography? Whatever stance we take, simply rejecting sexualization is unlikely to take us very far.

SEX AND MAINSTREAM MEDIA

The migration of porn from obscene to on-scene, demonstrated by its new accessibility and by pornographication, has been accompanied by a proliferation of representations of sex in the media. The second part of the book investigates mainstream representations in more detail. It begins with Greg Tuck's discussion of the way masturbation is now a subject for depiction in self-help literature and magazines, film, television and advertising. Yet despite its new visibility, masturbation is still often overlooked in discussions about sex and sexualization, and despite its prevalence and a growing acceptance of self-pleasure in Western cultures, forms of auto-sexuality continue to be the object of concern and fear. In particular, the old view that male masturbation is 'disordered' and harmful has persisted even in our sexualized culture. As this analysis of the mad, bad and sad masturbators that dominate popular culture shows, male auto-sexuality is still commonly presented as wasteful, exploitative and even horrific.

Interestingly, as the chapter shows, women's practices of self-pleasure find more positive representation in the mainstream, part of a wider celebration of women's sexuality in popular culture. Rosalind Gill's chapter looks more closely at contemporary representations of female sexuality, analysing the emergence of advertising which sells sex as a form of empowerment for women. In this kind of imagery the disciplined 'sexy' female body becomes the key sign of a contemporary femininity, and sexual display is presented as the source of women's pleasure and power. However, the exclusions of sexualized advertising – lesbians, older women, disabled women, fat women and any other women who cannot meet the narrow standards of conventional sex appeal – suggest that its real concern is with women's sexual attractiveness to men. Far from empowering women, it requires them to internalize and own an impossible and oppressive view of female sexuality.

The notion of sex as impossible – a norm to measure up to and a problem to resolve – is the subject of the final chapter in this section, which examines changes in sex advice since the 1970s. The sexualization of the media since then suggests that we live in a culture which is open about sex and which is characterized by widespread sexual literacy. However, media representations of sex are often very conservative, promoting sex as a way for women to please men, and presenting men with a view of male sexuality as a macho display which is nevertheless anxiety ridden. Petra Boynton shows that against this backdrop of misinformation, sex advisors and sex advice are increasingly being sexualized and commodified; unqualified 'sexy' counsellors are employed as agony aunts and sex help is often tied to commodities such as drugs or self-help publications. The solution to our sexual problems is increasingly something we have to pay for, and while the media offers a space for potentially accessible and helpful sexual information, this opportunity is currently being wasted. In the meantime, as the problem-page letters of both male and female readers suggest, some people are struggling to make sense of the way sex is presented to them.

ENGAGING WITH SEXUALIZATION

The final part of the collection turns to the question of social responses to sexualization, examining the ways different groups of people are engaging with the mainstreaming of sex and focusing on young people and women who are often seen as the 'victims' of sexualization. The first chapter considers the relationship between children, sex and the media in an era when children have unprecedented access to media technologies. Debates about sex and children generally exclude young people's voices, but a different starting point is taken here. The chapter investigates young people's responses to the media images of love, sex and relationships they encounter every day, and asks how they negotiate their way through a sex-dominated culture. Sara Bragg and David Buckingham show that young people present themselves as media literate and sex savvy and able to make their own decisions about sex. As the media replace the school as a classroom for sexual knowledge, an 'informed consumer model' of sexual citizenship and media literacy is emerging. This entails new freedoms *and* new forms of self-regulation which complicate our ideas about childhood and knowledge production, and about the relationship between social norms, the media and sexual individuality.

The following two chapters look at women's engagements with sexualization, examining how they are using sexual media in the privacy of the home and becoming sexual performers in public spaces such as pole-dancing classes. Dana Wilson-Kovacs shows how women's encounters with porn present them with a range of difficulties – women are concerned about the way they are represented in porn, anxious about other people's views of porn consumption, dissatisfied with their partners' lack of skill at integrating porn into their sex lives and guilt ridden if they enjoy it. But these difficulties are not present in their use of erotica, which they find liberating in quite practical senses – erotica appears to open up fantasy worlds and inspire sexual pleasure and the creation of a sexual self. Sexual self-creation is also examined in the chapter by Samantha Holland and Feona Attwood which investigates women's experiences of pole dancing and suggests that women are embracing sexualization in rather unexpected ways. Pole exercise is not only a means of feeling sexy, but a source of physical enjoyment, exuberance and exhilaration. It appears to offer women a way of embodying the feminine attributes currently prized in Western culture – hedonism, image-consciousness and feistiness – and a way of engaging with sexualization in ways that foreground skill, strength and power. While it may be easy to dismiss these kinds of practices, the chapter concludes that we need much more research in order to establish just what is at stake in women's engagements with sexualized culture.

The final chapter of the collection takes up this issue in a more explicitly political context, assessing recent calls for a 'sexed up' feminism focused on sexual pleasure and concerned with developing a sexier form of feminism itself. Rebecca Munford shows how third-wave feminism, young women's zines and a particular form of 'girlie feminism' have provided young women with a space to confess the problems and pleasures of 'feminism' and 'fucking', creating a joyful culture that appears to marry feminine pleasures and feminist politics. However, the chapter cautions that this may be limited as a starting point for political activism, especially in the context of a mainstream culture in which women are already hypersexualized.

DEVELOPING SEXUALIZATION STUDIES

As this collection shows, the mainstreaming of sex raises questions about the role of the media, technology, leisure, commerce, education and popular culture in producing sexual practices, identities, relationships and ethics. Sexualization is impacting on the way we think about sex. It is becoming central to the way we develop our sexual knowledge and to the way we see ourselves and the world. It has significant implications for sex education, media literacy, social and cultural analysis and political activism. It poses a series of interesting and important challenges for researchers, educators, legislators, policy makers and academics – and for all of us as individuals and as sexual citizens.

Public and popular debates about sexualization have so far focused on whether sexualization has the potential to democratize sexual discourse or whether it simply reduces sexual pleasure and energy to an empty and commodified performance – an impersonation of sex. Perhaps this is the wrong kind of question because it reduces discussion to an either/or response, the 'tired binary' which characterized debates about pornography until very recently (Juffer, 1998: 2), preventing the close and contextualized analysis which might have helped academics towards a more informed understanding of how to intervene productively in public debates about sex, the media and

culture. The recent resurgence of interest in sexual media, the development of sophisticated models of cultural analysis and the emergence
of a more thoughtful and varied diet of 'porn studies' should help us
to avoid making the same mistakes in our analysis of sexualization.

Rather than end here by passing judgement on sexualization,
as many commentators do, I would like to suggest three particular
themes that are emerging in the kind of academic work that makes
up this collection, and point to some specific gaps in our knowledge.
The first of these concerns the gendering of sexualization. Anthony
Giddens (1992) has described the uneven ways that intimacy has been
transformed in late modern culture, working to associate sexual intimacy and relationships with women, and commercial sex and sexual
hedonism with men. Although this is still apparent, especially in
magazine culture, there are signs that it may be changing with the rise
of the 'sassy, sexy and strong' girl that Rebecca Munford describes.
This new figure has been dismissed by many scholars, but I believe it
presents us with a real opportunity to examine how sexualization and
gender are entwined. More than this, we need to know much more
about how girls and women are responding to sexualization and we
need to move beyond the simple assumption that sexualization is in
the interests of boys and men and examine their experiences. We also
need a much clearer idea of how gender intersects with class, race
and sexuality in the sexualization of specific groups, how it becomes
part of the relationships between partners and across generations,
operates within peer groups and families, and how it works within
different political groupings and cultures of taste.

The second theme is how we develop a framework for making
sense of contemporary views of what sex is and what it is for, particularly given the new status of sex as a form of play. The process of
change in the meanings of sex is likely to accelerate given the increasing number of outlets for forms of auto-sexuality and sexual hedonism and the current trend for making sex over as a form of self-care
and self-development. How do we square this with its continuing
importance in the realms of reproduction and relationship and with
the expansion of commercial sex practices of all kinds?

This leads to the third theme which is the question of sexual
ethics. As the old frameworks we have relied on for regulating sexual

practices are thrown into question by shifting attitudes and developing technologies, the development of appropriate ethical frameworks is becoming more urgent. Sexualization is associated with the rise of neo-liberalism in which the individual becomes a self-regulating unit within society. This in turn is associated with an individualism that is often seen as a refusal of genuine social politics. Yet the most recent manifestations of sexualization have been accompanied by new and thoughtful notions of sexual citizenship (Weeks, 1998; Plummer, 2003), and by attempts to articulate a politics of intimacy. Critics argue that if sexualization is divorced from genuine social movements it can only ever be an occasion for individual lifestyle choices, and given that it is often underpinned by consumerism, that it will inevitably exclude many social groups, for 'only certain kinds of sexual identity are compatible with consumerism' (Arthurs, 2004: 147). However, we should not lose sight of the *potential* of sexualization for the 'democratization and diversification of sexual discourse' (McNair, 2002: 205), or the possibility of developing an ethics of sexualization. And, in a context where the meanings of commercial sex are shifting and the media is becoming a key resource for identity work and the development of communities, we need to ensure that we do not simply reproduce assumptions about what 'good' or 'correct' sex is. This will necessitate a careful contextualization of the ways and places in which sexualization takes place. The emergence of a new sexual ethics based on the values of honesty, happiness and personal freedom (Buckingham and Bragg, 2004) and the 'responsibilization' or self-governance of sexual matters should not simply be taken as an inevitable slide into neo-liberalism, but an opportunity to develop an 'informed citizenship' beyond 'state paternalism' or 'narcissistic individualism' (Arthurs, 2004: 149). This last point is perhaps the most important. Academic analyses are often invisible in wider public debates, perhaps partly because they are sometimes short on ideas about how to build on their critiques in positive and practical ways. Academics should enter more publicly into political debates, thinking more imaginatively about how to use academic work productively and creatively in other contexts, working with others who have different forms of expertise. In a context where individual and collective identity is increasingly bound up with contemporary forms of 'sexpertise' it is important that academic knowledge about sex and sexualization extends beyond the academy.

Part 1

PORNOGRAPHY AND

PORNOGRAPHICATION

Chapter 1

THE NEW PORNOGRAPHIES: REPRESENTATION OR REALITY?

SIMON HARDY

Most academic analyses of pornography have been predicated on a clear distinction between representation and reality, or the 'real' world. In the light of postmodern thought, the latter category cannot, as the obligatory quotation marks suggest, be taken for granted. We may perhaps, as Jane Gaines suggests, maintain a cautious distinction between mediated representations and the world of lived experience, which is *not just representation*, in order to 'temporarily get us around the problem of the ostensible "reality" of the world' (Gaines, 2004: 32). But the trajectory of pornography has always been towards the vanishing point of this distinction, and this is most evident in its newest manifestations. It is, above all, in the recently emerging pornographies of gonzo, amateur and sexblogs[1] that we seem to have reached the point at which any clear separation between the real and the representational has collapsed or been turned inside out.

These new types of pornography are heterosexual and essentially mainstream. I have chosen them because they carry forward into new media a longstanding tradition of pornographic representation, and it is therefore possible to see clearly how new media assist the objectives of that tradition. At the same time, they also demonstrate the broader process of the sexualization of contemporary culture – the preoccupation with confession, the public revelation of private

3

intimacy, the media exposure of the lives of 'ordinary people' and the everyday lives of celebrities. This chapter will trace the emergence of these new pornographies and consider the potential significance of these developments for the relation between pornography and 'reality'.

There has been a long history of concern that the obscene content of pornography will invade and corrupt mainstream culture, and a long history of legal and administrative attempts to prevent it doing so (Kendrick, 1987). The great research effort by social scientists, between the 1960s and the 1990s, to investigate the social and psychological effects of pornography was essentially a response to this anxiety. Here the problem was formulated in terms of a hypothesized causal relation between pornographic representations of sexuality and measurable consequences in the real world, defined as moral degeneration or increased rates of sexual violence. Yet this empiricism was never really able to bridge the gap between the real and the representational that its own epistemology insisted upon.

At the same time those who opposed the censorial implications of this type of research (Segal, 1993) and those who subscribed to a more sophisticated theory of mediated communications as having a limited, complex and negotiated impact on their audience (Hardy, 1998) also maintained the conventional distinction between representation and reality. They assumed that there were clear boundaries between the various points in the communication circuit of production, text and audience reception. Part of the reason why modern media theory sustains boundaries between these points is that each is a legitimate field of research in its own right, although the idea of a simple cause–effect relationship between media stimuli and human response has been rightly rejected. The representational text does not determine what happens in lived reality: human subjects may read texts in unexpected ways, use them for unintended purposes and know that the texts are not truth. From this viewpoint, audiences have been aware that they were looking at a representation and not at a truth about the real world. But can we still rely upon such a comfortable distinction between the representational and the real?

THE PORNOGRAPHIC QUEST FOR 'TRUTH'

One of the defining characteristics of pornography as a representational genre is the need for authenticity. This has driven it to attempt, by various strategies, to shorten its distance from real experience – a purpose for which it has recently and decisively been assisted by new media technologies. As this chapter will argue, pornography is a mode of representation that seeks to exceed its limits and thus can be seen as the 'limit case' (Gaines, 2004) for the theory of representation. The longstanding practices by which pornographers have sought to achieve greater realism include female first-person narration, the use of audio-visual media to document the performance of sex acts, and the exploitation of amateur participation. Although none of these practices are unique to new media pornographies, it is in the latter that they find their ultimate expression. It is worth considering the development of these practices, because they contribute important components to pornography as it functions today within the new media.

As a genre, pornography has always been characterized by a marked gender asymmetry in its circuit of communication. It has been produced predominantly by men for a male audience, and, material for gay men notwithstanding, with the primary object as female. Yet, pornographers have always sought to disavow this fact in order to produce a more authentic-seeming representation. In the case of written textual pornography, this disavowal has usually been affected by the adoption of a female narrative voice, which insists upon the content as a record of first-person experience. We see this even in the precursors of pornography: Greco-Roman sex manuals, Renaissance dialogues and the erotic novels of the eighteenth century typically all have the characteristic of being written by men in the assumed authorial character of a courtesan passing on wisdom gained from personal experience (Hunt, 1996). In those forms of modern pornography where the written word has remained the medium, this device is predominant. For example, the readers' letters and stories supposedly sent in to porn magazines by female readers are actually produced at the editorial office (Hardy, 1998). The truth is that pornography has almost always been the product of men as subjects of erotic discourse, who in the process of creation have also produced an imaginary female subject of erotic discourse. So deeply ingrained is this cultural pattern that even where the hand is known to be authentically female, the suspicion remains that the voice is male: for example, in the tradition of women's erotica from the 'beginning efforts' of Anais Nin, to such classics as *The Story of O*, to the modern Black Lace imprint (Hardy, 2001).

It is this long history of the male as subject and the female as object, and of the simultaneous denial of this fact, that today impels us towards the revelation of female erotic experience, now that women really are beginning to participate in the production and consumption of sexually explicit material on a significant scale. We see evidence of this compulsion to hear women speak about sex in the contemporary fascination with confessional memoirs, diaries and sexblogs written by women. For example, Catherine Millet's memoir, *The Sexual Life of Catherine M* (2002), reflects on a career of promiscuity and group sex and has been heralded by Edmund White on its cover as 'the most explicit book about sex ever written by a woman'. The text appears to combine elements of memory and fantasy that cannot be distinguished, but which together attest to a woman's guiltless abandonment of herself to a life of radical sexual adventurism. The diary of an Italian teenager, Melissa P. (2004), offers the experience of a younger generation of women, for whom, the blurb tells us, 'love may be hard to find, but sex waits at every turn'. This kind of episodic confessional text naturally lends itself to sexblogs, such as Abby Lee's *Girl with a One-Track Mind* (2006), where the record of events is ongoing and so has a stronger sense of the unfolding reality of someone else's life.

What all these narratives offer is the combination of frequent descriptions and references to sexual experiences with extensive passages of personal introspection. The latter element seems to establish a subjective identity and sexual orientation, which, although not marked as feminine, is clearly that of a real woman and in many ways bears a close resemblance to the narrative voice familiar from chick-lit. But these experiences are then rendered in the only available vocabulary, that familiar from textual pornography. In the book version of Abby Lee's blog (2006), the narrator describes a sexual encounter like this:

I finally got naked with a man for the first time in months. I ripped off my pants and begged Tony to fuck me hard from behind as he bent me over the edge of the bed. He was just as charged up as me; he'd made me climax four times before even entering me. We both came together and I felt like months of frustration were relieved in one go.

Here the subjective context of frustration and relief is combined with terse sexual description, including instant, pornotopian multiple orgasms. Works like this put explicit sex into the mainstream, using an authentically female voice to speak those very 'truths' about female sexuality that pornography has always claimed to express.

The use of female authorship and first-person narration is clearly one strategy by which the pornographic genre as a whole, within which we may now include women's erotic memoirs, attempts to invoke the *real*, and to close its distance as a representational practice from the empirical reality of its object: human, but especially female sexuality. This strategy applies, of course, to the written word, but for more than a century pornographers have also used the visual image as a medium. This, as Linda Williams (1989) has shown, offers a quite different avenue through which the truth of sexuality may be rendered into a knowable form. The essence of hardcore photographic and cinematic pornography is the literal documentation of bodies and sexual activity. There can be no literary devices or deceits here, just the plain facts recorded on film and thus captured and preserved for unrestricted contemplation. By its heyday in the 1970s, hardcore film had a clear formula of sexual numbers that were performed in the making of a movie: masturbation, genital intercourse, lesbianism, oral sex, threesomes, orgies, anal sex and sadomasochism. Here again there was an important gender asymmetry. The camera was not equally interested in all possible combinations: it focused on female masturbation, lesbianism and the anal penetration of women by men. This is not to deny that the image of the erect penis and of male ejaculation onto the face or body of the woman is of defining importance as proof of the truth and reality of the sex that is shown. But the ultimate limitation of hardcore, as Williams (1989) has pointed out, is precisely that it cannot deliver what it most desires: visual proof of the involuntary spasm of sexual pleasure in the female body.

The strategy of visual documentation is a second means by which pornography has attempted to eliminate the boundary between representation and reality. While the images themselves appear as a representation of sexuality, they invoke real sexuality in two ways: firstly, because they depict actual sexual acts that have taken place at some specific point in time between live performers, and, secondly, because the image is assumed to have the power to move the body of the viewer to arousal in an involuntary way. The real erection and ejaculation of the male performer is echoed in a second plain of reality by the erection and ejaculation of the male viewer. But the limitation of this strategy is also already apparent: we cannot know for sure whether the body of either the female performer or spectator is moved in a *real sense*.

Although this fundamental limitation of hardcore can never really be overcome, the advent of video technology in the 1980s opened up new avenues for advancing the project of realism, which digital technology and the Internet are now further assisting. These developments include gonzo and amateur porn. Both rely on the availability of increasingly cheap and accessible technologies of recording and distribution to close the gap between the producers and consumers of pornographic images. The gonzo format largely preserves the range of numbers from hardcore film but does not place them in a fictional narrative. If there is a narrative at all, it is a highly naturalistic one about what is actually taking place: a man or group of men with a camera 'picking up' a girl or girls and persuading them to engage in the various sexual numbers already cited. Typical of this type of format is John Stagliano's 'Buttman' series, including such titles as *Buttman's Rio Carnival Hardcore* (2002). There is obviously an element of artifice in so far as the girls will have agreed beforehand to participate in exchange for money, while the construction of the text makes it appear that the initially unsuspecting girl eventually gives herself for free. Nonetheless, gonzo gets closer to the experience of a one-off sexual 'conquest' as it might take place in everyday life. At the same time it should not be forgotten that the gonzo format, which is both financially and artistically undemanding, has provided the staple for a vastly expanded porn industry and a consequent proliferation in the number of people involved as producers, performers and consumers. Thus, in terms of both content and reach, gonzo has brought pornography closer to the lived realities of greater numbers of people.

If gonzo closed the gap, in some limited senses, between producers and consumers, amateur porn has done so in a much more radical sense. It is necessary to distinguish between the use of 'amateur' models and codes of representation by commercial pornographers, and genuinely amateur material. The former is simply another, well-established device for giving a sense of authenticity to the product. This practice is not new: it goes back to the glary, over-exposed realism of the 'Reader's Wives' section in downmarket porn magazines, which offer an image of the physical imperfection and therefore potential accessibility of the 'girl' or 'matron' next door. Even today a large proportion of 'amateur' porn on the Internet is professionally produced (Patterson, 2004). But the video revolution of the 1980s created the technical means for the development of informal networks for people to exchange videos of themselves having sex – a practice that was always going to be quickly absorbed by the facility of the Internet. The application of video to amateur performance helped to extend the transition from the *representation* to the *presentation* of sexual action, which hardcore film had begun. Amateur performers are seen to be acting for the intrinsic gratification of the act itself rather than for money; they become absorbed in what they are doing rather than consciously performing for an audience, or they perform in the expectation that any audience will themselves belong to the same coterie of amateur performers/viewers. Once again, what people are seeking from this material is not the *representation* of sex, but the *truth* of sex. What the hardcore image in itself cannot prove, namely the veracity of the female performer's erotic engagement, can instead be deduced from the circumstances surrounding amateur performance, where it is known that the motive of the performers is sexual rather than financial.

However, it is important to remember that the amateur performance of sex is still *performance*: people do not really act as they do when having sex in private. As Minette Hillyer (2004: 56) observes, 'the women perform their amateurism', looking into the camera or moaning and groaning for it. There is an inherent tension in amateur

porn between the two imperatives of authenticity and the visual gratification of the viewer. The more under-performed the sex, the less
gratifying the spectacle, and the more over-performed the sex, the
less authentic the action. As can be seen from any hardcore material,
the positions in which it is comfortable and pleasurable to have sex
are not necessarily the ones that make a good visual display of the
act to a third party of the camera and the audience it implies. The
celebrity sex tape of Pamela Anderson and Tommy Lee, discussed by
Hillyer (2004), is a case in point. Although obviously untypical of
anonymous amateur porn, it has many of the sub-genre's characteristics. Much of the tape takes the form of a home video. This provides
an authenticating context for the sexual action, but the action itself
must still exhibit the trademark sexual numbers of fellatio, fucking
for the camera and the external ejaculation of Tommy Lee's penis
over Pam's body, in order to function effectively as pornography. In
many ways the 'money shot' (capturing the moment of external ejaculation) can be seen as the ultimate distinguishing marker between
private sex and porn performance, insofar as it requires the sacrifice
of what many people would consider the crucial moment of tactile,
inter-bodily pleasure in exchange for the visible, outward significa-
tion of 'pleasure'.

This section has traced a series of authenticating strategies adopted
by the makers of pornography using the established media of writing,
film and video. It concludes that, in all these cases, there remains an
easily perceptible element of inauthenticity about the product that
ultimately marks it as representation rather than reality. But does
this remain the case when new media technologies are applied to the
most authentic-seeming format, amateur porn?

THE LIMITS OF CYBERPORN

It is in the new media technologies of digital cameras and the
Internet that amateur porn, and other forms of pornographic realism, find their true home. This is partly because these technologies make it possible for almost anyone to produce and distribute
their own pornography, with the result that in recent years amateur
porn, which is reckoned to be worth £1 billion in Britain alone,[2]

has advanced from being a niche in the market towards becoming one of its dominant formats. But it is also because these media seem to offer two things that pornography is apparently able to descend from the remote heights of mediated representation and get closer to the personal needs and lived experience of the consumer: choice and interactivity. The optimistic presumption is that these technologies allow greater freedom for the individual to explore his or her desires and to engage freely with others. Yet the impression of greater freedom may prove to be deceptive as, in fact, pornography simply employs these technologies to simulate sexual experience and structure desire in ever more sophisticated ways.

As far as choice is concerned, in theory Internet porn should offer limitless possibilities for subject positions, roles and identities. Yet as Zabet Patterson notes, 'in reality, what cyber porn tends to offer – especially with a rapidly consolidating market – is an environment in which desire and subject position are produced as "truths" of the self through a discourse of categorization and classification' (Patterson, 2004: 106). The options offered on corporatized websites are windows on a world of categorized desires, making a 'technology of desire both productive and regulatory' (Patterson, 2004: 107). There is an appearance of unlimited choice amid the vast maze of websites and windows, but only in terms of fixed and finite options. The catch is that what is in fact a strictly commodified set of options can be experienced as the expression of the inner desires of the self. Moreover, while giving the impression of fluidity, the technology also tends to habituate the choices once made through the process of signing up to websites and accessing 'favourites'.

Patterson (2004) points out that besides the limited range of representations available, there are also more direct ways in which technology structures our experience and desire. This concerns the material aspect of the computer and the physical habits it instils in the body. Most Internet pornography is not viewed on pay-sites, so that a key part of the experience is of waiting. There is the delay of logging on, the delay of finding a site, of the thumbnails loading, of waiting for the chosen image or sequence. The deferral of gratification and the process of seeking the perfect image work to structure the desire of the consumer. Indeed, even when the nearly perfect image is found, since none can measure up to the desired and unknown image, the viewer must decide whether this will be the last image or whether to continue the search for a more perfect one, accepting all the frustrations, as well as the pleasures, that it entails. This habituation to deferral and repetition in the search for satisfaction perfectly illustrates the way in which this new medium of pornography does not gratify any desires that it has not itself created.

The nature of the relationship between viewer and object, Patterson (2004) further argues, can best be seen in relation to amateur cyberporn on corporatized websites that exploit the Internet's potential for interactivity. In exchange for a monthly fee, amateur websites offer a space for very particular, pre-set forms of interaction. The viewer can follow the daily, routine activities of a 'girl', as well as her sexual action. All of this is filmed with low-resolution webcams, producing grainy images which have come to encode meanings of living immediacy and realism in contrast to the vivid images of 'fake' professional porn. Amateur porn trades in an abolition of the spectacular: it shows *real* bodies experiencing *real* pleasures. Unlike the professional performer, the amateur girl loses control and this guarantees the realness of the sex. The viewer sees something more than the performance of sex; something the girl does not intend to reveal; something as involuntary as the viewer's own response. Moreover, the viewer is able to interact with the girl and to be directly addressed by her, and it is this purchased intimacy that is a large part of what is being sold. Of course, the viewer is ultimately aware that the relationship is not real, but he disavows this knowledge in order to derive greater pleasure from the experience.

In summary, it seems that, no matter how sophisticated the technology, commercial pornography can never quite do what it promises to do for the consumer: reveal an external truth about sexuality and female sexuality especially. But there is one domain of pornographic representation that remains to be considered. This has been defined as 'realcore' by Sergio Messina (2006) who argues that it is deeply connected to the technologies of digital cameras and free web spaces. He contrasts realcore with traditional hardcore in a number of ways, claiming that it covers a much wider range of human sexuality and features 'real' people, unmade-up, without special lighting.

Filming techniques typically employ wide-angle views of situations rather than close-up detail, with long unedited shots and with the camera being addressed directly by those in front of it. Perhaps most importantly of all, realcore is mostly for free. Although it is not possible to draw hard and fast distinctions between the commercial and the non-commercial, at the very least realcore amateur pornography appears to blur the line between the two.

The non-commercial nature of realcore seems to be the essential point, because here at last we have a situation in which the motives of those producing the material are substantially the same as those viewing it: sexual rather than financial. In this sense, representation finally closes with reality. The makers of pornography have always tried to provide their audience with a more realistic product, and modern media technologies have brought this objective ever closer. Today the voyeuristic fascination with seeing 'reality' is also evident in the popularity of a range of other contemporary genres such as reality TV. But in realcore something further seems to be happening. We must ask what role the notion of 'reality' might play in the motives of the significant numbers of people who now engage in the making of realcore pornography.

It is likely that the appeal of the *real* also works for those who produce realcore as well as those who consume it. In an age without fixed identities, sexuality has become an important source of self-definition, giving a firm, relatively fixed sense of who and what we are. In a discussion of amateur pornography, Ruth Barcan (2002) sets the rising popularity of 'home-made' porn in the wider context of the search for 'authenticity' underlying the rise of reality and confessional genres. She invokes Michel Foucault's (1981) concept of the incitement to discourse on sexuality as a defining feature of contemporary culture. Here, we are encouraged by modern disciplinary regimes to discover the authentic 'truth' of the self. At the core of this self is its sexual essence. But we are also incited to express and externalize these truths of the inner self. To this extent, realcore is the perfect opportunity for which the Foucaultian self has been waiting.

It is arguable that in our media-saturated, celebrity-obsessed culture, putting oneself into the frame of representation is becoming a means of existential assertion. To be 'someone' one must be seen to *be*, on the screen of a television or computer monitor. So, why not combine in one moment these two means of self-authentication, sexuality and public display, by making and exhibiting an image of yourself having sex? By holding up the mirror of mediated representation people are able to see themselves and thus prove themselves as sexual subjects. If, as Linda Williams (1989) has argued, hardcore demonstrates the truth of other people's sexuality, the next logical step is that realcore demonstrates the truth of one's own. In short, it is not simply that realcore services or validates representation, but that representation begins to service and validate people's sense of their own reality.

Perhaps the crucial question we need to ask about the current democratization of pornography, especially as manifested in realcore, is to what extent these developments entail a disruption of the traditional patterns and power structures of the genre? Commentators such as Barcan (2002), Jacobs (2004) and Messina (2006) attest that amateur, reality porn is produced by people who have a much wider range of sexual identities than is the case in the established industry. Its makers are male, female, gay, straight, polyamorous and monogamous. Jacobs (2004) divides the material into a number of broad categories. There is 'peer-to-peer porn', which she argues works on the model of a mutually developing sexual interaction, as individuals share, exchange and collaborate with peer communities. There is 'pride porn', often associated with activist networks, and serving queer communities whose sexual bodies and scenarios are not adequately represented by commercial porn. And there is 'art porn', where digital media and networks provide a platform for diverse creative expression and communication on sexual themes. Although Jacobs acknowledges that the producers of peer-to-peer porn, pride porn and art porn have inherited the 'masculine power structures' and 'male fantasies' inherent in porn, she sees a general 'reclaiming of porn' through decentralized sexual platforms.

Pornography, in its many forms, has always claimed to reflect the truth of human sexuality, and has serviced a desire to see that truth represented. But it has also been claimed that pornography distorts that truth or that it represents only some aspects of sexuality: male, heterosexual, limiting. Now media technologies are making it possible for a far greater range of human sexual experience to be reflected. The impact of new media in closing the gap between reality and representation is surely neither inherently liberating nor oppressive. It may be worth concluding this discussion with some examples that seem to represent the best and worst of what is now accessible on the Internet, always bearing in mind that the vast majority of material lies somewhere in between.

On the one hand there is the website Positive Porn,[3] which makes a self-conscious attempt to challenge what it sees as the sexism of most existing pornography and to direct its audience to 'sex-positive' material. It observes that most porn advertises itself as 'nasty' for good reason, but insists that scattered among the bad are quite a few sites that show respect for their models, are honest in their portrayal of the personalities of their models, are positive in their depiction of female beauty and sex, and are produced by 'real people' who take pride in their work. The websites recommended do indeed seem to challenge, in a range of ways, the established structures of pornography. I Shot Myself offers nude and semi-nude images of young women that they have taken themselves with digital cameras. This does remove, in a real sense, the male-camera-subject that has been the key to the structure of so much pornographic representation, most obviously gonzo. The website Beautiful Agony features videos of women's faces during the full process of masturbation and orgasm. This is clearly designed to negate any notion of objectification, and even in the case of the related website I Feel Myself, which offers the full-body shot of the same theme, the emphasis is clearly on the subjective pleasure of the woman in view.

The images available on these sites are overwhelmingly of young women. It is significant that so many young women are keen to produce and exhibit amateur images of themselves, simultaneously acting as subjects while positioning themselves as objects of the erotic gaze. As one of Katrien Jacobs's (2004) informants suggests, the young women who display their bodies on such websites as SuicideGirls[4] are motivated by a desire for the 'fun' of self-expression and an 'ego-boost'. If, as I noted earlier, one of the defining power structures of pornography has been the relation of male-as-subject to women-as-object, it seems that in these examples the relation is fractured but by no means broken. Moreover this relation need not necessarily be underpinned by money or any coercive male power. Whether we like it or not, part of the normalization of pornography has involved the increasingly active internalization by women of their status within this dynamic.

At the other end of the spectrum, some of the realities pornography now shows us may be brutal and exploitative, and on occasion the new realism seems to service a desire to see brutality and exploitation. To take a rather dramatic example, a photo-shoot on the Iraq Babes[5] website shows porn actors dressed up as American troops and 'raping' Iraqi women, thus allowing the average American citizen to vicariously share in the tradition of invading armies that rape the women of a defeated power. These images were withdrawn once they began to circulate as authentic in the Arab world. Of course not all the atrocity images being generated by the current war in Iraq are pornographic, but both realcore and atrocity images service a similar preoccupation with seeing hitherto unseen realities of human behaviour. Moreover, the contemporary images from Abu Ghraib that evidently were authentic have been widely linked to pornographic representational practices.[6] We should be sceptical about this claim: it is difficult to believe that the images were meant to be arousing. But we must assume that, when asked to soften up their Muslim detainees, the American men and women staffing the prison drew on their established cultural repertoire of pornographic motifs to produce their grainy images of human pyramids, enforced fellatio and masturbation. The techniques of pornographic representation can and do inform the construction of real experience, and on occasion, real relations of power. We also see in this example that these disturbing realities can sometimes be fed back to us through pornography. The pornographic image is not innocent; it is efficacious. It can help to constitute and to amplify realities, which we may regard as progressive or regressive, desirable or undesirable.

We have reached a situation in which the old, accepted distinction between media representation and lived reality is breaking down, thus short-circuiting the debate about whether the former shapes the latter. People have been commenting on these developments for years, but they are nowhere more fully realized than in contemporary pornography. It is increasingly hard to tell what is real and what is representational. Pornographic texts have always sought to imitate experience, but now people's lived experience can be turned into a pornographic image.

Where does the collapse of the once axiomatic distinction between the 'real' and the representational leave us with regard to the concerns and debates, which were noted at the beginning of this chapter, about the possible effect of pornography upon the lives and sexual conduct of its consumers? Pornography has always promised to reveal sexual truth. But the concern, for some, was that it functioned to distort this truth by recasting sexual experience in terms of power relations between human subjects. Others claimed that mere representation could have no such capacity to create power relations that were not already there. On reflection, it seems likely that over the last 30 or 40 years the increasingly mainstream cultural presence of pornographic texts and images has made a contribution to contemporary sexual practice and experience. Pornography has surely influenced the way that men and women perform sex both on and off camera. There is a significant sense in which pornography *does* now simply record reality, just as it always promised to. But this is a reality that it has itself helped to shape. When we contemplate the content of amateur cyberporn what we see is less a case of pornographic representation affecting lived reality as a situation in which this reality itself is now available to be transformed into pornographic representation.

ACKNOWLEDGEMENTS

I would like to thank the editor for her patience and helpful editorial support, and Mike Webb at the University of Worcester for his encouragement and constructive comments when I was struggling with earlier drafts.

NOTES

1. Sexblogs are blogs devoted entirely to sex, and often are accounts of an individual's sex life. The most well known of these, both now bestselling books, are Belle du Jour: Diary of a London Call Girl,

http://belledejour-uk.blogspot.com, and Girl with a One-Track Mind, http://girlwithaonetrackmind.blogspot.com.

2.   Figure cited in a David Clews documentary, *Amateur Porn* (2005), for Channel 4.

3.   http://www.positive-porn.com (accessed 26.2.07). Positive Porn links to I Feel Myself, http://www.ifeelmyself.com/public/main.php; I Shot Myself, http://www.ishotmyself.com/public/main.php; and Beautiful Agony, http://www.beautifulagony.com/public/main.php, among others.

4.   http://suicidegirls.com. This is the most well-known 'altporn' site featuring women as pin-ups.

5.   For more information on Iraq Babes, see Sherrie Gossett, 'Bogus GI rape photos used as Arab propaganda', http://www.worldnetdaily.com/new/article.aspARTICLE_ID=38335 (accessed 19.3.07), and Sherrie Gossett, 'Fake rape photos infuriate Arab World', http://www.worldnetdaily.com/new/article.aspARTICLE_ID=38408 (accessed 19.3.07).

6.   For more information about the Abu Ghraib images, see Seymour Hersh, 'Torture at Abu Ghraib', http://www.newyorker.com/archive/2004/05/10/040510fa_fact (accessed 19.3.07). The images can be accessed at http://www.newyorker.com/archive/2004/05/03/slideshow_040503.

Chapter 2

PLEASING INTENSITIES: MASOCHISM AND AFFECTIVE PLEASURES IN PORN SHORT FICTIONS

CLARISSA SMITH

The escalation of sexual consumerism across multiple sites has been identified as a 'striptease culture' of 'self-revelation' (McNair, 2002: 81); essentially a good thing, sexualization frees up sexual feeling and offers a 'democratization of desire' through its expanded opportunities for sexual understanding and pleasure. Those products still institutionally regulated as 'pornography' figure in these arguments as the perverse 'other', occasionally capable of liberating sexual attitudes in their own right, but generally identified as the benchmark of 'undemocratic' media against which newer mainstream sex media are to be judged and designated good or bad 'representation'.

In this context it might seem rather perverse to turn to a more traditional sexual form – the top-shelf magazine – in order to examine its fictional characteristics. But that is what this chapter will do, focusing on stories in *Forum* magazine, one of the few spaces on the top shelves of UK newsagents still devoted to the written word rather than images.[1] Published since 1968, *Forum: The International Journal of Human Relations* was, until the recent sell-off, part of the Northern and Shell portfolio. Originally conceived 'to take the overspill from the *Penthouse* letters pages, which were dominated by a debate on whether or not one should spank one's wife' (Coldwell[2] quoted in Veitch, 2004), *Forum* offers in-depth features on what might be termed 'fetishistic' sexual practices alongside readers' letters, advice and fiction. My examination is necessarily truncated; there is only space to explore two stories from the 2000 volume of the magazine. My intention is to revisit erotic fiction and examine the ways in which it might be said to speak to its readers.

As theorizations of sexual media expand, problems remain in the implicit designation of pornography as an already too well-known category. Its forms of production, representation and consumption are too often assumed to perpetuate the objectification and fragmentation of sex and, most especially, women's bodies. This essentializing is made possible by the constant insistence on porn's 'phallic origins' (Williams, 1989), as if there is a quantifiable 'maleness' to its production, presentation and consumption. This is a key theme of Pamela Paul's recent discussion of 'pornified' culture and her claim that 'pornography is not about desire and fantasy; it's about hostility and shame' (Paul, 2005: 273) – a compounding of earlier rejections of porn on the basis of its aesthetic poverty and simplistic assumptions that porn narratives are *just* about fucking to spur male masturbation. The alleged narrowness of characterization and plot and the exaggerations of sexual prowess and anatomy in porn fiction are supposedly clear indications of their 'harmfulness' or, if we reject moralizing, their unimportance as a form of human expression because they are so goal (orgasm)-directed (Richard Dyer, 1992). Where connections are made between porn stories and other literary forms, it is generally only to reiterate the singular intentions of porn so that 'there is no need to examine individual books' (Sontag, 1969/2003: 403) unless they rise above the mass and do something new and innovative:

> The singleness of intention often condemned by critics is, when the work merits treatment as art, compounded of many resonances. The physical sensations involuntarily produced in someone reading the book carry with them something that touches upon the reader's whole experience of his humanity – and his limits as personality and as a body (Sontag, 1969/2003: 410).

Sontag looks for the particular prick[3] and innovative surprise of the obscene, capable of inspiring more than masturbatory impulse. This kind of account relies on the idea of the critic as a knowing scholar who can uncover the true meaning of stories and enable readers' perception of the 'radical' nature of texts they thought were just for titillation! Clearly issues of *quality* are being invoked here, and while there may be much to say about different forms and styles of storytelling, Bourdieu's (1984) critique of the social distributions and functions of taste should make us wary of citing quality as a guarantor of anything.

FORUM MAGAZINE

Forum claims an interesting status for itself, clearly signposting its interests in the 'scientific' exploration of sexuality and sexual practices – its board of consultants includes various health professionals, academics and sex educators. Its intentions to enlighten its audience are highlighted in each issue:

> *Forum* ... believes that because of ignorance, fear and guilt, the great majority of people in our country are today enjoying only a fraction of the potential joy and pleasure they could receive from their relationships ... by sharing the experiences of others, our readers gain a greater understanding of themselves as well as others through realising that no one is alone in their fears or frustrations or unique in their problems.

In *Forum*, sexuality is constructed as a repressed force to be liberated. Its stories and confessions of sexual experimentation and pleasurable possibilities are discursively staged within a 'progressive sexual politics' (Juffer, 1998: 123), and the invocation of a shared sexual community is articulated around the therapeutic good of educating and exploring desire. *Forum* claims 40 per cent of its readers are women, a statistic that challenges the received wisdom that top-shelf magazines can only cater to single-sex readerships. Articles, features and stories in *Forum* are aimed at a mixed readership and because of this the magazine offers an opportunity to think about the possible pleasures offered to men *and* women within its pages and how those may be similar rather than distinct gendered pleasures. In the analysis that follows I want to examine its stories' possible address to male *and* female readers through the invocation of bodily affects and a masochistic sensibility.

A cursory reading of *Forum* suggests a preoccupation with themes of power, focusing on experiences of bondage, domination and spanking. Other themes surface but the cover image of a woman in soft bondage costume, the editorial page outline of a safer sex code and articles on fetishist practices proclaim *Forum*'s focus on non-vanilla sex practices. Of the 24 stories examined for this chapter, 19, mostly told in the first person, featured women as the main protagonist. The remaining five focused on male characters (narrated in the third person, possibly reflecting a general scepticism about the reliability of men's sexual accounts[4]). Most featured some form of interaction between two or more people, often heterosexual – although five stories focused on women with women and no male protagonist; one story featured no sexual action, just flirting ('Prime Numbers', issue 5); one centred on masturbation ('Water of Life', issue 7); and in seven stories practices such as caning and spanking were described.

As with any other publication seeking nationwide distribution, *Forum* has to stay within the distributors' guidelines[5] which forbid any representation of banned sexual practices as outlined in the 1959 Obscene Publications Act and in the distributors' further interpretation of 'problematic' or 'unacceptable' sexual proclivities. Certain practices, including watersports, coprophilia, underage sex, and sadistic pleasures, are banned. However, many of *Forum*'s stories rely heavily on dramatizations of a masochistic sensibility: the erotic play of coercion, humiliation and pain and their interplay with sexual pleasure.

To describe the stories in *Forum* as masochistic need not be to re-enter the space of anti-porn theorizations of subordination. Instead, what I will argue is that expressions and descriptions of bodily discomfort, pain or shame are used in the stories to produce an emotional experience of sexual pleasure centred on bodily sensation. Where such experiences are explored in mainstream media – *9½ Weeks* (1986), *Crash* (1996), *Quills* (2000) and *Romance* (1999) – they are generally labelled 'sadomasochistic' representations, reflecting the traditional linkage of sadism and masochism. This linkage is predicated on the notion of a power relationship where one person inflicts pain on another. In Freudian thought this is an infantile form of sexual communication, inferior to properly mature forms of sexual conduct. Freud's assessment of masochism denies the link between its practice and sexual pleasure. As Phillips writes, 'Freud seems to be seeing ... the masochist ... [as] the willing victim, the person who docilely accepts punishment rather than standing up for himself' (1998: 27). The desire for other forms of connection – for example, stimulation of the skin – not tied to vaginal penetration is to be transcended in order to achieve fully adult sexuality. Thus psychoanalysis infantilizes physical and embodied experiences of sexual pleasure.

However, for practitioners, masochism is a form of human expression drawing on sexual dissidence, pleasure, escapism, transcendence and the refusal of normal genital sexuality, allowing for safer sex explorations of the lived body and its transformative potentials (Beckman, 2001). Such transformations need not be the exclusive property of one sexual identity and may well offer pleasures to those readers who would identify themselves as without masochistic tendencies. Unfortunately, the problematic conception of masochism as a passion for pain, submission and self-abnegation which is naturally aligned with femininity remains steadfastly alive in feminist debates and cultural theory. Because of this, feminist sexual ethics have often focused on the need for women to excise their 'incorrect' fantasies of submission (Bartky, 1990). As Grimshaw observes, this suggests:

> that somewhere there might be an 'authentic' female imagination, free of all the influence of male domination ... It also supposes that we have some clear means of telling what is and is not politically 'correct' – that the meanings of desires and fantasies are, as it were, written on their face, and that we can clearly separate those which are authentically feminine from those which are masculine, or the effect of social subordination (Grimshaw, 1993: 157).

I hope that an emphasis on feeling and affect, 'the corporeal intensifications' (Grosz, 1995: 199) of experiencing discomfort and pleasure, may help to explore the ways in which some pornographic fictions animate readers' responses without falling back on the claim that male readers have an inherent sadism and women an infantile desire to be punished. In the analysis that follows, I reject the fundamental misunderstanding of masochistic encounters as exclusively desirous of the receipt of pain, although that might form a part of some people's practices. I've chosen two *Forum* stories, 'Supermarket Slut' and 'The Ring', from volume 34, issues 2 and 1, 2000,[6] which demonstrate the importance of understanding how 'feeling' rather than power is conveyed in these fictional sexual imaginaries.

'SUPERMARKET SLUT'

Amanda's passion for flashing gets her into a sticky situation ...

'I like to tease the boys on the check-out.' With her 36DD breasts and blonde hair the female narrator of this story plays a game at the supermarket: she queries the price of her purchases, commanding the shop assistant's attention by placing the item between her breasts so that he touches them as he retrieves the item for price-checking. 'I laugh in their face and smile. And they smile as they look at my arse and I walk out of the store.' She's played this game for some time, but on returning from holiday she finds that there is a new system in place: a Client Privilege scheme has been introduced.

Amanda joins it and gets money to spend in-store, but when she next tries her price-check game, she's taken to the manager's office and told she's broken the rules. Ron shows her the contract she signed and tells her, 'You owe us privileges, my dear.' In the storeroom she finds out what her obligations are. She is told to strip off her top and climb up a pile of sugar bags. At the top, she's ordered to take off her knickers and then to come down again to fellate an assistant:

> Ron, I think it was then, he wanted me on the milk trolley and licked me between my legs. I kept my eyes shut but my pussy went up to meet his tongue, I couldn't help it, and then he entered me from behind, making me bend over a cold stack of butter bricks that made my nipples hard. I don't know who came after. I heard the plastic doors flap and breathe as someone else came in. Ron came inside me with a great sigh and let go of my hips with a last squeeze of my tits. Then this other one, I think it might have been the pimply boy from aisle seven, turned me round and wanted to suckle on my breasts. He sucked me till I came and then made me kiss his cock, just kiss it once or twice, till he came

on my face. That was the first night. I still go there sometimes.

On a superficial level, this story conforms to criticisms of porno-graphic fictions. It is written in prose that combines 'extreme fantasy with absolute cliché – as if the fantasy, however wild and excessive it may seem, had been gone through so many times that it had long since become incapable of being anything other than a weary and hopeless repetition of itself' (Marcus, 2003: 389). According to writers like Marcus, sexual couplings in pornography are a form of 'organ grinding' (Marcus, 2003: 392) in which language is limited to a constant reiteration of 'more, more, more', devoid of metaphoric power or emotional exposition. But, as in critiques of formulaic commercialized popular fictions like romance, this is condemnation, not analysis. The pleasures of reading become a pathological *use* of pornography, with little space for understanding *how* it works effec-tively upon the pulses.

There remains the necessary task of examining the text – not to get at its 'true' meaning, but to explore the ways its particular repeti-tions might be understood as enabling perception, and affective and physical engagements. This is not simply to challenge those accounts stressing porn users' passivity and an insistence on reader activity in the porn narrative. Instead I'm arguing that we need to understand the proposals of a porn story as more than a catalogue of particular kinds of stereotypical representations. This is especially true where analysis makes claims about the direct relation between representa-tion and the male sexual psyche and its eroticization of female vulner-ability.

The pathologizing of sexual relations between men and women as always turning on women's vulnerability is a key trope of anti-porn theorizing and is often replicated in 'analyses' of porn. The terms 'subordination', 'objectification' and 'stereotyping' have been used to explain the sexual pull of pornography, but these descriptive terms are not politically neutral and their status as tools of analysis has not gone undebated. They issue imperatives to the analyst to search for evidence of 'harm' or the reduction of individuals to the status of objects, thereby sidelining the idea of fiction as a dramatic expression of emotions, sensations, frustrations and pleasures. For example, in his analysis of the UK publication *Men Only*, Simon Hardy (1998) uses the insights of radical feminism to make the claim that the unequal power structure that is patriarchy is reflected, embellished and eroticized in the magazine's fiction.[7]

In order to sustain this claim, Hardy has to divide stories into scenarios defined as 'discrete sexual interaction between two or more people' (1998: 77). The sexual interactions turn on gender difference, 'for the Woman of pornography, to be aroused is to be powerless and to be powerless is to be aroused' (1998: 85). The Lover orders the Woman to remove clothing, threatens her with orgasm, sexual taunts and his Big Cock. The Woman usually adopts poses that stress her passivity and the 'dirtiness' of the act. Her submission to male desire is completed in her 'animalistic' and 'orgiastic' pleasure: a vital feature of the scenarios – 'the sexual conquest of the woman ... represents the conquest of the social self by natural essence' (1998: 95). Thus the narrative is assessed using 'scenario of degradation ... as the basic unit of analysis' (1998: 77). Sometimes 'scenario of degradation' draws on Andrea Dworkin's analysis of heterosex as inherently degrading for women (1981): a theoretical and methodological position which insists that any instance of sexual activity must be seen as 'damaging' to women. This analysis also claims that pornography eroticizes sexual activity as pleasurable because of its links to power and women's inability to freely choose. Pleasure comes from seeing women submit. Signs of women's submission to male sexuality are the *only* relevant indicators, confirming pornography's reflection of the real state of male/female relations. If male sexuality is conceived as dominating and bullying, and pornography 'tells the truth' about that sexuality, there is no point in looking for any other signs within the text. They are simply distractions or the disguising of real politics.

But this is a circular argument, in which 'sex scenes' are conceived as replications in print of *actual social relations*. Hardy draws the following conclusions: the Woman's verbal gestures are usually pleading in the face of the Lover's threats; her physical responses are 'forced' out of her in that she can't help but orgasm; and her appearance is submissive to the Big Cock and the effects of being fucked. Such conclusions absolutely refuse more complex conceptualizations of power as I shall go on to discuss. According to Hardy and other analysts who approach porn fiction through the concept of 'objectification', the subordination of women in the sex act is the only distinguishable and important 'fact' for readers, and their relation to the text is entirely gendered – the male reader inserts himself into the narrative space of the male protagonist. Therefore a certain welding together of the readers' lived 'reality' with the textual 'fantasy' is inherent in the use of pornography (Hardy, 1998: 123). However, this is a remarkably over-simplified explanation of readers' pleasures, dependent upon the notion of audiences' vulnerabilities and their desire to 'identify'.

Identification is a conceptual conceit that Martin Barker has argued 'benefits by remaining unclear' (2005: 354), and which has no real ability to grasp the complexities of the relationships readers have with their chosen media. Identification with the hero of the porn story is based on the simple equation that men identify according to gender and that the male character is simply there to fuck in place of the reader. To make such claims, it is necessary to remove any other elements as important to the reader – the narrative, propositions, form, conversations, motivations, and actions. All those features which mark it as a story have to be ignored to generalize about identification.

My suggestion is that porn stories are not identificatory tools; rather they are processual, requiring of readers that they accrete elements of the story as they read, and understand the characters, motivations and actions accordingly. Moreover, as Altman (1999) has suggested in relation to film, readers 'enter' stories and agree to engage with the 'rules' of the story even where these may conflict with other cultural norms. Fictions should therefore be understood through their specific modes of inviting readers to suspend 'realities' in order that the 'rules' of the particular form can be followed. A dialogic approach to stories (Volosinov, 1973; Martin Barker, 1989) is useful here, emphasizing as it does, the proposals of story forms and their invitations to an imaginative progression through their particular forms of sequence, unfolding and resolution. It is not that the sex has no importance – these are pornographic stories and by their very nature must be explicit about sexual detail and action – but sexual material cannot be directly mapped onto sexual intercourse in patriarchy. In other words, it is subject to the 'rules' of porn narratives, not 'real' life.

In a porn narrative, readers follow the 'rules' which allow for the imaginative exploration of recognizing desire, letting go and being seduced: the transformation of the ordinary into the sexually extraordinary. Porn stories are not documents of 'real' relationships, nor are they simply fictional and therefore entirely removed from the 'real'. Instead I am proposing that they should be understood as the means by which readers can experiment with various types of feeling, including those which might be understood to be risky or 'bad'.

The fundamental principle of much debate about the problems of porn and its relations to the 'real' has been the insistence on a one-dimensional relationship between reality and fantasy. Indeed, as Barker and Brooks have argued, 'if it were possible to insist, as the standard "scare" mode of argument does, that people respect and maintain a clear line between fantasy and reality, they would lose the power to imagine transformations' (1998: 288). Ang has argued that the 'internal' realism of the world within the soap opera is combined with its 'external' unrealism (1985: 47) in order to allow viewers the possibility of *playing* with reality within the confines of a fictional world. This is a 'game that enables one to place the limits of the fictional and the real under discussion, to make them fluid' (1985: 49). Searching for 'messages' encoded in the text and their 'decodings' by readers ignores the complexities of the interactions readers enjoy in all media forms, including pornography. Audience research has shown that readers and viewers are self-conscious about their media practices and the ways in which these are understood (Barker and Brooks, 1998; Barker et al, 2001; Hill, 1997; Smith, 2007). Readers and viewers don't simply decode messages, they 'rehearse the complex connections between forms of the imaginary, and [their] pictures of and plans for reality' (Barker and Brooks, 1998: 287).

So rather than assume gendered identifications, I want to suggest something different. Readers approach the porn story as a dramatization of the sexual moment and the possible pleasures of surrendering to sexual delight. Gender is less important to this process than the ability to give expression to libidinal intensities. In Hardy's account, the bodily and emotional experiences described in the stories are sidelined in favour of a focus on the ways in which the sexual encounter might be understood to replicate gender power relations. If, on the

other hand, we focus on the bodily sensations of exhibition, humiliation, shame and pain as 'vehicles ... for staging dramas of suspense,
supplication, abandon and relief' (Williams, 1989: 195), it becomes
clear that they are not just stories of domination by one gender over
another, but ways of expressing the intensifications of bodily experiences and feelings.

Grosz observes that 'erotic pleasures are evanescent; they are
forgotten almost as they occur', but porn stories attempt to recre-
ate pleasure as a textual formation and in the body of the reader
– to revivify 'the ache of desire' (1995: 195). How do they do this?
Reading is frequently a solitary activity and reading porn can be a
particularly private engagement with the text. All texts require that
the viewer, reader, listener orients themselves to the proposals of
that text (Volosinov, 1973). In a porn narrative we are invited to join
in the proposal offered to follow a narrative of desire expressed in
the sensations of the body and to engage with the quite wayward
expressions of motivation, sexual energy and sensitivities of particular bodily regions contained within the story. Often, as in the stories
I describe here, the narrative is offered as a first-person exploration
and explanation of the interiority of the experience of sexual arousal.
The story offers us ways of engaging with the body's responsiveness
to stimulation through the exploration of the feelings of the narrator. The reader engages in an empathetic relation with the narration
– this is how sex can feel, how it works on the body. It is a relation of
co-animation.

In 'Supermarket Slut' the story begins with a quite lengthy
description of the narrator's body, the ways she moves it and how
that makes her feel. Amanda's narration is charged with physicality
– from her description of her breasts through to her hyper-awareness
of her impact on the 'pimply young men' at the check-out:

> I lean my bare arm with the little blonde hairs on it that they'd
> love to kiss ... They have to get up, trying to hide the hard-on
> they've got in their little polyester supermarket uniform trou-
> sers.

The narration lays out the particular power game Amanda likes to
play, amusing herself as she arouses and embarrasses the check-out

boys. Things change when Ron the manager gets involved and here it is Amanda's turn to feel shame: 'I don't strip off like a common tart,' I said, blushing, my face burning, 'in a supermarket warehouse – what d'you think I am?'

The references to shame and humiliation are a way of bringing bodily experiences to the fore and they dramatize the reversibility of physical sensations: just like the check-out boys, Amanda is embarrassed *and* aroused. The story's erotic power depends upon the reversals of power and of bodily affect – the physicality of the body in all its relations to the social – so that shame brings a sensitivity and intensity to the sexual scene. The masochist sensibility of the story explores the borders and boundaries between painful emotions – fear, risk and shame – and eroticism: the interior voice tells us, 'I was still a little tearful, but I was flushed with excitement.' This ambiguity of sexual feeling and the contradictions of tearfulness and excitement dramatizes the capitulation to feeling. Pain, understood at its broadest to include emotional as well as physical pain and encompassing discomfort through to hurt, 'serves as a mode of corporeal intensification' (Grosz, 1995: 199). In dramatizing masochistic incidents these stories draw on vocabularies of intensity and demonstrate the ways in which the body has the potential to *really* feel. This is a corporeal intensification which requires going beyond the limits of 'ordinary, nice, well-behaved sex'; submitting to feeling, letting go, letting oneself experience sexual desire. Drawing on Bersani, Phillips insists that:

> Eroticism involves the sense of an interior self, a self that is always vulnerable to invasion from the outside – that defends itself yet longs for the invasion. Masochism lends itself to all erotic experience in this sense, since it involves the capacity to be shattered into joy or *jouissance* by an extreme pleasure that is also intense suffering (Philips, 1998: 150).

To explore this further, I turn to another story, where anger and social discomfort are the principal affects that drive the erotic play.

'THE RING'

Some presents are more intimate than others ...

A nameless woman anticipates her lover's arrival at a bar. She tells us that it's a favourite haunt of her successful, professional boyfriend, but she finds it intolerable because of the smugness and posing of the designer-obsessed clientele:

> Gleaming sports cars conspicuously glide into the car park, driven by people who have never had to look after their own possessions. They don't know what it is to cherish something ... They never get attached to a familiar item. It goes out of fashion and is discarded because *it fails to impress.*

As she waits, she meditates on her relationship with Jason – is she just a possession to be displayed? She looks at her Gucci watch, a present from him, and contemplates how she will dump him. He arrives, 'cocksure' and 'positively sizzling'. If only 'he wasn't so disarmingly horny'. No verbal greeting is exchanged but his hand goes up her skirt, discovers she's wearing knickers and insists she takes them off. Going to the toilet to do as he asks, she is angry but asks herself, 'Why am I so excited?' In the toilet she touches the small clit ring he gave her, and finds that the piercing is healed and that touching it gives her a shock of pleasure. Excitement mounting, she returns to Jason; he puts his hand up her dress to attach something to the clit ring. As she walks to the bar the something – a weight – pulls on the ring and sends 'pure pleasure down to my toes'. Other men show their sexual interest in her but she's irritated that she's 'suffering' sexual excitement while Jason is so unconcerned. Kissing him, she is pleased to find he has an erection:

> I can feel his hot breath against my shoulder and he really is getting quite worked up. He stands and takes my hand and I'm thinking. 'Hooray! I win, I win. Now give me my prize. Take me to that trendy apartment of yours, tie me to the four-poster and fuck my lights out.'

Instead of going home, they go into a club where she dances and, because of the clit ring and its weight, she experiences the most intense orgasm:

I can feel a great big shuddering heat starting to build up inside me. My legs are going and I'm falling, falling, falling, and suddenly Jason's there, catching me. He draws me to him and hooks an arm under my knee so that my dripping crotch is pressed against the huge bulge in his trousers. His tongue is in my mouth as the techno music drives me higher and higher. And I'm coming and coming and my eyes are stinging and - and ... I'm sucking his tongue and grinding my body into his. The first song mixes into the next, and its rhythm is faster, harder, meaner. The song is a blasting Prodigy track, my favourite one. I can hear Keith scream-ing - only somehow it's me. I shout as a final shudder heaves through me and I claw at Jason's jacket and rip the buttons from his shirt.

She sits down, has a cigarette and he walks away saying 'Give us a ring.' Irritated again, her final thought is '*Bastard!* I'll give him a ring all right. And I know exactly where he's going to wear it ...'

Both stories eroticize bodily affects that are not uncomplicatedly about pleasure. In 'The Ring' the narrator is burning with anger and resentment at her boyfriend, Jason, and her surroundings, but even as she feels anger, it constantly tips into recognition of her own bodily presence (how others are reacting to her) and feeling ('Why am I so excited?'). Several times the narrating voice says she is desperate for sex and yet she doesn't tell Jason: she lets him direct the action. In an analysis seeking to identify power relations, the focus would fall on Jason's orchestration of her orgasm, but that would be to side-line the description of sensations that animate her body (and that of the reader) - the flushed face, the weak knees, the tremendous orgasm. Power, here vested in Jason, is a device to ensure that she lets herself go entirely - no questions asked, no demurring, the narrator can surrender to an intense sexual experience all the more powerful because of her earlier sense of suffering.

Both stories hinge on the notion of a contract - in 'Supermarket Slut' this is expressly stated, in 'The Ring' it is implied - but in both the contract is an important 'psychological boundar[y] for good sex' (Langdridge and Butt, 2004: 40). Both women break the terms of the contract they've agreed to and both submit to the form of punish-ment dictated by their men. Yet, this is not submission as anti-porn theorizing would have it: the contract is a necessary fiction for the *illusion of powerlessness.* Arguments for the pleasures of sadomasochism stress the consensual nature of the practice (Califia, 1997; Taylor and Ussher, 2001; Beckman, 2001) and reject the pathologizing impulses of psychoanalytic and psychiatric accounts. In so doing, they reject the idea that sadomasochism is based on patriarchal power structures; social structures of power are institutionalized and rigid whereas the sexual practice of sadomasochism remains a 'fluid' relation – 'an acting out of power structures by a strategic game that is able to give sexual pleasure or bodily pleasure' (Gallagher and Wilson, 1984: 30). The practices of humiliation, bondage and excess are techniques for accessing and understanding the potentials of corporeal sensation. This refocusing refuses an emphasis on power as the defining charac-teristic of sadomasochism and insists on prioritizing the sexual affects of its practices. The women in the stories don't just submit; there is a level of self-reflexivity implicit in the questions they pose themselves because therein lies the possibility of exploring something new. Both women are motivated by a need to feel *something*: in 'The Ring' the woman complains about the complacency of those who have every material want satisfied, and Amanda, in 'Supermarket Slut', continu-ously pushes her luck at the supermarket. The 'inadvertent' breaking of the terms of the contract leads to the exploration of humiliation, of feeling exposed and vulnerable in the stories. But through this comes pleasure. The excitement of being caught out, of being made to take a punishment and the detailing of the sensate qualities of these feelings offer the exploration of a disturbing sexual pleasure.

As Califia writes, 'One of the things fiction can do for us is take us for brief journeys, even if they're just imaginary journeys, inside each other's bodies' (1997: 89). *Forum's* stories are interesting because they explicitly draw on particular issues of submission and dominance that have proved problematic for theorists of porn and sexual desire. These are narratives that are problematic to our wider culture (see, for example, 'Operation Spanner' in 1990 in which 15 men admitted to consensual acts of sadomasochism and were given lengthy sentences for unlawful bodily harm[8]), and to feminism in its exploration of female desire. Within anti-porn theorizing submis-sion is a pathologized and essentialized form of behaviour. This kind of theorizing refuses the possibility of a pain/pleasure dyad, arguing instead that any such insistence on a relation between discomfort/ pain and pleasure is to ignore and disregard women's suffering in forced sex (Dworkin, 1981).

The problem, of course, lies in the importation of an external form of worrying about effects and of searching for meaning and interpretations. What I am suggesting is that this has no relevance to understanding how and why readers gain enjoyment and masturbatory excitement from their fiction. In *Forum's* stories the pleasures described are of being overwhelmed by feeling and sometimes this is discomforting. How do involved and interested readers respond to these themes? How do they engage with the narrative progression and expression of bodily affect? The sexual excitement and masturbation that may be a part of reading porn fiction are processes of bringing the 'self' into the story, but existing audience research (Ang, 1985; Barker and Brooks, 1998; Barker, 2005) tells us they will be of a different order to those presumed by theories of textual identification. Future examinations of the ongoing processes and forms of sexualization will need to address a wide range of sexual practices, values and identities. They will also need to engage with the embodied experiences of reading and viewing sexual media. To do that we will need to understand the ways in which sexual representations articulate the ache of desire and be prepared to let go of some of our fondest assumptions about gender, power and pleasure.

ACKNOWLEDGEMENTS

My thanks to the editor of this book for her generous and insightful comments on earlier drafts of this chapter. I'd also like to thank Valerie Reardon who read earlier versions and Angela Werndly and Eliane Meyer for their cheerful conversations about masochism over lunch.

NOTES

1.   The magazine features very little pictorial material, with images used primarily to accompany articles, stories and letters. The sexu-

alization of mainstream culture has had a deleterious effect on the traditional top shelf. For three decades the top shelf was the UK's main source of sexually explicit short stories, but storytelling is in decline, a victim of the downturn in circulation and distribution of softcore magazines. The 1990s saw a major drop in purchases of softcore magazines such as Men Only and Penthouse, when men defected to the more respectable but saucy titles, FHM and Loaded. Porn publishers responded with segmentation and specialization – responses that have effectively done away with magazine short stories. Where titles like Men Only and Penthouse would once have featured at least one story each month, they are now included only infrequently. Publishers have cut back on written content because it is expensive and have focused on pictorial representations, a move which has rendered them particularly susceptible to competition posed by the Internet. For further discussion see Maddison, 2004 and Smith, 2005.

2. Editor of Forum since 1990 and a published author of erotic fiction.

3. This is similar to Roland Barthes' (1981: 45) idea of the punctum – the point in the photograph which takes us into the photo – the moment at which it 'annihilate[s] itself as medium to be no longer a sign but the thing itself'.

4. For example, in 'The Case in Question' (vol. 34, no. 12) by Frank Charnock, the third-person narration serves to ironize the unlikely scenario that two people mistakenly taking home the other's luggage should, on meeting, find themselves mutually eager for sex.

5. WH Smith and Menzies are the main channels of magazine distribution in the UK. For further discussion of their regulatory effects on content see Skordarki, 1991 and Smith, 2005.

6. I chose these two because on first reading I found 'Supermarket Slut' uncomfortable, but maybe that's the point! 'The Ring' was interesting because 'the action' has no mutually satisfying penetration.

7. Hardy's work is exemplary in offering bibliographic details of the stories analysed. A fuller critique of his arguments is developed in Smith, 2007.

8. See http://www.spannertrust.org/documents/spannerhistory.asp.

Chapter 3

'CHOKE ON IT, BITCH!': PORN STUDIES, EXTREME GONZO AND THE MAINSTREAMING OF HARDCORE

STEPHEN MADDISON

In her preface to the collection *More Dirty Looks*, Pamela Church Gibson notes the 'increasingly sexualised atmosphere of Western society, where ... sexually explicit images are to be found everywhere', and where 'pornography filters into the mainstream' (2004: vii, ix). Shops selling pornography can be found on most high streets and the growth of the Internet has made pornography more accessible. It has also facilitated new forms of pornography such as interactive sex shows via webcam, and new means of distributing and profiting from porn – major porn companies have been responsible for developing business models and software now used across the e-commerce sector. The Internet has revolutionized the choice of porn available and the ease with which it can be consumed – instantly, from home or workplace, and relatively unhindered by legal, social or geographical constraint. Crucially the Internet has also mainstreamed hardcore porn. As part of their daily routines most email users will view pornographic spam, and an increasingly popular and proliferating range of blogs and gossip sites such as Fleshbot treat the hardcore industry as just another form of celebrity culture.

In the USA in 2003, federal prosecutors began proceedings against Extreme Associates, a company owned by husband and wife, Rob Black (real name Robert Zicari) and Lizzie Borden (real name Janet Romano). This case has been described as the most significant legal case against the porn industry for ten years, not only because it represents the Bush administration's only notable attempt to make good on an offer it made prior to re-election in 2005, 'to make the investigation and prosecution of obscenity one of [our] highest criminal enforcement priorities', but because Extreme Associates' films eroticize violence and the subjugation of women.[1]

Extreme Associates' output represents one of the newly emerging porn genres, derived from the low-budget gonzo conventions established by John Stagliano in his *Buttman* series (1990–2005). Extreme Associates' films combine gonzo hand-held camera work and low-tech style with conventions derived from slasher movies, the reality TV genres of *Jackass* stunts and gross-out and fly-on-the-wall documentaries. Whilst the output of Extreme Associates is perhaps especially shocking, its films share many generic qualities with those of a growing number of other porn producers, such as Anabolic Video Productions (*Ass 2 Mouth 2*, 2005), Max Hardcore ('Throat gaggin, asshole drillin', hot gapin' holes, up chuckin' sluts'), and Evil Angel, who release films by Rocco Siffredi (*Rocco Animal Trainer*, 2000), Jonni Darkko (*Trophy Whores*, 2005) and others. Titles by these companies are coming to dominate adult video rental charts in the USA. And while some companies, such as Wicked and VCA, are continuing to cater to the couples market, making glamour-girl films,[2] the post-gonzo aesthetic offered by Extreme Associates is elsewhere increasingly replacing the high-budget narrative features that dominated the hardcore market in the 1990s and early 2000s.[3] In February 2002 the USA cable channel PBS aired a documentary called *American Porn*. In an interview with Black, published on the PBS website, he's asked, 'What's the nastiest stuff you guys do?' He replies that the nastiest is probably:

> a series called 'Cocktails' – it's pretty repugnant ... she's giving fellatio and she's hacking up boogies in a bowl. And they're spit-ting in the bowl ... and at the end they come in the bowl. And then she drinks it all down ... Sometimes ... the girl's giving

fellatio, and she's gagging so much she vomits.[4]

After *American Porn* aired, an undercover federal investigation began into Extreme Associates that culminated in their offices being raided in April 2003. In her seminal book *Hardcore*, published in 1989, Linda Williams offered an affirmative and detailed account of hardcore pornography, noting the growing importance of the couples market and domestic VHS consumption. As Lynne Segal has noted, Williams's book was important in arguing that hardcore is 'one of the few genres where women are not punished or made guilty for acting out their sexual desires' (1992: 85). The case against Extreme Associates offers an opportunity to consider the conditions in which porn is becoming more mainstream, both in the sense of being more visible and influential in popular culture and more meaningful in mainstream political debate. It also offers an opportunity to consider the gender politics that are coming to inform an increasing market for what could be described as extreme post-gonzo hardcore. In this chapter I will offer a detailed analysis of *Forced Entry* (2002), which is one of the films for which Extreme Associates is being prosecuted. My analysis will focus on the representation of women and on the organization of genital acts. The context of this analysis will be a wider consideration of the legal case against Extreme Associates.

In 1992, with the rising popularity of VHS, Williams was optimistic about the development of hardcore. In 2006 porn is more mainstream than ever, but, as I shall argue, critical engagement with hardcore, despite the emergence of 'porn studies', has failed to address the changing nature of porn representations.

UNITED STATES V. EXTREME ASSOCIATES

In November 2004 the hearing against Extreme Associates began at the District Federal Court in Pittsburgh. The trial concerned five films: *Extreme Teen 24* (2002), *Cocktails 2* (2001), *Ass Clowns 3* (2001), *1001 Ways to Eat My Jizz* (2002) and *Forced Entry* (2002). In January 2005 District Court judge Gary Lancaster dismissed the charges against Extreme Associates, effectively agreeing with their defence team that the constitutional right of individuals to view materials

in private cannot be meaningfully exercised without a corresponding right of companies to distribute such materials. The following
month, the Justice Department announced that it would appeal
against this ruling, and in April it filed an appeal with the Third
Circuit. In December 2005 the appeals court reversed the initial decision and reinstated the suit against Extreme Associates, questioning
the authority of the District Court in its reading of previous Supreme
Court decisions. In April 2006 lawyers acting for Extreme Associates
submitted their petition to the Supreme Court; at the time of writing, the Supreme Court has not yet made a ruling on whether Zicari
and Romano will go to trial. They face potential maximum penalties
of 50 years in jail and fines of $2.5 million.[5]

The case against Extreme Associates has been the occasion for a
re-articulation of familiar rhetoric that has played out along predictable political lines. Concerned Women for America, who engage in
activism against the so-called 'Gay Agenda', against abortion rights,
against sex education and the notion of sex before and outside
marriage, describe Extreme Associates as 'the worst of the worst
purveyors of obscenity' and have called the District Court's decision
'disturbing'. The National Law Center for Children and Families
(NLC) also criticized the decision. Both groups filed a friend-of-court
brief.[6] In the opposing corner, Adult Video News hailed the court decision in Pittsburgh as one 'that is bound to have enormous impact on
the Adult entertainment industry' and quoted one lawyer as saying
that 'this is a banner day for the First Amendment, and the equivalent
of Pearl Harbor for the Religious Right'.[7] Similar positions have been
taken up by the Free Speech Coalition, and the National Coalition
for Sexual Freedom.

In many respects this is familiar terrain: an apparent rehash of
the feminist porn wars of the 1980s and early 1990s, and the US
culture wars of the 1990s. The former saw feminism become increasingly defined by internal struggles over the politics of sexuality. The
latter saw the rise of the religious right in the USA as an activist political force, mobilized by an emerging neo-conservative movement that
targeted federal funding for arts and community projects by and for
so-called minorities. In his response to the legal action against him,
Rob Black has suggested that the US government is once again engag-

ing in a conservative culture war. However, his actions suggest an enormous amount of confidence about the eventual ruling – advertising the films cited by prosecutors as the 'Federal Five' and noting after the dismissal of the case, 'I ... have made fucking history ... *The business has been going great.'* [8] It would clearly be unwise to predict the outcome of the Supreme Court's decision, but Black's words are significant. Legal decisions on obscenity in the USA seem to be responding not to neo-conservative activism but to the demands of consumer culture (Maddison, 2004). Judge Lancaster's ruling was cognizant of the economic significance of the US porn industry, the widespread consumption of hardcore and what has been described as the pornographication of American popular culture, whereby pornographic imagery and the vernacular of pornographic representations become more integrated into mainstream political culture (cigars and stains in the Starr report) and popular culture (porn directors making videos for Britney Spears) (Maddison, 2004). One commentary on the Extreme Associates case, written for a resource site for adult webmasters, notes that 'technology has made many of the old concepts of obscenity obsolete'.[9] According to the industry journal *eMarketer*, retail e-commerce sales annually increased by an average of 26 per cent between 2001 and 2005, and it predicts they will increase by an average of 18.6 per cent per year between 2005 and 2009.[10] The economic significance of e-commerce in general, and of the porn industry in particular, brings considerable pressure to bear upon the US legal system.

PORN STUDIES AND POSTFEMINISM

In her recent collection *Porn Studies*, Linda Williams states that:

> Where once it seemed necessary to argue vehemently against pro-censorship, antipornography feminism for the value and importance of studying pornography ... today porn studies addresses a veritable explosion of sexually explicit materials that cry out for better understanding (Williams, 2004: 1).

Williams's rhetoric characterizes a predominant strain in current academic work on porn, which has not adequately dealt with the criticisms of anti-pornography feminists, the continuing expansion of the porn industry or the material conditions within which this has taken place.[11] The feminist pro-porn position, represented by writers and activists such as Gillian Rodgerson, Elizabeth Wilson, Mandy Merck and Lynne Segal in the UK, and Williams, Laura Kipnis, Susie Bright, Jane Juffer, Carole S. Vance and Pat Califia in the USA, has necessarily been characterized by a balance of political strategies. On the one hand, pro-porn feminists objected to the potential extension of state power demanded by anti-porn feminists, because they considered that legislative systems already enshrined patriarchal interests. They recognized the problematic affinity of anti-porn feminists with a wider coalition of right-wing politics, most famously demonstrated in Andrea Dworkin and Catherine MacKinnon's Minneapolis city ordinance of 1983. In order to try and pass legislation which defined pornography as sexual harassment, MacKinnon and Dworkin worked with right-wing politicians and invoked homophobic rhetoric – strategies which worked to violently split the feminist movement at the time. Such affinities can still be seen in the range of campaigns undertaken by anti-porn groups such as Concerned Women for America. Feminist politics of sexuality which informed anti-censorship positions rested on the presumption that in a patriarchal culture, women's access to affirmative cultural representations and women's ability to make sexual choices in their own interests had both been actively restricted by social institutions, and presumed that collective action was needed to understand and oppose such institutions. In the heated, polarized context of the porn wars this position necessitated strategic omissions and denials. The strategic need to argue for cultural outlets through which women, and especially lesbians, could explore sexual representation, meant that it became difficult to mount a sustained critical analysis of the overwhelmingly sexist nature of the porn industry.

This is especially urgent given the current power of the porn industry. Since the feminist porn wars began there have been enormous economic and technological shifts within capitalism: the deregulation of financial markets and the recession of state economic control, the deregulation of the media, the globalization of capital and the technological proliferation of media forms, most notably the

Internet, but also satellite, cable and digital TV. As a consequence, the range of financial and corporate institutions with interests in porn has grown considerably, significantly weakening right-wing calls for moral and social restriction in the very heartlands of neo-conservative power. It is clear that while Bush's team were happy to make strategic promises about getting tough on obscenity in order to secure the electoral support of groups like Concerned Women for America, once in power this agenda has effectively been mothballed.

In *Porn Studies*, Linda Williams notes the economic importance of porn, but accepts unproblematically the figures put forward by Frank Rich in the *New York Times* in 2001, where he estimates the value of the US porn industry to be between $10 and $14 billion.[12] The terms in which she notes the financial might of the porn industry indicate a kind of relief that the ground is now cleared for 'better understanding', rather than an acknowledgement that the sex wars weren't won in the field of feminism, in the name of social and sexual diversity, self-expression and female empowerment, but were rendered irrelevant by the growing economic power of porn and its importance in a context where state governments have long since abdicated responsibility to the market. Williams argues that:

> Where rape was once represented from a masculinist 'lie back and enjoy it' perspective in the old illegal stag films and in the early features, it has increasingly become taboo as women have become a component of the audience (Williams, 2004: 12).

There are two key issues to identify here: firstly, Williams suggests that porn has become less masculinist, and, secondly, she implies that this change is attributable not to feminist activism but to the market, in which women have become more visible as porn consumers. This position displays a troubling tendency towards a type of postfeminism which foregrounds individual rather than collective empowerment, and an entitlement to pleasure, where pleasure is not a function of political struggle, but of consumer choice (Sonnet, 1999). This is an ideological formation in which the rhetoric of female empowerment has been assimilated by capital, and where female empowerment becomes a function of consumer culture rather than one of a structural redistribution of gender power. And in this, postfeminism not only betrays the political potential of feminism but effectively forecloses the space for challenging the distribution of gender power, by displacing a collective political movement with individual and competitive instances of consumer power.

Is hardcore porn, which has undoubtedly proliferated over the last ten years, really less masculinist than it was? One key aspect of postfeminist ideology is its claim for women's 'right' to sexual pleasure. This 'right' works to naturalize heterosexuality: however economically and professionally emancipated the postfeminist woman is, this is culturally less significant than the continuing plausibility of her sexual desirability within heterosexuality, as a legion of iconic postfeminist texts, from *Bridget Jones's Diary* (2001) to *Sex and the City* (1998–2004), attest. Bridget Jones and Carrie Bradshaw offer a sexual politics that prioritizes romantic success in heterosexual relationships with men, where cute 'ditziness' is more important than professional and economic success. This 'right' to sexual pleasure is intricately bound up with the mainstreaming of sex, owing as much to commodification as to feminist sexual politics. But what constitutes the kind of sexual pleasures offered to women, or men, in contemporary hardcore?

FORCED ENTRY: LYING BACK AND ENJOYING IT?

The commercial release of *Forced Entry* consists of eight narrative scenes, framed by an additional introductory segment in which Rob Black directly addresses the camera, and by a short concluding segment, 'Behind the Scenes: Forced Entry', consisting of bloopers and shots from the set of the film. Of the eight narrative scenes, four contain sex acts and make up the bulk of the film's running time. The remaining four scenes feature Rob Black performing as spoof reporter Roberto Negro in pastiches of live news reporting. The four principal scenes depict the crimes of a fictional serial killer, played by the porn actor Luciano, who is inspired by the real-life serial killer Richard Ramirez, currently awaiting execution on California's death row. There is a significant generic disparity between the Roberto Negro scenes, which are facile, comic and relatively unscripted, and the sex scenes, which for all their use of gross-out techniques, lack humour. In the first sequence, Jewel DeNyle plays a woman who is attacked by a man (Luciano) who comes to her door to ask for directions. The film quality used here, as for all the sexual sequences, is grainy, deliberately lo-fi, with a slight fish-eye lens effect and darkened corners. The effect is to create a voyeuristic *mise-en-scène*, redolent of the conventions used in fly-on-the-wall documentaries. The man grabs the woman by the throat. When she screams, he slaps her, spits on her, pulls down her pants and fingers her. He then drags her up the stairs, spitting on her and slapping her as he does so. He tells her, 'I'm going to hurt you' and then rapes her. Throughout an *ad hoc* cycle of oral, vaginal and anal penetration, the female character cries and whimpers, while the male character verbally and physically assaults her ('you're not a virgin, you're a fucking teenaged whore'). The man puts his fingers in her mouth, stretching it wide, and spits in her face. He ejaculates on her face and then drags her into the bathroom, where he urinates on her face over the toilet, telling her he's cleaning the cum off to teach her a lesson. Back in the bedroom, on the bed, as his erection bobs about, the man takes a plastic bag from his jeans and wraps it around the woman's head. The film cuts to a series of slow-motion shots using gaudy coloured filters, and we infer that the woman is being suffocated. In the course of the scene, Luciano slaps Jewel 66 times.

The second scene works to establish the character of reporter Roberto Negro, played by Rob Black. The third scene opens with a girlish woman (Taylor St Claire) playing with a Yorkshire terrier on a couch, filmed in sepia tones. Two men, played by Luciano and Mickey G, enter, and the film switches to the same style of grainy colour used in the first scene. A battery icon temporarily appears in the corner of the screen, and there are frequent cuts throughout to a camcorder's blue screen. At one point Luciano's character turns to the camera and says, 'You getting this? Keep it rolling.' A voice off-camera replies that the woman is making too much noise, and it becomes clear that the images we're watching are supposedly being filmed by an accomplice of the characters played by Luciano and Mickey G. In the early parts of the scene, the cameraman expresses reservations ('I don't know about this, man') but as the scene progresses, he appears to become more excited and less apprehensive ('you're not fucking her hard enough'). The action proceeds very similarly to that in the first scene, with a few additions. The woman tells her attackers that she's pregnant and this becomes a motif throughout the scene, as they punch and slap her stomach: 'You're pregnant? Here's your abortion, you little cunt', and 'I'm going to punch the baby if you close your legs again'. The attacker played by Luciano again refers to Richard Ramirez, asking the woman if she knows the serial killer. Luciano pulls the woman's face towards the camera and tells her to 'say hello to Richard Ramirez'. At another point, Luciano looks into the camera and asks, 'Do you like what I'm doing to her, Richard?' The two men perform cycles of oral, vaginal and anal penetration on the woman, including a protracted sequence of double penetration. After they have both ejaculated on the woman's face, they shoot her and then the dog. In total, the two men slap and punch St Claire's character over 200 times in the course of the scene. This scene is again followed by one in which we see Roberto Negro outside the woman's home reporting the murder. In scene five, two men, one played by Luciano and the other by Brian Surewood, attack a woman, played by Veronica Caine, when her car breaks down. The sexual acts are similar to those in previous scenes, with similar levels of violence on the part of the men and distress on the part of the woman. In the course of the scene, Caine's character is slapped 69 times, and at the end the character played by Luciano stabs her in the stomach. As blood pours out of her mouth and wells up over her torso, he tosses a picture of Ramirez onto her body. Luciano addresses the camera as he rubs her blood up the walls: 'Did you like it?' The final three scenes of Forced Entry appear rushed and unfinished. They attempt to tie up the narrative of the film, and feature Rob Black in his persona as both Roberto Negro and a police officer. At the climax of the film, the killer played by Luciano is chased up an alley by a mob of men who stab and beat him to death.

In what appears to be a direct dialogue with the PBS documentary American Porn (2002), Black's opening monologue and the concluding 'Behind the Scenes: Forced Entry' segment both work self-consciously as justification of the film. In Black's opening segment, he tells us we are about to see the movie that's been causing all the controversy and which was featured in the PBS documentary. He tells us that there's a blooper reel at the end of the film in which we see one of the female actors get her hair piece accidentally knocked off, and in which the actors start laughing; as he speaks, we are shown the clip. Black tells us that the film crew we see in shot are in fact the PBS crew. He ridicules the fact that the documentary didn't discuss such relaxed and amusing moments on set, and instead implied that Extreme Associates take girls off the street and abuse them. He reminds us that the film only uses professional actors and is made as a fictional piece of entertainment, a movie. In the 'Behind the Scenes' segment, we see a variety of short clips, including one in which we hear a female voice, presumably Borden's, off camera telling DeNyle to fight back more, several in which we see the actors blocking out fight scenes and sex acts, and one in which we see the wrap of scene five, where Veronica Caine gets up off the floor, still covered in fake blood, with the picture of Richard Ramirez still stuck to her chest. She pulls it off, rips it up, and, wiping it between her buttocks, says, 'I'll wipe my ass with that fucker'. The inclusion of these extra-diegetic elements is noteworthy when one bears in mind that this is a porn film, and they were contained on the original VHS release of *Forced Entry*, and thus literally frame the film in a linear way, unlike the behind-the-scenes special features increasingly included on DVD releases of porn films.

Forced Entry raises a series of issues about the representational status of hardcore pornography. On the one hand, professionals perform within the confines of a script as in other kinds of narrative film; on the other hand, the distinctiveness of hardcore rests on an understanding that the sex acts undertaken for the camera are in some sense 'real' rather than simulated. In *Hardcore*, Linda Williams argues that the genre seeks to gain knowledge of 'female wonders', but instead discovers the limits of visibility. She suggests that we should avoid seeing hardcore as 'sex itself', and recognize the 'futility of assimilating hardcore to a simple case of escalating verisimilitude'; as such, the money shot is not documentary evidence of sexual pleasure, but a 'rhetorical figure that permits the genre to speak in a certain way about sex' (Williams, 1989: 94). It is clear that in some of the critical responses to *Forced Entry* there is a slippage in which the action depicted in the film is viewed differently from that seen in other kinds of narrative film. The catalyst for this critical slippage is *Forced Entry*'s conflation of sex and violence.

Each sexual scene depicts acts of rape and physical abuse, where the narrative and performative verisimilitude of the violence persists throughout the genital acts to the conclusion of the scene. This is in contrast to a more generically familiar depiction of rape, in both straight and gay hardcore, where the victim initially protests against the assault, but in the course of the genital acts becomes a willing participant. Such narrative coherence attests to the sophisticated production values employed in contemporary hardcore, and the self-consciousness with which representational conventions are employed by Borden. In *Forced Entry*, the recurring motif of Richard Ramirez and the use of direct address to camera by the character played by Luciano ('Do you like what I'm doing to her, Richard?') has the effect of reinforcing the narrative depiction of violence and implicating the spectator in the acts being committed. At times it appears as if the character of Luciano is addressing us as Ramirez, at others that we are members of Luciano's gang.

The Roberto Negro scenes featuring Rob Black are characterized by crude irony, but Borden chooses not to transpose this technique to the depiction of sex and violence. *Forced Entry*, like much of the rest of Extreme Associates' output, may derive its stylistic and generic cues from *Jackass* stunts and the parodic conventions of postmodern slasher films like the *Scream* series, but hardcore conventions rest upon an excess of literal genital display that constantly demonstrates the non-simulated nature of the sex acts. This literal genital display resists the potential for comedy and disrupts the potential *Forced Entry* might have had for becoming pleasurably parodic in its knowing use of postmodern devices. But the key issue here is gender power. Where *Jackass* offers male homosocial pleasures rooted in a self-consciously sadomasochistic masculinity, and *Scream* parodies tropes of female helplessness in slasher movies, *Forced Entry* is unwilling to risk alienating its porn audience by parodying the rigid conventions that constitute the genre of hardcore, and instead intensifies them, turning women into debased receptacles. Thus, instead of the gore and violence working to ironically deconstruct the phallic dominance implicit in the representation of genital acts, the slasher devices become less ironic and playful, precisely because *Forced Entry* makes no attempt to disrupt potential phallic identification. Crucially, the organization of genital acts offered by *Forced Entry* is emblematic of a contemporary style of hardcore, characterized by repetitive cycles of penetration, from mouth to vagina to anus to mouth, vagina and back again, the visual and affective pleasures of which lie in the performative supremacy of a large penetrating penis, and the denigration of women, whose bodies become mere collections of gaping orifices. Thus it is the extra-diegetic introduction and 'Behind the Scenes' segments that bear the weight of any parodic or ironic intent. While the figure of the rapist is killed by a mob at the end of the film, this appears to be a sloppy attempt to resolve the narrative presented in the Roberto Negro scenes and doesn't have sufficient meaning to dislodge the identification with the violence and sexual sadism of the character played by Luciano.

Forced Entry represents an exemplification of a current trend in porn, and one that is becoming increasingly prevalent and raises questions about the status of female pleasure and female physiology in hardcore. In *Hardcore* (1989), Linda Williams offers a historical analysis of the emergence of a linear progression of genital acts in the hardcore feature, culminating in external ejaculation. This progression, from arousal and foreplay, through to penetration and orgasm, is an organizing structure familiar to the hardcore spectator and offers a logic of human sexual physiology derived from Kinsey (1948, 1953). The linear progression of genital events has become increasingly reconfigured by current hardcore conventions. While scenes retain the climactic significance of external male ejaculation, this is often preceded, not with a linear progression from foreplay to penetration, but with mechanized cycles of penetration from one orifice to another. Rather than representing a series of genital acts that correspond to a recognizable accumulation of corresponding sexual pleasure in both parties, current conventions organize the depiction of genital acts solely according to the logic of penile stimulation, by hand, mouth, vagina or anus, and multiple combinations thereof. In *Forced Entry* and similar contemporary hardcore, women's bodies are penetrated cyclically, often with particular emphasis on double penetration or on female performers sucking a penis after having been anally penetrated by it (Luciano to Jewel: 'Are you going to taste your ass, you filthy cunt?'). Such cycles of penetration are usually performed without any clitoral stimulation, or any other kind of genital act that would signify female sexual pleasure that isn't a function of phallic performativity. Paul Willemen has recently suggested that:

> Phallic endurance ... is the defining dimension of the porn narrative ... women are the raw material required for this demonstration ... In the industrial production of porn films, the men figure as 'plant' along with other bits of machinery necessary to keep the factory going. The women function more like the different kinds of meat processed and canned for sale in the supermarkets (Willemen, 2004: 21).

As part of this non-linear, cyclical organization, acts of oral sex performed by female actors are invariably marked by signs of choking: gagging noises on the soundtrack, difficulty in breathing, facial redness, copious amounts of saliva. Rocco Siffredi, one of the most prominent and prolific male performers and directors in hardcore, is well known for the prolonged sequences of choking in his films and for his interest in anal sex. The box cover of *Rocco Meats Trinity* (2004) may have a tag line that tells us that 'Rocco is rough!! – And Trinity loves it!!' but it's clear in watching the film that Trinity becomes increasingly distressed by her inability to breathe as Rocco holds his penis down her throat. As the scene progresses, he has to work harder to get her to continue to suck him and her face becomes streaked with tears and saliva.[13] There are serious questions to ask here about the treatment of female performers in the industry and about the potential the genre has to realize Linda Williams's hopes for representations of female sexual agency. In a context where women's bodies have increasingly become 'meat' repositories for masculinist phallic display, we have to interrogate hardcore in a way that isn't foreclosed by what are increasingly becoming postfeminist preoccupations with entitlements to pleasure as a function of consumer empowerment: Williams's critical engagement with hardcore is limited by her faith in the idea of women as porn consumers. Consumer choice may be a potentially important mode of social and political citizenship, but the current state of porn requires other and more critical forms of engagement as well, especially if we consider that women's increasing consumption of porn runs parallel to the kinds of trends in extreme porn I've been examining here. As consumers, are the women Williams lauds buying porn, or buying *into* porn, and how are we to assess the effects of their consumer interventions?

Linda Williams is right when she suggests that we need an increased level of critical literacy in relation to porn, and yet it's frustrating that contemporary critiques of porn don't offer more biting critical engagement. I would argue that this project is especially urgent given the conditions that are driving the mainstreaming of sex. Censorship hasn't been held in abeyance by the liberationary potential many anti-censorship feminists recognized in porn, but by the interests of capital, as the case of United States v. Extreme Associates demonstrates. The mainstreaming of sex is in part being driven by a porn industry ideally placed to take advantage of the current conditions of capital. Pornography's asset base has considerable plasticity in terms of generating multiple commodities from one inexpensive production; it is a lean business in which profitability is high and overheads are low. And while politics and popular culture are key areas where we would note the impact of sex on the mainstream, this is actually a manifestation of underlying economic shifts whereby pornography has become a vital revenue stream not only for the world's largest entertainment corporations but for credit-card companies and high-tech businesses. Pornography is 'the handmaiden of new technology' (Maddison, 2004).

This necessitates a rather more urgent and material engagement with the real conditions of the porn industry than much of current academic porn studies offer. This is especially true in the context of the position of women in porn, both in terms of the meanings of pornographic representations of women and in terms of the position of women working in porn. The new extreme post-gonzo hardcore debases women in a way that is particularly disturbing given both the popularity of hardcore and its wider cultural significance in the context of mainstreaming. The genital acts required of female performers in the new hardcore genres are increasingly risky in terms of HIV transmission. Condom use in the heterosexual sector of the industry is negligible, and the gay sector is dispensing with them as well. Hardcore increasingly demonstrates a tendency to constitute women's bodies as 'meat' receptacles for phallic performance and this ideology isn't only being mainstreamed by pornography. The success of Viagra has led to a resurgence of biomedical discourses of sexuality, in which understandings of male sexual function have become synonymous with erectile performance, and female sexual function is defined by 'the viability of the vagina for receiving the erect penis (Marshall, 2002). The ubiquity of porn, and the increasing tendency of hardcore to constitute women as 'raw material' for demonstrations of phallic endurance, clearly requires further and urgent consideration. It may be the case, as Williams has said, that the new porn studies 'diverge markedly from the kind of agonizing over sexual politics that characterized an earlier era of the study of pornography' (2004: 1), but in the process they risk becoming irrelevant. The mainstreaming of sex, and the proliferation of porn require a political analysis that engages with the material and representational conditions driving them.

NOTES

1. Jake Tapper, 'Court Deals Blow to USA Anti-Porn Campaign', ABC News, http://abcnews.go.co/Nightline/print?id=433956 (accessed 2.5.06).

2. That is, films which focus on the sexual attractiveness of their female performers rather than the particular kinds of sexual acts that take place in them.

3. The *Adult Video News* top ten VHS and DVD rental titles in September 2006 included only one 'couples' film (*Taken*, 2006), the rest comprising titles such as *Jesse Jane: Sexual Freak* (2006), *Barely Legal Schoolgirls* (2006), *Ass Worship 9* (2006) and *Back 2 Evil 2* (2006), http://www.avn.com/index.php?Primary_Navigation=Charts (accessed 11.9.06).

4. http://www.pbs.org/wgbh/pages/frontline/shows/porn/interviews/black.html (accessed 2.5.06).

5. Greg Beato (2004), 'Xtreme Measures: Washington's New Crackdown on Pornography', http://www.reason.com/0405/fe.gb.xtreme.shtml (accessed 23.5.06).

6. An *amicus curiae*, or friend of court, is someone not a party to the case who volunteers to offer information on a point of law or some other aspect of the case to assist the court in deciding a matter before it. See http://courts.delaware.gov/How%20To/court%20proceedings/?ccpglossary.htm for a glossary of legal terms and http://www.nationallawcenter.org/current-news/extreme-associates-3d-circuit-decision.html. See also http://www.cwfa.org/radio.asp?broadcastID=2488&mode=detail for the relevant *amici curiae*. (All accessed 2.5.06).

7. http://www.avn.com/index.php?Primary_Navigation=Articles&Action=View_Article&Content_ID=214089 (accessed 2.5.06).

8. Jared Rutter (2005), 'Extreme Associates Case Dismissed', *Adult Video News*, http://www.avn.com/index.php?Primary_Navigation=Articles&Action=View_Article&Content_ID=214089 (accessed 2.5.06; my emphasis).

9. Eric Winston (2006), 'United States of America v. Extreme Associates: The Internet Misunderstood', http://www.ynot.com/modules.php?op=modload&name=News&file=ea_article&sid=10354&mode=thread&order=0&thold=0 (accessed 5.5.06).

10. http://www.emarketer.com/Report.aspx?ecom_USA_jun06 (accessed 5.5.06).

11. See also McNair, 2002.

12. Frank Rich (2001), 'Naked Capitalists: There's No Business Like Porn Business', *New York Times Magazine*, 18 May 2001. See Maddison, 2004 for a critique of Rich's figures, and discussion of the difficulty of estimating the financial value of porn.

13. It is worth noting that similar tendencies are emerging in gay porn. A recent film, *Gag the Fag* (2004), promises the spectacle of men 'face-fucked until they cough, choke, and even puke!' And while it is standard practice for heterosexual hardcore to be filmed without the use of condoms, in the last few years gay bareback porn has become increasingly visible and popular.

Chapter 4

FROM PORN CHIC TO PORN FEAR: THE RETURN OF THE REPRESSED?

BRIAN MCNAIR

An important strand in the ongoing sexualization of the mainstream cultures of advanced capitalist societies has been their 'pornographication' (McNair, 1996, 2002). The term refers to the cross-over of pornography from the private to the public sphere – what Linda Williams portrayed as a journey from the ob/scene of the back room, men-only stag reel to the on-scene of commercialized, industrialized porn made for every taste and perversion and consumed by women as well as men, gay as well as straight (Williams, 1989). It describes the fascination with pornography that emerged, from the late 1980s especially, in the worlds of high art and popular culture, in Hollywood cinema and literature, advertising and fashion, in journalism and the scholarly outputs of the academy. Porn became 'chic' in these contexts, insofar as talking about, referring to or borrowing from its codes and conventions had lost much of its transgressive, taboo quality and become acceptable, even fashionable. In the academy, it became possible to take the pornographic seriously without attracting opprobrium. Where pornography had been generally viewed as the 'pariah of representational practice' (Ellis, 1992: 158), now it was increasingly acknowledged as the appropriate object of scholarly work on sexuality and the media.

Where anti-pornography perspectives largely defined the feminist study of sexualized culture for most of the 1980s and into the 1990s (Itzin, 1992), more typical of feminist scholarship in recent times have been Pamela Church Gibson's edited collections of essays, *Dirty Looks* (1993), and its revised edition, *More Dirty Looks* (2004),[1] and Linda Williams's *Porn Studies* (2004). These volumes have explored, from within feminist theoretical frameworks, the often paradoxical pleasures of the pornographic. In Australia, Catherine Lumby's *Bad Girls* (1997) asserted women's right to participate fully in the liberalized sexual culture – including the consumption of pornography – which, in her view, feminism had by then done much to bring into existence. Camille Paglia (1990, 1993) and Laura Kipnis (1996) in the USA drew attention to what they read as the power embodied in female sexuality and its representation, even when that sexuality was expressed in ways which radical feminists of the 1980s would have regarded as deeply troubling, such as S&M imagery. These authors rejected the 'porn-fear' of the late 1970s and 1980s in favour of a more experience-based approach to understanding the factors underpinning the historic emergence and contemporary ubiquity of the pornographic.

There is growing resistance to the mainstreaming of porn, however, from those who resist many, if not all, of the phenomena associated with 'pornographication' and the broader, feminized sexualization of culture embodied, for example, in the rise of CAKE, a New York based social networking organization run by 'committed feminists' and dedicated to the 'women's sexuality market'.[2] A recent *Guardian* article reported that 'the mainstreaming of the porn and sex industries' had triggered a recent growth in anti-porn feminist organizations in the UK, such as Sheffield Fems at Sheffield University, dedicated to campaigning against top-shelf magazines, lad mags and the view, as anti-porn blogger Charliegrrl put it, that 'porn used to be men perving in their bedrooms, something hush-hush. Lads' mags and the attendant lad culture are normalising not just our objectification, but our harassment' (Bell, 2007).

Debates between anti-porn and pro-porn voices are not new, of course, but they have been fuelled in recent times by high-profile books by Catharine MacKinnon (2006), Ariel Levy (2005) and others, within and outside of the feminist movement (Paul, 2005). Against that background this chapter reviews the process of the pornographication of mainstream culture, and asks if the pendulum is now swinging away from porn chic.

PORNOGRAPHICATION AND PROGRESSIVE SEXUAL POLITICS

Since the cinematic release of *Deep Throat* (Gerard Damiano, 1972) and the first wave of porn chic in the 1970s, the pornographication of mainstream culture has parallelled a transformation of the sexpolitical environment of Western societies. Many observers have linked the two trends, viewing pornographication as a significant factor in the emergence of feminism, gay rights and other forms of hitherto marginalized sexual identity politics (Watney, 1987; McNair, 1996 and 2002). From this perspective the growing availability of gay and lesbian porn, for example, has played an important role in articulating and servicing 'the needs of still stigmatised communities' (McNair, 1996: 132). Likewise, the critical and popular success of artists such as Robert Mapplethorpe and Grace Lau, who have used the visual grammar and vocabulary of pornography as a tool in their work, has brought heightened cultural visibility to hitherto hidden lifestyles and subcultures.

The critical acclaim which attached to Mapplethorpe's homoerotic photography in the 1980s, for example, signalled and solidified a cultural climate in which the discourses and desires of homosexual men could begin to be accepted by mainstream publics. 'Gay art', it turned out – even Mapplethorpe's sexually explicit, sadomasochistic images – could henceforth be appreciated in galleries all over the world, with as much reverence as had traditionally been extended to the Great Straight Men of art history.

The validation of Mapplethorpe's porn-inspired art by the uptown New York arbiters of aesthetic taste, like the paintings of Keith Haring at around the same time, or the sexually transgressive installations of Gilbert and George in Britain, was both cause and consequence of the growing ease with which late twentieth-century capitalist societies were learning to live with the cultural articulation of sexual diversity. In Mapplethorpe's work, as in that of many other artists, the blurring

of the traditional art/porn boundary was linked to a political project
– in this case, the project of gay liberation. Just at the moment when
HIV/AIDS was threatening its existence, Mapplethorpe's work made
the underground world of bath houses and cruising visible and the
subject of public discourse. His sexually explicit photographs, which
he himself was entirely happy to compare in their form and function with porn, became a document of and testament to the cour-
age of a community under biological as well as political assault, part
of an environment within which pop stars like George Michael and
Elton John could come out, bands like Bronski Beat and Frankie
Goes To Hollywood have hit records, and gay villages be established
in cities all over the world. Homophobia persisted in many quarters,
of course, and still does, but it was no longer the default position of
respectable straight society. Just as sexism has become a recognized
wrong, even though there are still sexists, homophobia moved from
the realm of broad social consensus to that of acknowledged ideological dysfunction, routinely contested in many arenas of cultural
and public life. In Britain in 2007, the Conservative Party leader was
defending same-sex civil unions, discriminatory laws on pension and
adoption rights were being repealed, and the traditional homophobia
of institutions such as the military and the churches was being challenged to an unprecedented degree.

   While it is impossible to prove direct cause-and-effect connections
between the artistic contribution of a Haring or a Mapplethorpe and
the gradual public acceptance of homosexuality as an identity and a
lifestyle, it is equally difficult to argue that there is no relationship
between the two. What is clear is that one consequence of the process of emergence of homosexual identity into mainstream culture
was the heightened visibility of homoerotic sexual representation,
and this included the explicit imagery contained in gay porn and the
art/culture which referenced or drew on it. Mainstream coverage of
these images in turn raised all manner of sex-political issues in the
public sphere, such as the social meaning of HIV/AIDS.

   A similar relationship with sexual politics characterized the
frequently explicit, sexually transgressive work of artists such as
Cindy Sherman[3] and the later waves of 'bad girls' with whom she was
grouped (Institute of Contemporary Art, 1993). In the sphere of popu-

lar culture, the publication of Madonna's *Sex* (1992), with its references to and borrowings from porn, was a global media event, albeit one accompanied at the time by much moral and critical disdain. From this distance it is arguable that the book, and her music and video work in general, have been a major influence on art and popular culture in the last two decades, without which younger generations of performers such as Kylie Minogue, Christina Aguilera and Britney Spears would look and sound very different.[4] While assessments of Madonna's contribution to feminist politics diverged widely then, and still do, there is no doubt that she herself, and those who championed her, saw *Sex* and the rest of her sexually transgressive output as a sustained attempt to redefine female sexuality in the postfeminist era (Frank and Smith, 1993). For Camille Paglia, writing in 1993, Madonna's engagement with pornographic imagery represented 'a new kind of feminism, one that stresses personal responsibility and is open to art and sex in all their dark, unconsoling mystery' (1993: vii).

By the early years of the new millennium, pornographication had proceeded to the point where porn chic often acquired a parodic quality that was not necessarily intentional. In September 2001 the *Australian* newspaper reported with characteristic 'ozzie' irreverence on artist Lee-Anne Richards' *Arseholes* exhibition at Photo Technica in Sydney, 'featuring a series of chicks chucking what can only be described as brown eyes' (Tom, 2001). Richards's intention, as she put it, was 'to challenge the idea of the male gaze in pornography. What is unsettling about the photos is the fact they follow porn conventions up to a point and then fall short, or perhaps go a little too far in some directions. The effect is a bit unnerving.' In London a year later the Turner Prize was won by Fiona Banner for works including *Arsewoman in Wonderland*. Banner, explained the blurb accompanying *Arsewoman*, 'uses pornographic film to explore sexuality and the extreme limits of written communication'.

One could cite many more examples of women discussing and working with the conventions and discourses of porn, sometimes to critique its heterosexist and masculinist content, but more often to explore and comment on its transgressive appeal *to* women, or to subvert its patriarchal origins and applications in pursuit of a more satisfying porn-*for*-women.

The success of artists like Mapplethorpe and Madonna in the mainstream cultural marketplace may be read as an index of the emerging political and cultural power of gay men and women – and of women in general – as consumers and sexual citizens. Through their work, and its frequent celebration of the pornographic, these and other artists made visible in mainstream culture sexually defined communities whose desires, demands and discourses were not necessarily those preferred by patriarchy, but could still be accommodated and marketed within a culture which remained predominantly patriarchal.

And this was not only a Western trend. In the case of photographer Nobuyoshi Araki, the huge success of his transgressive S&M-themed images (2005) – which often deliberately set out to look like pornography – has reflected what many observers have identified as a profound change in the sex-political environment of Japan. The enthusiastic participation of Japanese women as models in Araki's work, and his status as an impish, Dionysian celebrity artist, has accompanied the transformation of women's socio-economic status in that country, a shift reflected also in the growth of the women's porn market. A recent study notes that eromanga made for women accounts for about 10 per cent of the Japanese porn market (Shamoon, 2004).[5]

PORN IN THE MULTIPLEX

A further dimension of pornographication has been the expansion of that sub-genre of films which, though they do not present themselves as pornography, reference or pay homage to it in various ways. This trend should be viewed as distinct from the broader liberalization of film censorship regimes over many decades, and the fact that mainstream Hollywood became more sexually explicit in 1980s and early 1990s as can be seen in films such as *The Postman Always Rings Twice* (1981), *Henry and June* (1990) and *Basic Instinct* (1992).

The more specific category of porn chic exemplified by movies such as *Boogie Nights* (1997) and *The People Versus Larry Flynt* (1996) emerged in the 1990s, reflecting in mainstream cinema the changed attitudes towards and heightened interest in the pornographic fuelled by Mapplethorpe, Madonna and others. Where films such as *Basic Instinct* can be viewed as products of a more general pushing of the boundaries in cinematic sexual representation, these 1990s works directly addressed pornography as a subject, even if they did not – could not, given their marketing as mainstream commercial fare – show penetrative sex or other activities associated with hardcore pornography. Where *Deep Throat* – and the first wave of porn chic which it initiated – was an explosion into mainstream culture of 'authentic' porn, the second wave can be so described because it was *about* porn, often focused on the industry that produces it. Porn chic in the 1990s broke with hitherto prevalent anti-porn perspectives by portraying pornographers, performers and consumers, not as depraved deviants, but as ordinary people, with all the flaws and imperfections of other people and other businesses. Where a late 1970s movie like Paul Schrader's *Hard Core* exemplified the porn fear of that era, with its tale of a deeply religious patriarch searching for a daughter lost to the LA porn industry, *Boogie Nights* and *The People Versus Larry Flynt* made the porn business the backdrop for often tragic but ultimately redemptive human dramas. Porn chic of a less critically celebrated kind has continued in films like *The Girl Next Door* (2004) and *The Moguls* (2005), two comedies where the fact of a porn industry in which decent human beings might work is taken for granted.

After the critical and commercial success of *Boogie Nights*, porn chic migrated to television. *Rated X* (2000) took elements of *Boogie Nights* and *The People Versus Larry Flynt* to craft a bio-pic of San Francisco based porn pioneers, the Mitchell brothers, while *Dirty Pictures* (2000) dramatized the anti-censorship battles fought by the curator of the Philadelphia Art Museum when he tried to mount a Mapplethorpe retrospective in 1989. British TV in the late 1990s and early 2000s broadcast a wave of documentaries about pornography, such as Louis Theroux's sympathetic study of the LA porn scene for Channel 4 (2001), the docu-soap *Porn: A Family Business* (2003) and *Pornography: The Musical* (2003), in which original musical numbers were performed by real-life porn stars, punctuated by graphic visual and verbal accounts of what it felt like to be in a watersports or bukkake movie. The German beer manufacturer Grolsch ran a TV ad campaign pastiching a porn set, complete with mustachioed plumber and sex-obsessed housewife. The Jerry Bruckheimer produced *Skin* (2003), about the porn industry, premiered on Fox in the US in October 2003, followed by HBO's reality show *Pornucopia* in 2004. A stage musical version of *Debbie Does Dallas* toured the world in 2005. Few of these manifestations of porn chic had the critical or commercial impact of *Boogie Nights* or *The People Versus Larry Flynt*. They indicated, however, the extent to which the subject of pornography had, by the early twenty-first century, migrated even into the worlds of primetime TV and musical theatre.

A form of pornographication was also evident in art-house cinema, in films such as Catherine Breillat's *Romance* (1999), with its episodic structure of girl-seeks-sexual-satisfaction-from-increasingly-perverse-encounters-with-a-succession-of-men. Breillat followed *Romance* with two further sexually explicit works, *A Ma Soeur* in 2001 and *Sex Is Comedy* in 2002, and then with *Anatomy of Hell* (2004), featuring Italian porn star Rocco Siffredi in another episodic tale of sadomasochistic desire. The French new wave of cinematic transgression, in which Breillat had been a key figure, included the rape-revenge drama *Baise Moi* (2000). The film, based on Virginie Despentes's novel of the same name, combined the nihilistic violence directed against men and women which characterizes many of the more boundary-breaking French films of that period with explicit sex scenes of the type normally found only in porn, including slow-motion money shots, cheap video effects and group sex scenes. Lucas Moodyson's *A Hole in My Heart* (2004) depicted the making of an extreme 'DIY' porn video in a bleak Danish housing estate. Moodyson's film, though very different in tone from P.T. Anderson's big-budget Hollywood production, echoed *Boogie Nights* in its depiction of the porn industry as a surrogate family structure.[6]

Distinct from porn chic, but a related part of the processes of pornographication and cultural sexualization which produced the former, were cinematic works of unprecedented explicitness such as Patrice Chereaux's *Intimacy* (2001), based on Hanif Kureishi's confessional novel and depicting various sex acts including fellatio. While representations of blowjobs are not new to mainstream cinema

(Warhol's *Blow Job* was screened in 1966), this one was shown in full frontal, and performed by the highly regarded actress Kerry Fox. Not intended to be read as pornographic, insofar as its explicit sexual content was mediated by the austere realism of the film's *mise-en-scène*, *Intimacy* was nonetheless a radical break with the tightly censored sexual content of films classified for 18 year olds and older in Britain up to that time.

Subsequently, directors such as Michael Winterbottom have pushed the boundaries of the sexually explicit still further. Winterbottom's *9 Songs* was described on its release in 2003 as 'the most sexually explicit mainstream film ever made' (Higgins, 2004). Comprising a series of sexual encounters between its two protagonists, punctuated by their attendance at live performances by the Dandy Warhols and others, the intention and effect of the piece is, like *Intimacy*, far removed from that of pornography. The sex is just as explicit as one would find in what was once regarded as hardcore porn, however, and the episodic, narrative-lite structure of the film is clearly influenced by the porn genre. At Cannes, the film's producer went to some lengths to deny any suggestion that, blowjobs, penetration scenes and come shots notwithstanding, the film could be regarded as 'some kind of kinky porno flick'.[7] Nonetheless the appearance of a film like *9 Songs* in early twenty-first century Britain would have been inconceivable without the climate created by the pornographication of the previous decade.

In 2006 the US-produced *Shortbus* toured multiplexes across the world, presenting audiences with still more graphic sex scenes involving its gay, straight and bisexual protagonists. *Shortbus* was marketed as a comedy, and is indeed a charming, genuinely funny film, in which the sex scenes are embedded in a narrative about personal development and sexual discovery. But from the first scene, in which we see one character perform fellatio on himself and including a money shot, to a gay threesome involving analingus, this is a film which presumes an audience comfortable with explicit sexual representation.

One measure of the extent of cultural sexualization evident by the early twenty-first century was the fact that none of these films attracted anything like the public controversy that greeted David

Cronenberg's *Crash* as recently as 1996. Benefitting from a more liberal classification regime introduced by the BBFC at the turn of the millennium, *Baise Moi*, like *9 Songs* and *Shortbus*, was given an '18' rating in the UK and screened all over the country with no significant protest. My copy was purchased for £5 in a high-street record store, where it nestled next to *Bewitched* (2005). As with *9 Songs* and others, attempts by the producers to generate publicity with media pieces declaring that here was 'the most sexually explicit mainstream film ever made' failed to generate significant moral opposition, or indeed substantial audience interest. Despite widespread coverage of its sexual content, *9 Songs* earned only about £200,000 at the UK box office, as compared to the £45 million earned by the average Harry Potter movie in the same market. Art-house movies are not often big earners at the box office, of course – my point is that while films such as *Last Tango In Paris* (1972) became global cultural events in the 1970s because of their transgressive sexual content, 30 years later we had become so immunized to the shock effect of explicit sexuality that much more graphic works could routinely be shown at the local multiplex without attracting attention, let alone the kinds of protests which made Cronenberg's *Crash* notorious.

If the response to films such as *9 Songs* and *Shortbus* indicated the declining capacity of the sexually explicit to shock, there remained visible throughout this period a critical media discourse on porn mainly focused on the harms caused to performers. A 2001 Channel 4 documentary, *Hardcore*, explored the disturbing world of LA-based producer Max Hardcore, whose speciality is the verbal and physical degradation of the women who appear in his movies. Novelist Martin Amis, whose 1980s novels frequently used pornography as a metaphor for Thatcherism, penned an accompanying essay in the UK *Guardian* (2001) expressing his revulsion for Hardcore's output. In 1998 Joel Schumacher's *8mm* remade Paul Schrader's *Hardcore* (1979) with Nicholas Cage as the wounded father in search of a child – lost, in this case, to the underground world of the snuff movie. Coming after *Boogie Nights* and *The People Versus Larry Flynt*, *8mm* was clearly intended as a riposte to the promoters of porn chic.

Gough Lewis's *Sex: The Annabel Chong Story* (1998) started off as an apparent endorsement, even celebration, of porn's artistic and academic legitimacy, before veering off into a study of the damaged psyche of its subject and the disturbing spectacle of her participation in 'the world's largest gang bang' which gives the film its narrative structure. *Autofocus* (2002) dramatized the destructive effect on the marriage, career, and ultimately life, of an interest in do-it-yourself porn by the real-life TV actor Bob Crane, star of 1960s US sitcom *Hogan's Heroes* (1965–71). Set in the era when domestic video recorders were just becoming available, the film's sleazy milieu and stern moral tone make a neat companion piece to Schrader's *Hardcore* of two decades before. Around the same time *Wonderland* (2003) provided a more fact-based account of the incident in *Boogie Nights* involving drugs and guns which marked the low point of Dirk Diggler's descent into Hollywood hell. In contrast to *Boogie Nights'* surrogate family of quirky but sympathetic characters, the pornosphere depicted in *Autofocus* and *Wonderland* is a world inhabited by the unredeemably sleazy, the dysfunctional and the criminal.

Where porn chic downplayed or contested the darker side of the porn industry, these films, whether in documentary or fictional form, put them at centre stage. But where, a few years before, such perspectives occupied the default position for most debate on the role and impact of pornography, now they were received as somewhat peripheral commentaries on a process of pornographication which, by the start of the new millennium, looked irreversible.[8]

PORNOGRAPHICATION AND THE SEXUALIZATION OF CULTURE

While the market for mediated sex, and porn in particular, continued to be dominated by materials produced for and consumed by men, pornographication was a trend in which women were increasingly prominent both as producers and consumers. In February 2002 A.C. Grayling observed that 'one of the marks of the age is the sexual liberation of women, whose magazines never fail to discuss aspects of it, and for whom elegant sex shops and subtle pornography are now mainstream'. Away from the galleries and art-house cinemas where Breillat and others presented their porn-influenced wares, a feminized culture of sexual consumption and expression flourished in Ann Summers high-street stores, reported to be turning over £150 million a year in the UK, mainly to female customers (Davidson, 2006), and in the phenomenon of social networking organizations such as CAKE. In November 2005 the *Guardian* newspaper reported the efforts of *Scarlet*, 'the magazine that turns women on', to secure distribution in Tesco stores in the UK.

Susan Faludi (1991) famously used the term 'backlash' to describe what she argued was a patriarchal reaction to the growing power of women in the 1980s. There is evidence of another kind of backlash now under way, which targets the pornographication of mainstream culture.

On the one hand, the rise of the religious right, and its widely acknowledged influence on the Bush White House, has increased opposition to cultural sexualization in the United States, and to pornographication and the advances in sexual identity politics which I am arguing have accompanied it. But in 2004 when Janet Jackson revealed a stud-adorned breast as she performed with Justin Timberlake in front of a stadium full of football fans and a television audience estimated at 80 million, 200,000 viewers complained. The incident was interpreted as another landmark in the inappropriate sexualization of popular culture. The US Federal Communications Commission launched an investigation, and MTV, the organization responsible for the broadcast, responded by pushing the transmission of promotional videos by Britney Spears and others back into the late night schedule, citing as the reason the emergence of a more censorious cultural environment.

One month before the Jackson incident, Paul Verhoeven and Brian De Palma had complained to Linda Ruth Williams in *Sight & Sound* that the golden era of cultural liberalism in the American cinema was over (Williams, 2004). In their view as working filmmakers, mainstream Hollywood in the era of George W. Bush was becoming increasingly nervous about funding the kind of boundary-breaking films which had made both directors' reputations in the 1980s and 1990s.[9]

There had of course always been opposition to pornographication and its associated trends in the USA, as exemplified by Senator Jesse Helms's brandishing of some of the more transgressive Mapplethorpe photographs in a 1989 speech denouncing the 'National Endowment for the Arts' funding of these and other sexually transgressive works. The difference, as some commentators perceived it, was that the culture warriors of the 'moral majority' were now installed securely in the White House, at a time (post-9/11) when religiosity and moral conservativism were in the ascendant in the West. Alongside US government crackdowns on the porn industry went renewed efforts to restrict abortion rights, to halt or roll back the legalization of gay civil unions and adoption, and strengthen the family.

These signs of renewed 'culture wars' around sexual representation, accompanied by resistance in many of the same quarters to the acceptance of diverse sexual lifestyles, were in part a response to major changes in the sex-political environment since the 1980s in which pornographication played a role. They were given added impetus, however, not just by the ascendancy of moral conservatism in the White House, but by the heightened visibility of sexual morality issues produced by 9/11 and the subsequent 'clash of cultures'. Research has still to be conducted on the nature of the link, if indeed there is any, which exists between the global rise of religious conflict and the resurgence of Christian-led opposition to sexual liberalization in the West. That there might be such a link seems a reasonable working hypothesis, however. And while there is little evidence of concrete success in attempts to roll back the progressive sexual politics of the recent past, even in the USA where the campaign is most intense, there are no grounds for complacency as the global cultural and political environments continue to be shaped by a 'clash of civilizations' in which one form of religious extremism squares up to another, with sexual liberalism often the focus of the battle.

It is not only moral conservatives who have expressed heightened anxiety around pornographication and related trends in sexual culture, however. Within feminist commentary and scholarship, too, there has been a resurgence of debates around the meaning of cultural sexualization, and in particular the sexualization, objectification and commodification of the female body by women themselves. The rise of what Ariel Levy calls 'raunch culture' (2005), and what Paglia, Lumby and others characterized in the 1990s as displays of female sexual empowerment, is undergoing renewed scrutiny from a range of voices within feminism.

Some of the arguments being made are familiar to those which followed the intra-feminist 'porn wars' of the 1980s. For example, 2006 saw the publication of Catharine MacKinnon's *Are Women Human?* Here, as in earlier writings, she blamed pornography for everything from the desensitization of people to violence against women to Serbian war crimes.[10] She argued that the situation was worse now than in the 1980s because the pornography industry had 'extended its reach' and women and children were 'being increasingly violated to make it' with more and more of them 'being abused through its use'.[11]

MacKinnon's familiar critique of pornographication as the extension of predatory male power is regarded as unhelpful by many contemporary feminists seeking to understand the complexity and contradictoriness of human sexual desire and its representation in culture, but its echoes can often be detected in the public sphere. In the UK the Labour government's proposals to ban 'violent' pornography, including simulated sub-dom and S&M images, for example, are reminiscent of those anti-porn feminists who in the 1980s focused attention on alarming if unrepresentative S&M imagery as evidence of the genre's misogyny, whether or not the images involved consensual adults, and whether or not women were portrayed as the dominant parties in the action.

The porn addiction model advanced by some feminists in the 1980s has also been revived. A 2003 essay in the *Guardian* cited the Ted Bundy case as evidence for the claim that 'pornography, like drugs and drink, is an addictive substance'. In the USA, Naomi Wolf (2003) has claimed that the ubiquity of porn is leading young men on American campuses to expect their girlfriends to behave like porn stars in the bedroom:

> The young women who talked to me on campuses about the effect of pornography on their intimate lives talked about feeling they could never measure up. They could never ask for what they really wanted; and if they did not offer what porn offered, they could not expect to hold a guy. The young men talked about what it was like to grow up learning about sex from porn and how it was not helpful to them in trying to figure out how to be with a

real woman, let alone meet her needs.

The Girl Next Door (2004) satirized this notion with a plot about a young man enthralled by a porn star. For Naomi Wolf the normalization of porn was no laughing matter, however, but a disease eating away at the emotional health of the nation. Pornographication, indeed, justified for Wolf a positive re-evaluation of cultures which 'condemn the wide dissemination of sexual images', such as Islam. Such cultures urge men not to look at porn, she noted with approval, because 'they understand what it takes to keep men and women turned on to each other over time', and 'because they place a high value on erotic married stability'.

Accompanying the resurgence of traditional anti-porn feminist discourses were new arguments about the pornographication of female sexuality in the twenty-first century, focused not so much on what men were doing to women as what women were doing to themselves. Ariel Levy's *Female Chauvinist Pigs* (2005) presented the feminization of sexual culture – or 'raunch culture' – as the unwelcome victory of two anti-female trends: the acceptance of patriarchal definitions of what it is that women want sexually and how they should perform to get it, and the intrusion of market forces into the private realm. She argued that 'raunch culture is not progressive, it is essentially commercial' (Levy, 2005: 33), apparently assuming that the two qualities are mutually incompatible. In this respect, her critique was founded on the assumption that commercialization is a bad thing. But as I have argued, an alternative view is that it is the commodification of previously marginalized sexualities that has contributed substantially to their mainstreaming.

Levy observed that women's participation in raunch culture 'has only grown more extreme and pervasive', despite 'the rising power of Evangelical Christianity and the political right in the United States' (Levy, 2005: 5). She argued that although women now have 'staggeringly different opportunities and expectations' from previous generations because of feminism, they are misusing this freedom and that this isn't 'some kind of triumph, it's depressing' (Levy, 2005: 44).

Ros Gill has identified the 'construction of a *new femininity* ... organised around sexual confidence and autonomy' in which women are constituted as 'knowing, active, and desiring subjects' (Gill, 2003:

103). She argues that we can understand raunch culture as one ambivalent consequence of a shift 'from an external, male judging gaze to a self-policing narcissistic gaze'. Women are 'invited to become a particular kind of self, and endowed with agency on condition that it is used to construct oneself as a subject closely resembling the heterosexual male fantasy that is found in pornography' (Gill, 2007a: 258). The auto-objectification of the female body, be it in the performance of a lap dance for a boyfriend, or the wearing of a 'porn star' t-shirt in the street, is less about the exercise of female choice than 'the requirement to transform oneself and remodel one's interior life' (Gill, 2007a: 261). This self-transformation is linked in turn to a neo-liberalist injunction 'to render one's life knowable and meaningful through a narrative of free choice and autonomy' (Gill, 2007a: 260).

The entrepreneurs behind CAKE, meanwhile, have defended themselves by arguing that 'Telling a woman that by exposing herself she is a victim of male sexual pleasure doesn't talk to our generation, because we own more of the public space than we used to' (in Krum, 2006). From this point of view, feminism has been successful in transforming patriarchal societies into spaces where women have more power and opportunity. Women are freer to look and to be looked at in conditions where they have control and autonomy over their own bodies. In this sense, the new sexualized culture can be seen as an assertion of a particular kind of female sexuality which, if by no means compulsory and certainly not representative of how most women behave most of the time, is at least a legitimate expression of sexuality for some, in some circumstances.

The long history of the 'porn wars' suggests that arguments about the meaning of contemporary cultural sexualization are unlikely to be resolved any time soon. It is possible to conclude, however, that the processes of sexualization, including the pornographication of mainstream culture, have created new spaces for female sexual display. Nor is there any dispute about the emergence of a hugely expanded market for feminized sexual consumption, often trading in products and services such as pole-dancing kits which would have appalled earlier generations of feminists. The participation of many young women in this market need not be taken to mean that feminism has failed, however. On the contrary, the gaudy, in-your-face political incorrectness of so much that is associated with cultural sexualization is a problem arising from feminism's political success and the opportunities it has given women to be 'bad girls'. The consequences of this shift have been controversial and often uncomfortable to watch, especially when the culture market in its profit-hungry blindness has seemed to encourage the inappropriate sexualization of younger and younger girls. This is not a return to pre-feminism, however, but one of the challenging paradoxes of a commercialized cultural environment re-made by feminism. Largely owing to the efforts of second-wave feminists, patriarchy, as we have known it for centuries in the West, is dissolving, producing tensions and unpleasant surprises not just for the men who stand to lose out on the deal, but those feminists who anticipated a very different outcome for their efforts than the excesses of raunch culture.

I referred above to Camille Paglia's call for a 'new kind' of feminism capable of exploring the 'dark, unconsoling mysteries' of sex. Ros Gill has argued that 'the challenge now is to articulate the politics that can engage effectively with this new sensibility, and move forward' (2007a: 271). Effective engagement, if it is to have any chance of success, will have to acknowledge the truth in Paglia's observation. Part of that is an acknowledgement of the legitimacy of diverse responses, from both women and men, to the processes of pornographication and cultural sexualization.

NOTES

1. A revised edition of the earlier collection, containing several new essays.
2. Sharon Krum (2006), 'No more faking', *Guardian*, 15 May. CAKE's mission statement was described in this article in the following terms: 'i) women like to initiate sex; ii) we get turned on every day of the week; iii) we are visual; iv) we fantasise; v) we know how to get ourselves off; vi) we like sex; vii) we know how our bodies work; viii) sex isn't over until we orgasm'.
3. See her *Centre Folds* and *Sex Pictures*, for example.
4. Today Madonna is widely celebrated as a pioneering popular artist, and a feminist who has transformed conventional understandings

of female sexuality as she evolved from New York disco queen to English country lady in a narrative which included rape, rebellion, domestic violence, bisexuality, motherhood, but through it all, power and control exercised through the exploitation of her sexuality. She was a key figure in the mainstreaming of homosexuality, using her stellar profile to familiarize her audience with images of gay men in *Sex* and in many of her most enduring videos. In academia, the 'Madonna phenomenon' generated a substantial literature.

5. Shamoon argues that the 'very existence' of this material 'denies many common myths about pornography, such as that women are not visually stimulated and that hardcore pornography necessarily proves harmful to women' (2004: 99).

6. In a press interview to promote the film's release the director noted that porn performers 'are stigmatised by both sides – the feminists and the moral majority. But they have a good reason to be in porno.' Quoted in Xan Brooks (2005), 'Dirty Business', *Guardian*, 4 January.

7. Comment by actress Margo Stiller, in Charlotte Higgins (2004), 'Why I made that film', *Guardian*, 20 May.

8. J. Harlow (2006), 'Booming porn faces backlash', *Sunday Times*. As of 2006 the US porn industry was reported to be worth $12 billion, a figure 'higher than all the money generated by the combined professional American football, baseball and basketball franchises'. Twelve per cent of all net traffic, or 4.2 million sites, and 13,500 video titles released that year, were classified as pornographic.

9. This might be thought to conflict with the example of *Shortbus*, but independent movies of this kind tend to operate in a different economy, free of the constraints imposed by big multinational media and their political interests. Precisely because they are 'arthouse' films, unlikely to be viewed by the mainstream multiplex audience, they may transgress in ways which a De Palma or a Verhoeven would find more difficult to sell to their backers.

10. She argued that because of this, 'you need more violence to become sexually aroused if you're a pornography consumer. This is very well documented.' Interview in Stuart Jeffries (2006), 'Are women human?', *Guardian*.

11. While the pornography industry has certainly expanded since the Mackinnon–Dworkin campaigns of the 1980s, and the accessibility of the Internet has undoubtedly 'extended its reach', Mackinnon presented no evidence for her claim about the abuse of women and children.

Part 2

Sexualization and

Mainstream Media

Chapter 5

THE MAINSTREAMING OF MASTURBATION: AUTOEROTICISM AND CONSUMER CAPITALISM

GREG TUCK

'... a man gives up his personality ... when he uses himself merely as a means for the gratification of an animal drive ... when one abandons himself entirely to an animal inclination, he makes himself an object of unnatural gratification, i.e., a loathsome thing, and thus deprives himself of all self-respect' (Immanuel Kant,
The Metaphysics of Morals, 1785).

'Don't knock masturbation, it's sex with someone I love'
(Woody Allen, *Annie Hall*, 1971).

SEX FOR ONE: VICE OR VIRTUE?

At one level the claim that there has been a sexualization of our contemporary culture seems obvious. As our own experience of consumer society and scholarly research make clear, we live in a culture imbued with sex. The entertainment, advertising and marketing industries rely heavily on sexualized images (Lin, 1998) and many of the canonical works of both modern and postmodern art and literature employ explicitly sexual tropes and imagery (Pease, 2000). In late modern culture, we are also witnessing the sale of sexual pleasure in a range of 'mediated' sex industries which, unlike the direct sexual gratification offered by prostitutes, sells sexual pleasure *outside* of a physical sexual encounter with another person.

The mediated sex industries are part of the mainstream, an established part of the pleasure industries of contemporary capitalism. As such they repeat and reflect capital's ready adoption and development of technology, its prodigious capacities for production and its exploitation, alienation and injustices. However, we must do more than recognize that sex can be bought and sold or simply condemn, condone or celebrate the commodification and mediation of sex. We must ask a more fundamental question, one that is surprisingly absent from much discussion about the mediated sex industries. That is, what sort of sex is mediated sex, and what types of sexual pleasure are invoked by sexual images, products and services? The answer, I would suggest, is that it is essentially masturbatory, one in which an autoerotic mode of consumption dominates. Even though pornography, as well as other sexual commodities such as phone sex lines, deliver indirect and mediated sexual encounters with others, they do so by relying on the masturbatory potential of the consumer. Even though this sex is not entirely 'otherless', its masturbatory status is confirmed by the requirement of the consumer to self-stimulate, as well as by the fact that the encounter is not with a subject so much as an object. Sexual consumers see an image not a body, hear an electrical transmission not a voice, and whether they touch themselves directly or through a mass-produced sex toy, the flesh of the other remains absent.

We are a profoundly self-pleasuring society at both a metaphorical and material level; without self-pleasure, much of our contemporary sexual culture would not exist. Furthermore, as masturbation is the most common and generally the first *type* of sexual activity that we experience, it *must* be included within a properly conceived notion of human sexuality. Yet the amount of scholarly attention paid to masturbation compared to other aspects of our sexual lives is extremely limited. This is despite the fact that evidence from sex surveys suggest that close to 100 per cent of men masturbate at some time in their lives (Giddens, 1992: 16) with a figure of 82 per cent being reported for women (Hite, 1993: 54). In the infamous Kinsey reports of 1948 and 1953 only 90 per cent of men and 62 per cent of women admitted to having masturbated at some stage in their lives. How much the increases reported in more recent literature mark an actual increase or represent a willingness to admit to the practice is hard to tell. Either way, the visibility of masturbation has increased. Furthermore, in addition to the growth of the technologies and industries of masturbation, in the last decade or so, masturbation has gained a far greater representational visibility across a range of media. For example, mainstream television programmes such as *Men Behaving Badly* (1992–98), *Sex and the City* (1998–2004) and *Desperate Housewives* (2004–) make reference to or more directly represent the practice. Teen comedies such as *There's Something About Mary* (1998) and *Scary Movie* (2000) and critically acclaimed films such as *American Beauty* (1999) and *Mulholland Drive* (2001) seem more willing to represent male and female adult masturbation. Mainstream advertising also links masturbatory orgasmic satisfactions to the most ordinary of products such as shampoo and chocolate. However, we must be careful not to confuse visibility with acceptance.

GOOD SEX, BAD SEX, NOT SEX

Outside of the work of medical/social historians (Porter, 1997; Allen, 2000; Laqueur, 1990, 1995, 2000, 2003) there has been little consideration of masturbation in relation to contemporary sexual identity or representation. Historically, its status as a solitary act has raised concerns over its precise 'sexual' status; being unpartnered, masturbation seems to be not-sexual or even anti-sexual (Tuck, 2005). Paradoxically, it has also been seen as worrying evidence that our 'natural' sexual reproductive functions do not determine our sexual pleasures, and in this sense masturbation deeply troubles functionalist accounts of sexuality. It is the strange status of masturbation as something both inside and outside the normative concept of sexuality that makes it such a rich source of enquiry. It brings into question or seems in excess of many of the binaries associated with hegemonic sexual ideology, not least because it seems beyond the processes of identity formation usually linked to our sexual behaviour and desires. While intensely visceral and embodied, a material physical event, masturbation is not limited to any particular type of body by age or gender, and while linked to the sexual imaginary, it is not limited to any one sexual orientation. Almost every 'body' masturbates. An analysis of masturbation therefore offers a way of understanding our sexuality outside of the usual binaries of biology (male and female), culture (masculine and feminine) and sexual orientation (heterosexual and homosexual), but one that is still firmly grounded in the visceral realities of our actual sex lives. Beyond or prior to our sexual identities, masturbation offers potential evidence of a more fundamental sexual capacity at odds with the binary oppositions that dominate mainstream understandings of sexual difference and orientation. Indeed, it could be argued that the negative attitudes associated with masturbation are evidence of a patriarchal anxiety that people will reject its normative demands and the linking of sexuality with 'natural' function.

Until fairly recently, most accounts of the mediated sex industries have tended to leap from text to effect without much of a pause to consider the precise mode of its consumption. Anti-pornography campaigners such as Andrea Dworkin and Catherine MacKinnon focused on what they saw as the heterosexist, exploitative and violent nature of heterosexual porn, while other anti-censorship feminists have produced a range of more nuanced and considered, although not necessarily uncritical, responses. Despite their differences, however, both are concerned with the *subsequent* effect of pornography rather than its more immediate embodied affects (see Williams, 1989; Church Gibson, 2004). Likewise, non-straight porn has been analysed in relation to its representation of a range of gay sexual identities, but again in a way that seems outside or beyond the actual material encounter with pornography itself (Mercer, 2003). There is no doubt that such studies offer provocative political readings of pornography and valuable dissections of the processes of representations. However, the body as opposed to the subjectivity of the pornography user has remained curiously attenuated, indeed absent from much of the argument and the analysis.

While it is undoubtedly the case that pornography carries and produces meaning, it is not manufactured to mean but to arouse, and while it is used and watched by couples and groups, the assumption is that most porn is watched and enjoyed alone. Although accurate empirical evidence about the consumption of pornography is hard to come by, its use as a masturbatory prop during solitary sex would seem self-evident. Indeed, in the West it has been the 'solitary' nature of the masturbatory pleasures offered by pornography that has attracted the most concern and vilification (see Laqueur, 2003: 333–58). So in contrast to the anti-pornography maxim that 'porn is the theory, rape is the practice', I would suggest that the practice encouraged and elicited by porn is masturbation. Effects research misses the fundamental fact that what unites all porn consumers is that they are *all* masturbating. The masturbatory consequences of pornography are profoundly levelling. It could, of course, be argued that this reveals our mutual alienation as much as our liberation, but either way it seems an articulation of sexuality that is particularly contemporary, a potential democratization of pleasure which materializes Descartes' individual *cogito* as an autonomous visceral self. In masturbation, I think, I act and I pleasure myself – therefore I am.

MASTURBATION, MODERNITY AND LATE MODERNITY

The supply and demand of autoerotic sexual pleasure is linked to late modernity at an industrial level and it has undoubtedly been a driver of new media forms and technologies, particularly during their initial development. The novel, photography, film and video, and the Internet have all grown by feeding our autoerotic needs (see Juffer, 1998; O'Toole, 1998; Mudge, 2000). Masturbatory sexuality has been co-opted and encouraged by the needs of the market, and the supply of solitary pleasures reveals the fundamentally masturbatory logic that drives consumption-based market economies. It is in these orgasmic commodities that the sexual and the economic most clearly converge. But arriving at an understanding of the status of masturbation within contemporary culture is not an easy task. The evidence is contradictory and ambiguous. There is ambivalence and anxiety in the way masturbation is portrayed and there are as many negative representations of the practice in mainstream media as there are goods and services that seem designed to elicit it.

Compared with the anti-masturbation hysteria that arose during the Enlightenment and continued on and off into the middle of the twentieth century, current attitudes towards masturbation seem more accepting, if not always celebratory. Gone are the days of toothed anti-erection rings, genital cages and barbaric surgical intervention such as suturing, castration and clitoridectomy to prevent masturbation (Allen, 2000: 79–118). Likewise, Kant's depiction of masturbation as animalistic yet unnatural has given way to a culture where in sexual 'self-help' literature one is likely to find masturbation 'widely recommended as a major source of sexual pleasures, and actively encouraged as a mode of improving sexual responsiveness on the part of both sexes' (Giddens, 1992: 16). Yet it would be wrong to assume that the hysteria has entirely abated. As recently as 1992 the Vatican was still describing masturbation as an 'intrinsically, and gravely, disordered act' in its revised *Catechism of the Catholic Church* (Stengers and Van Neck, 2001: 168). Alongside religious censure has grown up a psychological discourse about the infantile nature or even the potential harm of masturbation. Freud (1905) and Lacan (1973) described masturbation as a lesser form of sexual practice for either sex, and both claimed men risked reducing their sexual potency if they masturbated (Tuck, 2003). As this fear does not stand up to the obvious reality that sexually potent men masturbate, have partnered sex lives and father children, the question is why do such fears persist?

The idea that masturbation is detrimental to male potency is linked to far older beliefs regarding the 'spermatic economy' and the role semen plays in engendering masculinity. It developed from the ancient classical medical model that good health was a consequence of the proper balance between the four bodily humours, which meant that semen, like all other 'vital fluids', could not be depleted without risk; semen was believed to be a purified form of blood and its loss mimicked the effects of extreme blood loss. To lose too much seed, according to the second-century physician Aretaeus the Cappadocian, necessarily leads to 'enfeeblement, inactivity, stupidity, torpor and effeminacy' (cited in Allen, 2000: 83). Under the influence of Christian thinking, particularly the writings of St Augustine, the other aspect of this classical belief – the equally negative effects of abstinence – were ignored.

Although the censure directed towards masturbation was based on an economic/medical model of loss and balance, centring on the essential scarcity of semen, it was theologians rather than doctors who led this assault until the early eighteenth century. At this point, alongside the rise of the market economy, moral and medical attitudes to masturbation became deeply intertwined. In particular, the synthesis of existing religious notions of sexual sin with a crude functionalist concept of 'science' produced the new disease of 'Onanism', drawing on the anonymous publication around 1712 of an pamphlet called *Onania, or the Heinous Sin of Self-Pollution, and all its Frightful Consequences, in Both Sexes, Considered*. Over the next 50 years this new disease was blamed for all manner of illnesses and even deaths. According to Thomas Laqueur, the argument that developed went as follows:

> Semen, money and energy are all in short supply and are profligately expended at the wastrel's peril. Just as in the world of trade and commerce one must discipline one's use of scarce resources, so in the spermatic economy men need to save and to husband their precious bodily fluid ... The economic realm maps nicely onto the corporeal one (2003: 194–5).

The figure of the sallow-cheeked, pale and consumptive masturbator became a commonplace of eighteenth-, nineteenth- and early twentieth-century medical opinion. Interestingly, a number of contemporary sexologists continue to raise similar concerns, but couch them in terms of the 'addictive' nature of the practice, an addiction fuelled by what they refer to as the 'triple A Engine' – access, affordability and anonymity – of the Internet (Cooper, 2000). However, this triple A engine undoubtedly describes the more general logic of the 'free' market of consumer capitalism. Again this looks like masturbation taking the blame for the consequences of a consumption-based economy in which 'restraint' must be a property of the individual rather than the market, which must remain 'free'. Other sexologists question masturbation's ability to improve sexual response and fear it damages our capacity for intimacy (Christensen, 1995: 87–99). But there is little to demonstrate that masturbation is specifically or intrinsically capable of causing harm, or being symptomatic, let alone the cause of physical, moral or psychological decay. In reality 'people who have regular sex partners, and/or are married, are more likely to masturbate than people without sexual partners and/or who live alone' (Michael et al, 1994: 165). The myth of the lonely compulsive masturbatory is just that – a myth.

This, of course, is only one aspect of the story and the last 30 years has seen the development of less damning, even celebratory readings of masturbation. Outside of the dubious sexual politics of pseudoscientific enquiries, other theories, particularly feminism, have championed masturbation's role in granting sexual satisfaction and autonomy. Indeed, it is undoubtedly the case that contemporary attitudes are asymmetrical in relation to their concerns over 'wasteful' male masturbation compared with 'empowering' female masturbation. In the early 1970s, with the publication of Nancy Friday's *My Secret Garden: Women's Sexual Fantasies* (1973) and the Bodysex Workshops of Betty Dodson, many feminists developed a discourse of female masturbation as a form of self-love. In 1974, the woman's magazine *Ms.* ran an article that widely publicized Dodson's views and later became the groundbreaking book *Liberating Masturbation: A Meditation on Selflove* (1974). Masturbation was championed as a political act, evidence of women's sexual liberation. The social stigma and difficulties women encountered in accessing sexually explicit texts have, of course, been lessened by the access, affordability and anonymity of the Internet. Women can now feed their erotic imaginations and masturbatory desires within the safety and autonomy of their domestic environments.

Jane Juffer has suggested that the masturbatory use of mediated sex products has become a far more 'mainstream' practice for women (1998: 69). However, while evidence from sex surveys suggests that the promotion of female masturbation has taken root, these positive attitudes are by no means universal. Feminists sympathetic to psychoanalysis, such as Luce Irigaray (1985), promote a less orgasmic and more polymorphous reading of feminine sexuality, while others worry about the 'phallicization' of promoting an overtly genital form of female masturbation, in particular through the potentially alienating use of sex toys. The dildo has been a topic of much debate, particularly among lesbians, as to whether it is inherently 'male-identified' or not (Findlay, 1999: 466–76). However, beyond the issue of whether the dildo is a substitute penis is a deeper concern about whether 'subjects' should have sex with 'objects' at all, and an anxiety about the feared price we may pay when sex becomes solitary, mediated and mechanical rather than intersubjective, immediate and sensual. An episode of *Sex and the City*, 'The Turtle and the Hare' (1998), plays out these concerns when Charlotte (Kristin Davis) is introduced to a vibrator called 'the rabbit'. While initially reticent to use an unnatural device, Charlotte confesses to Carrie (Sarah Jessica Parker) that the rabbit has allowed her to achieve the longest and most intense orgasms of her life. She begins staying at home at nights and her friends suspect she is becoming addicted to her vibrator. After they confront her, Charlotte reluctantly gives up her rabbit and returns to the dating scene. Despite the reputation of the programme for promoting the right to individual sexual pleasure, Charlotte's duty to engage in sexual 'relations', which emphasize her heterosexual identity rather than indulgence in autoeroticism, wins out.

PLEASURE, PROFLIGACY AND PROFIT

What seems to link many of the negative attitudes towards masturbation is the metaphorical relationship between commodity consumption and masturbatory pleasure. Consumer capitalism is, after all, driven by the activities of individuals who seek self-satisfaction. The masturbatory subject and the commodity consumer are, in this regard, similar. Indeed as Laqueur has suggested:

> the debate over masturbation that raged from the Eighteenth century onwards might best be understood as part of the more general debate about the unleashing of desire upon which a commercial economy depended and about the possibilities of human community under these circumstances – a sexual version of the classic 'Adam Smith problem' (Laqueur, 1995: 157).

The problem identified by Smith in his *Theory of Moral Sentiments* (1759) was how society would survive the self-interest unleashed by a market economy. Smith held that our 'reason', the ability to put ourselves in the position of a neutral observer, tempered our natural economic selfishness and allowed an acceptable level of self-interest to drive capitalism. However, this model appeared less applicable to matters of sexuality which seemed beyond or outside such reason. Smith claimed that the self-interest cancelled itself out like an 'invisible hand' that calmed the workings of the market. But it did so at the cost of exciting the individual in the sexual sphere, feeding irrational and insatiable private desires. However, worse than the potentially limitless nature of the autoerotic desires unleashed, was the autonomous mechanism through which such pleasures could be gained. That is, masturbation also indexed a withdrawal from social interaction, a self-satisfaction and a failure to exchange. This profoundly threatened the workings of the market.

This is the paradox at the heart of the model of masturbation that continues today. On the one hand it appears self-determining, while on the other it seems isolated and alienating. As a moment of pure consumption masturbation seems to generate exactly the type of individual consuming subject required by capitalism. Yet at the same time it appears a wasted production and a failure to invest, particularly for men. Worse, the fact that it is cost free is also anathema to a society in which only those goods and services that are exchanged have value. We are both encouraged and condemned for enjoying ourselves and it can come as no surprise that current psychological and sociological surveys suggest that many people are still deeply anxious about masturbation – '50 percent of Americans still feel guilty about masturbating' (Allen, 2000: 80). In 1994, the then United States Surgeon General, Doctor Jocelyn Elders, was dismissed from her post for suggesting that teenagers should be reassured as to the normality and utility of masturbation in order to help prevent sexually transmitted diseases (Bennett and Rosario, 1995: 2). Of course, with the publication of the Starr report, the masturbatory pleasures of the president who dismissed her, Bill Clinton, later became the focus of intense cultural interest.

REPRESENTING THE PARADOX

A comparison of two very different representations of masturbation, one, an Internet viral advert – a form which can be considered to be on the leading edge of mainstream visual culture – the other from a Hollywood feature film that undoubtedly occupies a position in the centre ground of what is deemed representable and permissible, helps map out the terrain.

The viral advert, made to promote the mobile telephone texting service Hotxt (2006), begins with a close-up of a young woman's face. The image is of web-cam quality and does not suggest a professional or corporate production. Likewise, the woman is ordinary rather than glamorous. She looks directly into the camera as if she is about to record a video diary entry and then lies down. We see her head on a pillow and the naked tops of her shoulders. She starts to look down her own body and from the noise she is making and her facial expression it is obvious that she is masturbating. In the background is a frequent beeping noise that suggests she is using some sort of device to assist her. A fade provides a temporal ellipsis and she now appears close to orgasm. However, at this point we hear the familiar ring of a mobile phone and see the woman's anxiety as to whether to answer it. With a mixture of exasperation and frustration she lifts her right arm into view and we see she is holding a mobile phone rather than a vibrator. She has been using the text alert vibrate setting to the same effect. She answers the phone and says 'What? – just text me alright' and ends the call. Before answering it, she wipes the phone on her shoulder, a gesture which undoubtedly adds a degree of 'gross-out' comedy and explicitness to the scene. After hurriedly finishing the call she returns to her previous activity as another string of text alerts provide her with masturbatory pleasure. The image fades and the caption 'The Joy of TXT' appears on screen, which itself then fades to a message about the texting service and Hotxt Company. We briefly return to a now calmer and satisfied woman who wipes her mouth, sighs and says 'Yeah!'

Compare this scene of masturbation to that offered by the mainstream horror fantasy *The Cell* (1999). The film follows the activities of a serial killer, Carl Stargher (Vincent D'Onofrio), who abducts and incarcerates young women in the cell of the title. This is a glass-fronted sealed room that slowly fills with water until his captives drown. After every murder, which Carl films, he takes the corpse home and bleaches it. The body is laid out on a slab in Carl's cellar.

Using metal chains connected to piercings down his back and legs, we see Carl use a hoist to suspend himself above the corpse. He masturbates over them while watching the videotape of their ordeal, timing his own orgasm to coincide with their last terrified gasps of life. Carl has fully objectified his victims, turning both image and corpse into little more than a masturbatory prop.

Between them, these two representations map out the range of conflicting attitudes towards autoerotic pleasure in contemporary Western culture, a pleasure that seems self-determining and autonomous as well as frighteningly automatic, alienated and machine like. They also link masturbation to unnatural and/or manufactured pleasures that augment or abuse our natural embodied capacity. In this regard, both of these subjects are enjoying 'cyborg' sexuality, but it is their differential relationship to the means of orgasmic production, the metaphoric 'price' of their consumption and production, that seems at issue. For the woman, technology unleashes new embodied capacities, perfecting her mode of private consumption so she may more fully have and enjoy herself. For the man, however, masturbation is not enjoyed as a form of personal pleasure, but presented as a wasted *production*, one that demands the most elaborate and terrible consumption of another person. His is not a solitary vice, but one that mimics in extreme form the mediated consumption made available by the sex industries. He is a producer as well as a consumer, and beyond the sadistic horror of these scenes the dominance of machine technology and a factory system of production seems particularly crucial. That is, the process of objectification and exploitation is not simply sexual, but also industrial.

In this regard the figure of the masturbatory serial killer is a bad, but not illogical, subject under capitalism. His desire to mediate the other into a commodity, to consume an abstraction rather than directly engage with a person, is to do no more than the capitalist mode of production does to us all. However, what makes him truly obscene from this perspective is that he consumes his own production and therefore does violence to the concept of market exchange as well as to his victim. The 'productive' element of male orgasm – the waste of semen – links male masturbation to bad/wasteful masculine production as opposed to good/unwasteful feminine consumption. After all, our woman phone user is still engaged in a market exchange as well as a moment of self-pleasure and is therefore not a threat to capitalism but its ally.

MASTURBATION AND SEXUAL DIFFERENCE

According to the sexual ideology of texts such as *The Cell*, when male sexuality is so fully colonized by the masturbatory economic logic of capitalism, it is lived somewhere between insanity and addiction: a hideous materialization of the atomized, alienated consumer *and* the instrumentalism and exploitation of the most callous producer. Mad male masturbators are frequently represented in mainstream culture and have appeared in films such as *Silence of the Lambs* (1991), *Quills* (2000) and the remake of *Psycho* (1998). So, despite the existence of industries and technologies that promote male masturbation, at a representational level much of the logic of the anti-masturbation hysteria of the last three centuries persists. This is not to say that representations of insane female masturbators are not in circulation. Mad masturbating women have appeared in a number of films such as *Haute Tension – Switchblade Romance* (2003), *Eye of the Beholder* (1999) and *Mulholland Drive* (2001), all narratives concerned with the inability of women to form non-exploitative relationships. While none of these women use a victim as a direct masturbatory prop, they all murder their lovers – lovers who they feel they can never fully 'have'. Masturbation indexes this inability and their masturbatory priorities are as consuming of others as Carl's is in *The Cell*. Interestingly, compared with more positive representations of female masturbation, these portrayals are far more explicit in that we see their actual hand movements. Here, as is frequently the case with the representation of male masturbation, the *mechanical* mode of orgasmic production is made clear. Marie (Cécile De France), the chainsaw-wielding lesbian psychopath of *Haute Tension*, is a case in point. As she lies on the bed, her personal stereo blocking out her sense of contact with the outside world, we clearly see the repetitive movement of her hands which are thrust down the front of her undone jeans. It is, of course, only after she has masturbated that the carnage begins. The 'damaged' masturbatory sexuality of such cinematic serial killers takes them beyond a normative sexual orientation, but not an economized reading of their exploitative desire. They are still the sexualized version of the 'Adam Smith Problem' writ large (Tuck, 2005).

While I have been able to find representations of mad, bad and sad masturbators of both sexes, and neutral even positive representations of female masturbation, I have been unable to locate any unequivocally positive or even unconcerned representations of heterosexual male masturbation in mainstream texts. Furthermore, many of the most negative representations of male masturbation show the abuse or consumption of another during the act, and other people, especially women, are turned into little more than pornographic props. This is not confined to the fantastic and sadistic fates of victims of serial killers, but also involves the more mundane abuses of obscene telephone callers and voyeurs. As well as obvious issues of power, there seems to be an implication that men lack the imaginative capacities of women, and in some sense need forms of material stimulation to elicit their autoerotic capacities.

These representational differences raise a number of questions that demand further investigation, not least of which is how we are to account for the difference in the way male and female masturbation is presented. After all, both are related to forms of self-stimulation, though the way men and women arouse their autoerotic desires might at first seem different. For example, masturbation and visual pornography is more usually associated with men, while written erotica is associated with women. Another assumption is that sex toys are vastly more popular with women than with men. In both cases male desire seems linked to more exploitative relations involving mediated bodies, whereas female sexuality appears more genuinely independent and reliant on fantasy. This is undoubtedly one of the main reasons why masturbation has been championed by feminists as a materialization of female autonomy. How much these assumptions reflect material reality and how much they reflect the ways male and female sexuality are perceived more generally is a moot point. None of these behaviours are gender exclusive, particularly once the full range of human sexual orientation is taken into account. Women enjoy porn and men enjoy fantasy and we would do well to question the essentializing consequences of assumptions of 'difference' in this regard. Indeed, the fact that the notion of male sexual autonomy seems entirely absent from the debate as well as from the representations discussed seems particularly telling. That so many media texts represent self-stimulation allied to an abuse of another person suggests that these are not properly autoerotic behaviours. This seems to be the real horror of male masturbation, a fear that it is neither properly independent nor socially or emotionally productive. It is not just 'not partnered sex', it is 'anti partnered sex'. Sexual ideology works hard to disavow the potentially levelling effect of the recognition of our universal masturbatory desires, behaviours and potential. As soon as this capacity to free us from the functional sexual logic of reproductive patriarchy is evoked, it becomes re-colonized by the logic of consumer capitalism. In this respect masturbation is too productive a drive not to be harnessed, but the price of the pleasure it offers is seen as radically higher for men than it is for women.

A reassessment of the value and status of male masturbation, allowing it a more favourable comparison with the positive readings of female masturbation, could have profound political consequences. For a start, an acceptance of the reality of women's use of pornography and the reality of male masturbation without the use of pornography would help counter the imposed binary of exploiting/wasteful versus liberatory/productive masturbation that is currently mapped onto gender. It would allow us to recognize that masturbation is part of a fuller, richer sex life and not an activity that reduces or detracts from our partnered sexual pleasures. Masturbation is not engaged in instead of, but as well as partnered sex. Rather than isolating us, an acknowledgement of the masturbatory aspect of our sex lives would encourage a championing of our shared sexual capacity for autonomous pleasure, a pleasure not based on gender, reproduction, exploitation, scarcity or market logic.

In this regard masturbation is inherently 'queer' in the most positive and celebratory sense of this term. It lets us be sexual persons rather than identities or destinies. Furthermore it breaks the link between sexual and economic ideology as a pleasure that indexes the cost-free generosity of the flesh. Against the current emphasis on the insatiable character of sexual and commodity desire, as well as the hysterical and ridiculously exaggerated fear of loss and waste, an acknowledgement of masturbation allows us to reinstate the *satiable* possibilities of the body. Indeed once we acknowledge the ubiquity and pleasure of masturbation, the lack of evidence that it becomes compulsive or addictive would suggest that people are well able to regulate their masturbatory behaviour and that, rather than always wanting 'more', we want 'enough'.

As with our sex lives more generally, few of us think that more sex is necessarily the same as good sex, and the value we derive from our sexual being is beyond that which may be simply quantified or counted. If contemporary attitudes to masturbation suggest the colonization of our sexual lives by our economic ones, this reappraisal of masturbation might even help reverse the ideological influence. Instead of the insatiable desires of the market being imposed on our sexuality, the more limited reality of embodied physical pleasure might be seen as a more fundamental driver of economic human activity and community as well as a measure of 'value'.

Of course, no form of sexual practice is in itself revolutionary, exploitative, enriching or degrading. However, it seems remarkable that the potential for masturbation to offer and reveal our shared capacity for simple embodied pleasure is still so difficult to contemplate for a society which is supposedly based on the pleasure of the individual. Indeed, it may be the potential materialization of truly free individuals who know and enjoy their own limits and recognize the same in others that really troubles normative sexual and economic logic. But what is more troubling if we are to counter repression and exploitation is the near absence of more positive accounts of our masturbatory potential within supposedly more oppositional discourses. In particular, why have the positive accounts of masturbation offered by feminism for female masturbation not been extended to men? If we are really to encourage or demand a revolution in sexual politics for both genders and all sexualities, men who identify themselves as heterosexual are in as much need of liberation from sexual stereotyping and patriarchal functionalism as everyone else. This is not a luxury but a necessity.

Chapter 6

SUPERSEXUALIZE ME![1]: ADVERTISING AND THE 'MIDRIFFS'

ROSALiND GILL

It might be Venice Beach in California or any other similar board-walk, with white sand, blue sky and the ocean in the background. A tall, slim, blonde young woman is pictured turning away from the viewer. She is bending over to tie the laces on her rollerblades, and the tops of her tiny red shorts rise up to reveal the cheeks of her buttocks. The pose is familiar to anyone who has ever glanced at heterosexual pornography and is known to scholars of animal behaviour as 'presenting'. The only thing stopping us from seeing the young woman's genitalia is a contrasting blue g-string worn over the shorts. Either side of the image, runs the following text:

Q: Why do you run?
A: One word. Thong.

And then comes the brand: Puma running.com.

'Fancy a smack?' says another advert. It shows a tall, slim, PVC-clad, blonde dominatrix holding a man tethered on all fours, with a collar and leash around his neck and his trousers pulled part way down. The woman holds a hard paddle/slipper in her right hand and her arm is raised: she is poised to beat his naked, exposed buttocks. A small box in the right-hand corner reveals that the image is advertising Gym Box, an exercise centre in central London.

'Home slave' reads a third advert – this time for an apartment block in Manchester. Here yet another tall, blonde young woman is shown, tightly tied up from head to toe, while an attractive, chisel-jawed businessman regards her coolly from behind his state-of-the-art laptop computer.

Pornographic poses, sadomasochism, bondage. These have all become regular parts of the iconography of advertising in the early twenty-first century. Arched backs, exposed breasts and simulated orgasms are so routine as to rarely provoke comment. Porn chic has become a taken-for-granted mode of representation in a context in which advertisers believe they have to produce ever more arresting and stimulating images to get consumers' attention in the crowded, sign-saturated mediascape. Hypersexualized imagery is one way of achieving this, as is the use of graphic representations of violence. Both have increased dramatically in the last decade (Carter and Weaver, 2003).

In this chapter I want to consider advertising and sexualization through an examination of a related shift: the emergence of the figure of the 'midriff', which has become an iconic part of advertising targeted at young people. I will suggest that in the period since 1994 there has been a marked shift in the manner that women's bodies are depicted sexually, in ways that emphasize pleasure, playfulness and empowerment rather than passivity or victimization. This chapter will document and interrogate this shift from a feminist perspective.

First I will review some of the traditional concerns about the representation of women's bodies in advertising and highlight some significant changes. Then I will look specifically at the rise of midriff advertising, using examples to discuss its key features. Finally, I will evaluate the significance of this shift in political terms and offer a critical assessment of midriffing. The chapter's aim is not straightfor-wardly to weigh into the debates either for or against explicitly sexual representations – the so-called 'sex wars' of feminism – but to explore the *nature* of contemporary sexualization in advertising, to reflect upon the ways in which women's bodies are depicted sexually and to critically examine current constructions of feminine subjectivities and desires.

ADVERTISING AND FEMINISM

Advertising is inescapable and ubiquitous in Northern/Western societies, and increasingly elsewhere too. It is estimated that the average US citizen sees or hears 3,000 adverts each day (Kilbourne, 1999). When you translate that into the notional time spent 'interacting' with adverts, and work it out as a fraction of a lifetime, the results are sobering; Kilbourne puts the figure at approximately three years in the average lifetime of a North American, and citizens of other developed countries are not far behind. Adverts are at the heart of social existence in the West. Indeed, the magnitude of advertising's influence has been compared to that of education and organized religion (Lazier-Smith, 1989). It constitutes a 'vast superstructure' (Williamson, 1978) and is, according to Leiss et al (1986), perhaps the most important body of material in the mass media.

It is not surprising, then, that in the wave of *feminist* scholarship and activism that swept through Western countries in the 1960s and 1970s, advertising was a key target for analysis and critique. The short, condensed nature of adverts predisposed their creators to rely heavily on crude, easily recognizable stereotypes, and research highlighted the narrow range of degrading and trivializing images of women: the dumb blonde, the unintelligent housewife, the passive sex object, and so on. Throughout the 1970s and 1980s, content-analytic studies documented the same consistent pattern of gender stereotyping in adverts: women were predominantly shown in the home (indeed, in the kitchen and bathroom); depicted as housewives and mothers; they were frequently shown in dependent or subservient roles; their appearance – looking beautiful and sexy – was more important than anything else; and they rarely provided an argument in favour of the advertised products – voice-overs were generally provided by men, indexing their greater authority. In contrast, men were portrayed in a range of settings and occupational roles, shown as independent and autonomous, and presented as objective and knowledgeable about the products they used (Dyer, 1982; Livingstone and Green, 1986; Lovdal, 1989; Furnham and Bitar, 1993; Gunter, 1994).

A landmark study by the sociologist Erving Goffman (1979) provided another way of coding gender representation in advertisements, concentrating on the way in which *non-verbal signals* communicated important differences in male and female power. Examining magazine and billboard advertising, Goffman concluded that adverts depicted ritualized versions of the parent–child relationship, in which women were largely accorded child-like status. Women were typically shown as lower or smaller than men and using gestures which 'ritualised their subordination' (Goffman, 1979: 43), for example, lying down, using bashful knee bends, canting postures or deferential smiles. Women were also depicted in 'licensed withdrawal' (1979: 29), slightly distanced from a scene, gazing into the distance, not quite there. The predilection of advertisers for showing women looking into mirrors was another way of presenting this withdrawal, additionally conveying the message that women are narcissistic.

Goffman's work was developed by many other writers to examine the body's presentation in advertising. Perhaps the major insight of subsequent feminist work has been the analysis of how 'cropping' is used in adverts. Many studies have highlighted the way in which women's bodies are fragmented in adverts, visually dissected so that the viewer sees only the lips, or the eyes or the breasts (Dyer, 1982; Coward, 1984a). This frequently mirrors the text in which women's bodies are presented simply as a composite of problems, each requiring a product-solution. The effect is to deny women's humanity, to present them not as whole people but as fetishized, dismembered 'bits', as objects.

For the last four decades the notion of objectification has been a key term in the feminist critique of advertising. Its centrality to the feminist critical lexicon lay in its ability to speak to the ways in which media representations help to justify and sustain relations of domination and inequality between men and women. In particular, processes of objectification were held to be the key to understanding male violence against women:

> Adverts don't directly cause violence ... but the violent images contribute to the state of terror. Turning a human being into a thing, an object, is almost always the first step towards justifying violence against that person ... This step is already taken with women. The violence, the abuse, is partly the chilling but logical result of the objectification (Kilbourne, 1999: 278).

It is difficult to over-estimate the importance of this argument for feminism (and also for understandings of racism and other relations of brutality); it has been central to feminist activism around advertising and media representations more generally. However, I want to suggest that a number of significant changes have taken place in the regime of representation that mean that the notion of objectification no longer has the analytic purchase to understand many contemporary constructions of femininity. Increasingly, young women are presented not as passive sex objects, but as active, desiring sexual subjects, who seem to participate enthusiastically in practices and forms of self-presentation that earlier generations of feminists regarded as connected to subordination. Perhaps the advert that most vividly captures this shift and marks its inception is Trevor Beattie's famous 1994 poster for the Playtex Wonderbra in which model Eva Herzigova is shown regarding her own Wonderbra-uplifted breasts under the slogan 'Hello Boys'. The humorous and direct address to male viewers marked a profound change: Herzigova was positioned not only as an object of the male gaze but also as an active subject, knowingly playing with her sexual power.

This shift was emblematic of a wider transformation happening in advertising in the early 1990s. Robert Goldman (1992) has argued that advertisers were forced to respond to three challenges at this time. First, there was the growing experience of 'sign fatigue' on the part of many media audiences fed up with the endless parade of brands, logos and consumer images. Like its millennial sibling, compassion fatigue, sign fatigue showed itself in what we might call a weariness of affect, an ennui and a disinclination to respond. Secondly, advertisers had to address increasing 'viewer scepticism', particularly from younger, media-savvy consumers who had grown up with fast-paced music television and were the first generation to adopt personal computers and mobile phones as integral features of everyday life. To get through to this generation, who regarded themselves as sceptical and knowing in relation to commercial messages, advertisers had to adapt. They increasingly came to produce commercials that mocked the grammar and vocabulary of advertising and effaced their own status as advertisements. Thirdly, advertisers needed to address feminist critiques of advertising and to fashion new commercial messages that took on

board women's anger at constantly being addressed through representations of idealized beauty.

Goldman argued that advertisers' response to this third challenge
was to develop what he called 'commodity feminism'[2] – an attempt
to incorporate the cultural power and energy of feminism whilst
simultaneously domesticating its critique of advertising and the
media. Commodity feminism takes many different forms. It consists
of adverts that aim to appease women's anger and to suggest that
advertisers share their disgruntlement with images of thin women,
airbrushed to perfection. It is found in adverts that attempt to
articulate a rapprochement between traditional femininity and characteristics which are coded as feminist goals: independence, career
success, financial autonomy. It may be identified in gender-reversal
adverts or in revenge adverts that mock or turn the tables on men.
Elsewhere I have considered a number of shifts in the representation
of gender in advertising in some detail (Gill, 2007a).[3] In the remain-
der of this chapter, however, I will turn my attention to perhaps the
major contemporary shift in the sexual representation of women: the
construction of a young, heterosexual woman who knowingly and
deliberately plays with her sexual power and is forever 'up for it': the
midriff.

SEXUALIZATION AND THE MIDRIFFS

The midriff is a part of the body between the top of the pubis bone
and the bottom of the rib cage. This part of the female body has been
the site of erotic interest in many non-Western cultures for a long
time. In the West, the recent upsurge of interest in the midriff can be
traced back to the visual presentation of Madonna in the late 1980s in
which her pierced belly button and toned abdomen became features
for erotic display in dance routines. For almost a decade, between the
mid-1990s and the mid-2000s, revealing the midriff was central to
young women's fashion in the West, with low-hung hipster jeans and
cropped or belly top, exposing a pierced navel at the front and the
familiar 'whale back' (visible g-string) from behind. Increasingly, the
lower back has also become a site for elaborate tattoos.

This style was so widespread for such a long time that the term 'midriffs' has become a shorthand employed by advertisers and marketing consultants (Rushkoff, 2001; Quart, 2003). In one sense it signals a generation – primarily women in their 20s and 30s, but sometimes also girls in their teens and women in their early 40s – defined by their fashion tastes. More tellingly, the midriffs can be understood in relation to a particular *sensibility*: a sensibility characterized by a specific constellation of attitudes towards the body, sexual expression and gender relations.

Advertising aimed at the midriffs is notable for its apparently 'sexualized' style but this is quite different from the sexual objectification to which second-wave feminist activists objected. In today's midriff advertising, women are much less likely to be shown as passive sexual objects than as empowered, heterosexually desiring sexual subjects, operating playfully in a sexual marketplace that is presented as egalitarian or actually favourable to women.

Midriff advertising has four central themes: an emphasis on the body, a shift from objectification to sexual subjectification, a pronounced discourse of choice and autonomy, and an emphasis upon empowerment.

Perhaps the most striking feature of midriff advertising is the centrality of the body. If in the 1950s the home was the ideal focus for women's labour and attention, and the sign used to judge their 'worth', in the new millennium it is the body. Today, a sleek, controlled figure is essential for portraying success, and each part of the body must be suitably toned, conditioned, waxed, moisturized, scented and attired. In advertising, more and more parts of the body come under intense scrutiny: Dove's summer 2006 campaign alerts us that the newest must-have accessory is beautiful armpits, lest we forget to use all the products necessary to render this part of the body acceptable.

Today, the body is portrayed in advertising and elsewhere as the primary source of women's capital. This may seem obvious and taken-for-granted, but it is, in fact, relatively new. Surveillance of women's bodies constitutes perhaps the largest type of media content across all genres and media forms. Women's bodies are evaluated, scrutinized and dissected by women as well as men and are always at risk of 'failing'. This is most clear in the cultural obsession with celebrity which plays out almost exclusively over women's bodies. Magazines like *Heat* and *Closer* did not even exist a decade ago, but today offer page after page of colour photographs of female celebrities' bodies, with scathing comments about everything from armpit hair to visible panty lines, but focusing in particular upon the crimes of being 'fat' and, more recently, 'too thin' (McRobbie, 2004; Gill, 2007b). In the very recent past, women's cooking, domestic cleanliness or interior design skills were the focus of advertisers' attention to a much greater extent than the surface of the body. But there has been a profound shift in the very definition of femininity so that it is now defined as a bodily property rather than a social or psychological one. Instead of caring or nurturing or motherhood, it is now possession of a 'sexy body' that is presented as women's key source of identity. This is captured vividly in an advert for Wonderbra, which shows a young woman wearing only a black, cleavage-enhancing bra. Situated in between the breasts is the following slogan: 'I can't cook. Who cares?' - making the point that her voluptuous body is far more important than any other feminine skills or attributes she may or may not have.

There has also been a shift in the way that women's bodies are presented erotically. Where once sexualized representations of women in the media presented them as the passive, mute objects of an assumed male gaze, today women are presented as active, desiring sexual subjects who choose to present themselves in a seemingly objectified manner because it suits their liberated interests to do so. A 1994 advert for Wonderbra pictured model Eva Herzigova's cleavage, and hailed us with a quotation from Mae West: 'Or are you just pleased to see me?' The first part of the quotation - 'is that a gun in your pocket?' with its implication that the male viewer had an erection - was left out, for us as viewers to fill in. This was no passive, objectified sex object, but a woman who was knowingly playing with her sexual power. A Triumph advert from the same period has the same confident and assertive tone: 'New hair, new look, new bra. And if he doesn't like it, new boyfriend.'

This advert, like others in the series, has a feminist veneer, but represents the idea that women can gain control through the commodification of their appearance - that by acquiring a particular look they can obtain power (Goldman, 1992). The notion of objectification does not seem to capture this; a better understanding would come from the Foucaultian idea of (sexual) subjectification, which speaks to the way that power operates through the construction of particular subjectivities.

A crucial aspect of both the obsessional preoccupation with the body and the shift from objectification to sexual subjectification is that this is framed in advertising through a discourse of playfulness, freedom and, above all, *choice*. Women are presented not as seeking men's approval but as *pleasing themselves*; in doing so, they just happen to win men's admiration. A South African advert for She-bear lingerie in 1999, for example, featured an attractive young white woman wearing only her lingerie and a nun's habit and rosary. The slogan, 'Wear it for yourself', ties the brand identity to women who dress for themselves rather than for men – even if they are not nuns. 'If he's late you can always start without him', declares another lingerie advert in which the *mise-en-scène* constructs a picture of seduction, complete with carelessly abandoned underwear, but in which a sexual partner is absent. This seems not to be genuinely celebrating the pleasures of masturbation for women but is designed to show how arousing the product is, and how sexy it will make you feel. Of course, this raises all kinds of difficult questions. What is the difference between self-pleasure and feeling sexy? How is it that women's arousal has come to be tied so closely to pleasing men? And how precisely is this connection signified in the adverts – that is, is the link made in the text or in the reading of it by normatively interpellated heterosexual feminine subjects, in which case other, resistant readings might be possible?

Dee Amy-Chinn (2006) eloquently captures this double-edged postfeminist emphasis on women pleasing themselves, in the title of her article about lingerie advertising: 'This is just for me(n).' Such advertising hails active, heterosexual young women, but does so using a photographic grammar directly lifted from heterosexual pornography aimed at men. The success – and this is what is novel about this – is in connecting 'me' and 'men', suggesting there is no contradiction – indeed *no difference* – between what 'I' want and what men might want of 'me'. This is clearly complicated. There is no necessary contradiction or difference between what women and men want, but equally it cannot be assumed that their desires are identical. What is most interesting is the sophisticated 'higher' development of ideology and power relations such that the ideological is literally made real. This takes the form of constructions of femininity that come straight out of the most predictable templates of male sexual fantasy, yet which must also be understood as authentically owned by the women who produce them. Part of their force lies precisely in the fact that they are *not* understood as ideological, or indeed are understood as *not* ideological. Janice Turner (2005: 32) has referred to this as the idea that straight porn has 'come true':

> Once porn and real human sexuality were distinguishable. Not even porn's biggest advocates would suggest a porn flick depicted reality, that women were gagging for sex 24/7 and would drop their clothes and submit to rough, anonymous sex at the slightest invitation. But as porn has seeped into mainstream culture, the line has blurred. To speak to men's magazine editors, it is clear they believe that somehow in recent years, porn has come true. The sexually liberated modern woman turns out to resemble – what do you know! – the pneumatic take-me-now-big-boy fuck-puppet of male fantasy after all.

In a 1995 advert for a Gossard bra, a young woman is depicted lying dreamily in some straw or grass, wearing only a black translucent bra and pants. The text reads: 'Who said you can't get pleasure from something soft'. This emphasizes women's pleasure, and directs us to the redundancy of men in achieving it, but uses a form of representation which is familiar from pornography: the woman is pictured from above, almost naked and pleasuring herself, or at least being pleasured by her underwear. In 'pleasing herself', she is also of course pleasing the many heterosexual men who may have consumed very similar images in porn.

This apparent dual address to 'new' women and to 'old' or unre-constructed men is captured brilliantly in Jacky Fleming's (1996) satirical cartoon about advertising of this kind. In the first frame a heterosexual couple is shown standing in front of two large images of young attractive women in their underwear. The woman says: 'I don't know why you're staring like that, Adrian, these adverts aren't FOR men. They are meant to be for WOMEN and they make us feel

cheekily confident about being sexy in a raunchy but fun loving postfeminist sort of way ... And there's a lot of humour involved too.' In
the second frame, the same man is shown again in front of the post-
ers, but this time with a male friend. We assume he has just reported
his partner's explanation. 'Tell you what mate,' says his friend, 'if this
is feminism we've been backing the wrong horse!'

Almost as central to midriff advertising as the notions of choice
and 'pleasing one's self', is a discourse of feminine *empowerment*.
Contemporary advertising targeted at the midriffs suggests, above all,
that buying the product will empower you. 'I pull the strings', asserts
a beautiful woman in a black Wonderbra; 'Empower your eyes', says
an advert for Shiseido mascara; 'Discover the power of femininity.
Defy conventions and take the lead', reads an advert for Elizabeth
Arden beauty products. What is on offer in all these adverts is a
specific kind of power – the sexual power to bring men to their knees.
Empowerment is tied to possession of a slim and alluring young body,
whose power is the ability to attract male attention and sometimes
female envy. Wonderbra's 2006 campaign, 'Experience WonderYou',
signals this particularly vividly, in a shot of an escalator designed
to allow the viewer to situate herself imaginatively as the object of
universal male admiration and female mistrust, competitiveness and
envy. A US advert for lingerie dares to make explicit that which is
usually just implied. Showing a curvaceous woman's body from the
neck down, clad in a black basque and stockings, the advert's text
reads, 'while you don't necessarily dress for men, it doesn't hurt, on
occasion, to see one drool like the pathetic dog he is'.[4] This is 'power
femininity': a 'subject-effect' of 'a global discourse of popular post-
feminism which incorporates feminist signifiers of emancipation and
empowerment as well as circulating popular postfeminist assumptions
that feminist struggles have ended, that full equality for all women
has been achieved, and that women of today can 'have it all' (Lazar,
2006).

SUPERSEXUALIZE ME: MIDRIFF ADVERTISING
AND POSTFEMINISM

What, then, are we to make of the shift in the way that women are presented sexually? In offering up representations of women who are active, desiring sexual subjects, who are presented as powerful and playful, rather than passive or victimized, has advertising pointed to more hopeful, open or egalitarian possibilities for gender relations? I do not think so. On the contrary, I want to argue that midriff advertising *re-sexualizes* women's bodies, with the excuse of a feisty, empowered postfeminist discourse that makes it very difficult to critique.

Let us examine first some of the exclusions of midriff advertising. Most obviously this includes anyone living outside the heterosexual norm. Contemporary midriff advertising operates within a resolutely hetero-normative economy, in which power, pleasure and subjectivity are all presented in relation to heterosexual relationships. Indeed the parallel growth of a kind of 'queer chic' (Gill, 2008) seems to locate homosexuality in terms of style and aesthetics rather than sexuality. A cynic might suggest that the greater visibility of hyper-feminine/hyper-sexualized lesbians in advertising may be a way for advertisers to evade charges of sexism whilst continuing to present women in a highly objectified manner.

Others excluded from the empowering, pleasurable address of midriff advertising are older women, disabled women, fat women and any woman who is unable to live up to the increasingly narrow standards of female beauty and sex appeal that are normatively required. These women are never accorded sexual subjecthood. The figure of the 'unattractive' woman who seeks a sexual partner remains one of the most vilified in popular culture. Indeed, returning to the first image discussed in this chapter, it is worth noting that a parallel advert featured in the same magazine highlighted the alter-ego of the micro-shorted leggy blonde: her mother. 'Why do you run?' asks the advert again. But this time, the answer: 'I love my mother. But I don't love her thighs.' An unflattering shot shows the behind of an older woman, her wrinkled hands placed on her hips, her upper thighs dotted with cellulite. Here in the figure of the older woman is the repressed of midriff advertising: she who you do not want to become. Unlike the midriff, she has no voice, is accorded no sexual autonomy or playfulness and is put on display as an object (not a subject), a warning.[5] Sexual subjectification, then, is a highly specific and exclusionary practice, and sexual *pleasure* is actually irrelevant here; it is the power of sexual *attractiveness* that is important. Indeed, the two are frequently and deliberately confused in midriff advertising.

The practice is also problematic for what it renders invisible, what Robert Goldman has called the 'diverse forms of terror experienced by women who objectify themselves'. He explains:

> There is the mundane psychic terror associated with not receiving 'looks' of admiration – i.e. not having others validate one's appearance. A similar sense of terror involves the fear of 'losing one's looks' – the quite reasonable fear that ageing will deplete one's value and social power. A related source of anxiety involves fear about 'losing control' over body weight and appearance ... and there is a very real physical terror which may accompany presentation of self as an object of desire – the fear of rape and violence by misogynist males (1992: 123).

Midriff advertising is notable not only for its success in selling brands but also – much more significantly – for its effective rebranding or reconstruction of the anxieties and the labour involved in making the body beautiful, through a discourse of fun, pleasure and power. The work associated with disciplining the feminine body to approximate the required standards is made knowable in new ways that systematically erase pain, anxiety, expense and low self-esteem. See, for example, the way that the application of boiling wax to the genital region and then its use to pull out hairs by their roots can be discursively (re)constructed as 'pampering' (Sisters, I don't think so!).

Goldman is correct, too, to point to the erasure of violence in such advertising. It seems literally to have been conjured away. In one advert, an attractive young woman is depicted wearing just a bra, her arm stretched high in the internationally recognized gesture for hailing a taxi. 'I bet I can get a cab on New Year's Eve 1999,' she declares, laughing. Here, again, exposed breasts are a source of male attention-grabbing power, a way to defeat the notorious concerns about taxi queues on the millennium eve. But the representation is entirely shorn of any suggestion of the violence that might threaten a woman so scantily attired, late at night, in the midst of large numbers of men who are drinking heavily. More generally, the depiction of heterosexual relations as playful, and women as having as much – if not more – power as men in negotiating them is at odds with statistics which give an extraordinarily sobering picture of the levels of violence by men against women.[6]

Midriff advertising is notable for articulating notions of women's self-determination and agency, yet it is precisely the construction of the subject as autonomous that constitutes another set of tensions. First, it is notable that women's agentic capacities are confined to the 'aestheticisation of their physical appearances' (Lazar, 2006) and, moreover, their power as agents is directly tied to consumerism – points that suggest there is rather less to celebrate about this shift than some (for example, Scott, 2005; Taylor, 2006) might have us believe. More fundamentally, however, the notions of choice and autonomy as they are articulated within advertising are systematically eradicating any space within which we might think about ourselves as social beings. In short, any notion of cultural or political influence is disavowed.

Midriff advertising articulates a thoroughgoing individualism in which women are presented as entirely autonomous agents, no longer constrained by any inequalities or power imbalances. The pendulum swing from a view of power as something obvious and overbearing which acts upon entirely docile subjects towards a notion of women as completely free agents who just 'please themselves' does not serve feminist or cultural understandings well. It cannot explain why the look that young women seek to achieve is so similar: if it were the outcome of everyone's individual, idiosyncratic preferences, surely there would be greater diversity, rather than a growing homogeneity organized around a slim, toned, hairless body. Moreover, the emphasis upon choice sidesteps and avoids all the important and difficult questions about how socially constructed ideals of beauty are internalized and made our own.

The notion of choice has become a postfeminist mantra. The idea that women are 'pleasing themselves' is heard everywhere: 'women *choose* to model for men's magazines', 'women *choose* to have cosmetic surgery to enhance the size of their breasts', 'women *choose* to leave their children in Eastern Europe or in the Global South and come and make a better life in the rich countries'. Of course, at one level, such claims have some truth: some women do make 'choices' like this. However, they do not do so in conditions of their own making, and to account for such decisions using only a discourse of free choice is to oversimplify both in terms of analysis and political response. We need urgently to complicate our understandings of choice and agency in this context (Gill, 2007c).

Finally, I would argue that midriff advertising involves a shift in the way that power operates: it entails a move from an external male-judging gaze to a self-policing narcissistic gaze. In this sense it represents a more 'advanced' or pernicious form of exploitation than the earlier generation of objectifying images to which second-wave feminists objected – because the objectifying male gaze is internalized to form a new disciplinary regime. Using the rather crude and clunky language of oppression, we might suggest that midriff advertising adds a further layer of oppression. Not only are women objectified as they were before, *but through sexual subjectification they must also now understand their own objectification as pleasurable and self chosen.* If, in earlier regimes of advertising, women were presented as sexual objects, then this was understood as something being done *to* women. In contemporary midriff advertising, however, some women are endowed with the status of active subjecthood so that they can 'choose' to become sex objects because this suits their liberated interests. One of the implications of this shift is that it renders critique much more difficult.

In the documentary *The Merchants of Cool* (2001) the cultural theorist Douglas Rushkoff argues that the term 'midriff' should be used as a *verb* to refer to the actions of advertising executives. *To midriff*, according to Rushkoff, is to wrap old sexual stereotypes in a new feisty language of female empowerment. It is an entirely cynical exercise dreamed up by the advertising industry in order to continue using women's bodies as sexual objects while evading legitimate charges of sexism.

Rushkoff has a point. Whilst I do not subscribe to the more conspiratorial aspects of his critique, preferring instead to see advertising as a networked, mediated practice whose images are the outcome of multiple, often contradictory, determinants, his emphasis upon the way that midriff advertising creates an excuse for sexism is important and resonates with Robert Goldman's analysis of commodity feminism discussed earlier in this chapter. Both stress the ongoing struggle between advertising and feminism, and both suggest that, so far, it has largely been resolved in favour of the advertising industry, with feminist ideas ransacked, cannibalized, incorporated and 'domesticated'.

To contest this, there are three fronts on which feminists must engage: first, to articulate a language and cultural politics of resistance to midriff advertising, preferably one that is funny, feisty, sexpositive and inclusive; second, to rethink agency and choice in more sophisticated terms that reject the existing dualism; and, finally, to push for – or create – more diverse representations of gender and sexuality.

ACKNOWLEDGEMENTS

I am very grateful to Meg Barker and Merryn Smith for their very helpful and insightful comments, and hope to develop their important suggestions in subsequent work on this topic.

NOTES

1. This title owes a debt to Morgan Spurlock's powerful critique of the fast-food industry, *Super Size Me* (2004).

2. Commodity feminism is, of course, a homage to Marx and Engels's notion of commodity fetishism.

3. See also Gill (2008) for a discussion of sexualization that looks at the rise of 'queer chic' in advertising, the erotic depiction of men's bodies, and the increasing use of the grammars of heterosexual pornography in advertising.

4. Elsewhere (2007a) I have considered the offensive depiction of male sexuality in such adverts.

5. I am grateful to Angela McRobbie and Valerie Hey for pointing out to me the significance of this woman being represented as the mother. Unfortunately, there is not space here to explore the psychoanalytic implications which follow from this.

6. It is estimated that there were 190,000 incidents of serious sexual assault and 47,000 female victims of rape in 2001 in England and Wales. See Walby and Allen (2004). Research by Amnesty

International in the UK published in November 2005 found that a blame culture exists against women who have been raped, with up to one-third of people questioned seeing a woman as responsible if she was wearing revealing clothing, had been drinking or had had a number of sexual partners.

Chapter 7

WHATEVER HAPPENED TO CATHY AND CLAIRE?: SEX, ADVICE AND THE ROLE OF THE AGONY AUNT

PETRA BOYNTON

In the past two decades there has been a dramatic expansion in the sources of sex advice, particularly for young people. These now include telephone and text advice, websites offering advice and information, charities tackling sexual health, reproductive and relationship problems and specialist agencies campaigning for the rights of young people, LGBTQ groups and adults. The linking of sex and relationships, both as 'health' and 'lifestyle' issues, has worked to further expand the range of advice sources available. All of these developments have added to the increasing variety of media representations of sex.

Despite the glut of advice in contemporary society, advice and advice giving is under-researched and agony aunts – the people in an 'expert' position to give advice – are not taken seriously by social science researchers or journalists (McRobbie, 1991; Boynton, 2006). This is partly due to the fact that sex and relationships are often overlooked in the social sciences and dismissed as 'lite' topics in journalism (Boynton and Callaghan, 2006). This chapter explores the history of sex and the problem page, reflects on issues affecting contemporary advice giving and predicts future trends in this important area for sex information.

NO MORE CATHY AND CLAIRE

Twenty years ago the main sources of advice were magazines aimed at girls and women (Ehrenreich and English, 1979; McRobbie, 1991). The advice given there on sex and relationships was generally conservative, designed to complement rather than question the status quo (Ehrenreich and English, 1979; Walters, 2000; Naish, 2005). As a teenage consumer of magazines in the 1980s – and particularly of *Jackie* magazine – I avidly read Cathy and Claire's problem page each week, noting their advice on how I should obey my parents, use sanitary towels instead of tampons and not let kissing get out of hand. I was very drawn to Cathy and Claire, who seemed to be a combination of big sister and aunt, and who you felt you could ask things you probably would not be able to ask your mum, teacher or best friend. Before I read their replies I always liked to try and have a go at answering the questions myself, and although I usually deferred to their judgement I longed for a day when I could be an agony aunt myself.

Fast-forward 20 years and I am now working as an agony aunt, drawing upon my experience as an advisor and as an academic who studies sexual health and media. Unlike Cathy and Claire, I am asked by teenage girls how to give a blowjob, what anal sex is and how to tell if they are bisexual (see also McRobbie, 1996). These questions might suggest a growing sophistication about sex amongst young people. However, many people – regardless of age and gender – lack access to or do not fully engage with sex education, and because of this have poor sexual knowledge. Indeed, levels of sexually transmitted diseases, sexual problems, coercion and dissatisfaction with sex amongst all age groups remain high.

In the past two decades the Internet, increased access to more television channels and the sexualization of the media has meant that teenagers and adults are exposed to much more sexual information. Developments in technology have affected both the sources and forms of advice seeking and giving. Problems no longer arrive in the form of handwritten letters; they are more likely to be sent by email or text and may include photographs (Baker and Boynton, 2005). But despite these changes, the problem page continues to be a place where people can ask for advice they are unable to get from other sources such as teachers, counsellors or healthcare staff. As Angela McRobbie notes, 'advice columns exist because of so much that cannot be said, or cannot be discussed elsewhere' (1991: 157). They are a place to raise issues that are too dangerous to voice elsewhere – domestic violence, sexual abuse, rape, bullying and self-harm – and they are also a place to talk about sex in the absence of other reliable sources. Sex education is patchy, parents may not be able or willing to offer advice, and in some cases fear of punishment may make it too risky to ask (Vuttanont et al, 2006). The problem page is increasingly a resource for those who are disadvantaged within society, those who do not have access to friends or colleagues, those who are too embarrassed or afraid to seek advice elsewhere, or those who live in countries or communities where advice is not freely available or easily accessible (Baker and Boynton, 2005).

In this context, the quality of advice on offer in the media is an important issue. This is particularly so, given that advice in magazines, newspapers and websites is often Westernized and aspirational in tone. For example, standard advice given to a woman who has gone off sex is that she should make time for herself, enjoy hobbies or indulge herself with a bath and a bottle of wine – practices that may be unsuitable or impossible for a reader in the developing world (Baker and Boynton, 2005) and often not ideal for Western women either.

It is worrying, then, that many experienced sex advisors are now being dropped to make space for a new breed of celebrity advisor. The celebrities chosen are often highly sexualized figures such as porn stars or glamour models. Abi Titmuss, Jodie Marsh and Jordan have presided over advice pages in FHM, Zoo and More magazines (Boynton, 2006). It is well known within the media that such columns are ghost-written by existing magazine staff, thus dispensing with the need to employ qualified advisors. Celebrities may be paid a large retainer but this will cover being available for photographs as well as fronting an advice column, thereby generating more revenue for the magazine in terms of associated publicity (Boynton, 2006). In the past few years there has also been a shift away from paying qualified experts to write columns to inviting contributors to write for free – the trade-off being the opportunity to promote their books, websites or products such as sex toys. This has resulted in an increase in under-qualified or unqualified 'sexperts' occupying columns and offering advice. Two recent examples indicate what magazines are now looking for when appointing an 'agony aunt':

> Real Magazine is in the process of a very exciting re-launch and is extending its sex/relationship features ... If you look after a well-established attractive female relationship and are a sex expert/ psychologist or counsellor, please get in touch!

> Company magazine is looking for a young, enthusiastic qualified psychologist, willing to tackle a broad range of topics ... It's unpaid, but is a great way to boost your public profile, and of course a fantastic opportunity to talk about any books or products you're currently working on.

Increasingly, advisors are expected to be young (aged under 35), conventionally attractive and to have a product to promote. It is becoming particularly difficult for women offering media sex advice to do so in ways that are not sexualized (Boynton, 2006).

The sexualization of advisors is part of a broader shift in the way information about sex is presented in the media. The mass of sexual content in the media is often seen as a sign of an open sexual culture, but sex coverage itself is actually often limited and much of it is repetitive and conservative (Boynton, 2003; Attwood, 2005b). Indeed, the problem page is potentially challenging to magazines because it is a place where people admit to having sexual problems and needing information, contrary to the image of the sexually competent reader that magazines prefer to promote. It may be for this reason that many magazines strive to give the appearance of very spicy content, while they keep a tight control over the problems they include, ensuring that they never detract too much from the overall lifestyle and sensibility they are trying to promote (Boynton, 2003, 2006). It is important that problem pages and advice giving are included in wider debates about sexualization because the problem page is a place that constructs and subverts mainstream representations of sex and a space where sexual commercialism can be most aggressively maintained or challenged.

SEX, GENDER AND THE PROBLEM PAGE

Underlying all the questions people ask of agony aunts, regardless of age, gender or sexuality, is the question, 'Am I normal?' (Christian, 2006). However, what counts as normal is radically different in the way sex is represented to women and men. Angela McRobbie has argued that since the 1970s girls' magazines have had much more sexual content and that they present sex as being of paramount importance to a teenage girl's life. The focus is still resolutely hetero-sexual, but it has abandoned its concern with 'how to get and keep your man through romance' for an anxiety that 'if you do not have sex he will leave you' (Boynton, 2006). However, contemporary girls' magazines place relatively little emphasis on sexual desire or pleasure. It is often assumed that girls have lower sexual desires than boys, and little effort is made to encourage them to consider what might arouse them. Fears about encouraging girls to have sex mean that many magazines run very negative features, telling girls not to have sex or emphasizing the terrible things – pregnancy and sexually trans-mitted diseases – that will befall them if they do. There is little posi-tive information that might encourage girls to consider masturbation, fantasy or confidence-building around body image, personal skills or ambition. Most magazines focus on sex, relationships and beauty, and there is little room for celebrating girls' and women's achievements or for appreciating bodies that come in sizes bigger than zero.

In girls' and women's magazines a key theme is often the perform-ance of sex to get, please and keep a male partner (Boynton, 2003; Tyler, 2004; Jackson, 2005a, 2005b) – a theme that derives from a more general emphasis on women's appearance rather than their pleasure in mainstream media. This is often played out in the prob-lem pages where girls worry about how best to pleasure a partner, but not how to please themselves. In many magazines, agony aunts advise girls and women who do not like the idea of a particular sexual prac-tice to give it a go for their partners' sake, and readers who report a low sex drive are often encouraged to make themselves have sex rather than address other issues that may be causing them problems. Magazine features are littered with information on how to give the perfect blowjob, what to wear to turn him on or guarantee he'll never stray. They rarely mention the clitoris, masturbation or the exploration of sexual fantasy (Boynton, 2003). Nor do they address other factors that may impede a woman's sexual desire – stress, being overloaded with housework, childcare, health problems or problems with partners. Sex is something that women do to prove their attrac-tiveness, improve themselves and maintain their relationships with men.

Magazines for young men are similarly sexualized, though this takes quite a different form. The characteristics of the old 'top-shelf' softcore porn magazines – the explicitly sexual display of women's bodies and a tone of macho bravado about sex – have shifted to the 'middle shelf' in 'lad mags' such as *Loaded, Maxim, FHM*, and latterly *Nuts* and *Zoo* (Attwood, 2005b). Men's sexuality is repre-sented as active and aggressive, while a sexual double standard is still maintained – women are desired for sex, but those who have sex are judged negatively (Boni, 2002). Homosexual discourses are largely absent (although there is a growing genre of gay magazines and websites). The male body is represented as a machine that can be measured for speed, shape, size and performance. This portrayal also extends to the way male sexuality is imagined (Jackson et al, 2001). Men are depicted as always interested in sex. Sex is not routinely linked to relationships or domesticity, as it is in women's magazines, but is represented as a hedonistic and selfish pleasure. Men's task is to persuade women to give in to sexual practices that they either don't want, or may want if they are shown how. Men's magazines are full of tips on things to do to ensure women put out, where to find the g-spot (less often the clitoris), and positions to guarantee that women ejaculate, as a means of 'proving' male sexual skills. It is rarely suggested that a woman might show a man where her clitoris is or how she likes it touched. There is no mention of the skills of talking to partners about sexual needs or wants, and when a woman has gone off sex men are advised to use a combination of romance (candles, flowers, music) and patter (tell her she's beautiful) to get her to want more sex. It is never imagined that a woman may have gone off sex because her partner is unskilled or that she is bored and wants a raunchier sex life. Instead, the assumption is that women are not as 'naturally' sexual as men, that they lose interest in sex fairly soon after a relationship begins and that they are somehow deficient if they take 'at least 20 minutes to orgasm' or do not orgasm through penetrative sex alone.

Moreover, in all these discussions of sex there is no place for men to appear ignorant. Features tell men how to add to their existing skills base – they do not assume they lack skills to start with. It is not acceptable for men not to want or enjoy sex, or to worry about their bodies or sexual performance. Nor is it acceptable for men to have concerns about their relationships. Improving the quality of a relationship is only described in relation to an opportunity to get more sex, not because men may seek an enjoyable partnership. Because male sexuality is constructed in this manner, the inevitable result is increased anxieties and insecurities for men – with fewer opportunities to ask for help and support.

Problem pages themselves also occupy quite different places within magazines for men and women. They are less likely to appear in men's magazines, and when they do they are often hosted by traditionally feminine, non-threatening advisors such as 'the girls in the office', 'the girl next door' or porn stars and glamour models (Boynton, 2006). Often these mock the reader or retell sex stories rather than focusing on problems, reinforcing a view that men don't or shouldn't have problems or talk seriously about sex.

What is immediately striking about the letters sent to agony aunts is the repetition of particular problems. Angela McRobbie's analysis of teenage girls' magazines identified four common themes: peer pressure, conflict with friends and parents, physical and sexual abuse, and concerns about the body – weight, spots, body odour, physical appearance and breast size (1991: 158). The letters I receive from teenage girls are still focused on these problems. However, I also increasingly see questions from girls and young women that are outside the range of problems identified by previous analysis and which often indicate a shift towards greater levels of sexualization (McRobbie, 1996; Vuttanont et al, 2006). Anecdotal evidence from agony aunts suggests that the number of questions relating to sexual abuse is increasing. This may be a reflection of a greater awareness of abuse as a problem and of young people's ability to recognize and report sexual abuse. Other letters demonstrate a range of questions about sex topics that were not being asked 20 years ago. Alongside other new questions about eating disorders and self-harm, teenagers ask about pornography, how to perform oral or anal sex and negotiate threesomes.

These are typical examples of the more 'sexualized' questions I am asked:[1]

> hi, im sixteen and im going out with a guy thats eighteen. i was playing with his phone and decided to have a look in his pictures, which to my disgust were mainly graphic pictures of another girl. i got really upset and then later found out that the girl that had sent him them also phones him everyday. im a really insecure person and i feel like he is just using me and laughing at me behind my back. i tried to confront him about it but i got really upset and he said i was being really immature and childish.

> I sed to my boyfriend I had kissed a girl before and I liked it. Now he is on at me for a threesome all the time. He wants me to get my best mate over for a threesome with him but she is straight and I don't want to. He says I'm being unfair not having a threesome since I did kiss a girl before. I don't want to lose him or seem boring but I don't want to have a threesome either. Help!

> Is anal sex normal? My boyf really wants to try it (on me). He says it will be a big turn on. I heard it really really hurts tho. Does it hurt? Is it okay or will I get an STD from it? He thinks there are creams you can use so it won't hurt – should I do that?

These questions show how sexualization may cause new problems for girls. Technologies such as camera phones offer new opportunities for sexual expression but they may also be a new source of sexual insecurities. Girls feel under pressure to avoid being seen as 'boring', 'immature' or 'childish' by refusing to indulge in a threesome or to tolerate boys' liaisons with other girls. The normalization of anal sex and girl-on-girl action elsewhere in the media is also evident in the way teenagers talk about sex, and these seem to be practices which are now expected by boys and which girls worry about refusing. At the same time an old-fashioned view of sex as something that boys want and girls resist or give in to remains intact. Girls also appear to feel they should take responsibility for sexual problems:

I recently slept with a guy, but everytime we went to actually have sex he lost his erection. I know that he was attracted to me because he was hard during foreplay, and it wasn't to do with a condom either. I haven't spoken to him since, but i've been paranoid that it was something to do with me that he didn't like. Is there any advice you can give me?

I've had sex with my current boyfriend a few times now, I lost my virginity to him and I love him very much and he loves me too. I was quite excited about having sex, but have been dissapointed, sometimes its great but other times its just boring, i just lie there on the bed, is there something I should be doing to make the exsperience more pleasurable?

These girls are made to feel 'paranoid', 'disappointed' and 'bored' – concerned about their inability to make sex work or make it pleasurable. Girls also continue to worry about their lack of sexual experience, as they have in the past, but this has become complicated by the range of practices they now feel expected to perform:

Hi, I'm 15 and have just recently got together with a boy. We've not been together long, but I've been with boys before and put off things like giving head because I don't really know what to do. I would however just rather have sex. Is it bad to want to skip out other 'bases' and go straight to sex? I would of course be making sure it was safe sex and all of that kind of thing. I'm not saying I want to have sex straight away, I want to wait until I know he's the one I want to lose my virginity to, but in the mean-time, I'm worried about other bases!! please give me some advice!

Where girls do talk about desires and pleasures that are not focused on heterosexual interaction, they frequently experience them as problematic (see also Jackson, 2005a, 2005b):

i think i might be bisexual. i know for definite i'm not totally gay because i'm still attracted 2 boys, but recently i've been attracted 2 breasts and kissing girls. i kissed my girl mate the other day and i was turned on by her. any advice?

i have a really big masturbating problem i get turned on by nearly everything and i am happy going down on a guy but i don't like it when they go down on me! is there something wrong? i prefer giving myself pleasure!

What is interesting about the letters I receive from young women is that they are frequently very clear about what they already know and about the kind of advice they might like. However, their concerns and worries are often due to a lack of basic sex education or a lack of communication and negotiation techniques – the ability to know what they would like in their sex lives and how to ask for it. They perceive themselves as relatively powerless in their relationships with boys or unnatural if their desires do not revolve around boys.

Letters from boys and men are somewhat different. A content analysis of one year's worth of email problems I received when I was the sex editor at *Men's Health* magazine showed that 27 per cent were about sexual techniques – particularly how to give a partner an orgasm, or how to be sure they had achieved this; 23 per cent were about sex problems – erectile dysfunction and premature ejaculation; 17 per cent were about penis size and shape; 17 per cent were about dating; 11 per cent were about body image; and 10 per cent were about relationship problems. These are typical of the questions I get from men generally, and, in contrast with questions from girls and women, they include less information about their problems, cover a far narrower range of issues and tend to focus on a 'quick fix' to their problems. These are typical of the questions I receive from boys and men:

I am very short (4 inches) and it [the penis] is in a curved shape when erect. I feel very low about this. What can I try to make it straighter and longer?

I have a date with a girl next week. I'm worried I won't get it up – will Viagra help?

When I have an erection should my penis bend upwards, point straight up?

When I see flaccid penises on the t.v. the foreskin is folded back and the head exposed. When flaccid mine is small and thin and appears to have loose foreskin on the end which looks like a spout. I am slightly overweight at the moment and also a virgin. Would this explain my loose foreskin?

I cum in about 3 mins and I'm scared to have sex coz I might not last long enough. How long does a normal 16–22 year old have to last in sex?

How can I cure coming too soon, is there any medications I can take to stop me doing this?

When I see someone I like my mouth goes dry and I can't speak. If it's someone I don't fancy I can chat away like anything. When it is someone I do fancy I cannot say a word and look like I have a really stupid sheepish smile on my face. How do I get over this? What do I say when I like someone so I don't sound like an arse?

As these letters show, boys' and men's problems tend to be much more specific and focused on the body and the problems their bodies cause them – their questions often focus on physical size and shape. Apart from the last question here which shows a broader concern with shyness and communication, the readers seem to be entirely preoccupied with their bodies, or, more specifically, their penises. They are concerned with an ideal of what their penises 'should' look like and often have measured and examined them carefully. They worry about erections and ejaculation and see 'medication' as a potential cure for any problems they may have with these. Men's concerns and the way they express them are often interpreted by journalists as evidence that men require a more 'factual' approach to their problems. My interpretation is that men are often not given as many sources of information about the body as women are and that they are overwhelmed with images of the perfect penis which they worry they do not live up to. It is not uncommon for men to contact me having avoided relationships for decades because of a fear they simply do not 'measure up'.

This may not be surprising, given the way sex is represented in men's media – as something men do to women and assuming a high level of competency, confidence and a willing partner who would be happy to try anything without complaint. In many ways, the problem page offers a space to subvert this representation, allowing men to express their lack of knowledge and technique and their sexual fears. But many men's magazines continue to be unwilling to allow readers to show themselves as having difficulties with sex. It is not uncommon for serious questions to be cut from the magazine or even for letters from gay readers to be edited to appear as though they have been written by straight men. In this way, a view of male sexuality as straight, simple and mechanistic, and of men as confident and competent sexual beings, is perpetuated. This is in stark contrast to the view the mainstream media often presents of girls' and women's sexuality as anxiety ridden and focused almost entirely on men and relationships. Both sets of representations are also in line with the gendering of contemporary sexual relationship styles as Anthony Giddens has described (1992). Sex combined with romance in a 'pure' relationship based on mutual self-interest is increasingly associated with women, while an 'episodic' form of sexuality, based on the hedonistic pursuit of sex and the avoidance of intimacy and emotion, is associated with men. The problem page may either reinforce or subvert this message depending on the publication.

TWENTY-FIRST-CENTURY AGONY AUNTS

Alongside gender differences in the way young men and women articulate their experiences of sex and sexual problems, there is a general shift towards more explicit sexual discussion and a high level of anxiety in both male and female readers' letters about sex, confidence, body image and negotiating interpersonal relationships. Young people may have a greater awareness of sex-related topics from living in a sexualized culture where sex is synonymous with lifestyle and consumerism (Tyler, 2004; Attwood, 2005a; Elliott and Lemert, 2006), but this does not mean they are necessarily comfortable with the situation or able to effectively negotiate the culture they find themselves living in. It seems that teenagers are increasingly anxious, confused and bewildered by the ways in which sex is represented to them.

Despite what appears to be a growing need for reliable sex information in print, online and in broadcast media, there is currently no regulation of advice giving, nor is there any support for advice givers (Boynton, 2007). There is no formal training for agony aunts, although charities such as the Family Planning Association and organizations such as the Department of Health do organize training events focused on specific issues such as teenage pregnancy or HIV. These are often well attended, but celebrity advisors and counsellors who use their columns for self-promotion rarely take advantage of this kind of support.

There are concerns that young people are increasingly under pressure to have sex when perhaps they do not want to, or in ways that do not always appeal to them, in order to keep a partner or prove sexual prowess, rather than for reasons of desire, passion or sexual curiosity. Although sex is everywhere in the media, it is often reduced to information about a limited repertoire, and imagination, exploration and adventures are not encouraged. Magazines serve to maintain and construct our views of sexuality, and often they simply represent the views of journalists who have a limited and often conservative view of sex (Boynton and Callaghan, 2006). This problem is compounded because of the low status of sex as a topic, the fear of losing advertising revenue and the common practice of basing sex coverage on existing features in other magazines. Because of this, the range and format of problem pages and sex features remains limited and suggestions of change are resisted.

We know very little about why people become agony aunts, but discussions with a number of my colleagues indicate two main reasons for writing. For one group – usually those who are older, more qualified and more established – advice giving is a personal and political act, something you do for love, often for little or no money, and something you use another career, for example, as a novelist, doctor or psychologist, to fund. Many of the 'aunts' in this group also have personal experience of childhood trauma or abuse, eating disorders, unwanted pregnancies or abusive relationships. The second group – the new generation of advisors – see themselves as columnists rather than agony aunts, and use their roles to promote their products or services to a wider audience, or, in the case of celebrity advisors, to reach a wider fan base.

This commodification of advice giving in which advisors are

increasingly people who have something to sell is highly problematic. Discussions with 'aunts' from the first group show that most answer all the letters they receive, and they often break with the policy of not entering into personal correspondence with readers to make contact with individuals they are concerned about. Many of the newer gener-ation of advisors do not see all the letters they are sent, instead rely-ing on what the magazine gives them. Perhaps unsurprisingly, the older generation see this new group of advisors as less dedicated and professional. But it is not surprising that they take quite a different approach to their roles as agony aunts in a climate where advisors and advice are sexualized and commodified.

There are now numerous opportunities for advice giving. The expansion of advice giving online – in advice pages, sites, blogs and podcasts – presents us with opportunities to subvert the idea of only 'experts' being able to give advice. It makes more space available for the discussion of problems and it allows for the creation of search-able archives of information and advice. However, the sheer volume of sites offering advice, many only a cover for commercial ventures, is problematic. Glossy sites that feature photographs of doctors in white coats may look reputable but are often a front for sales of untested or ineffective pills, patches or other products. Men in particular are targeted by sites posing as advice sources but advocating penis enlargement or related products (Boynton, 2004; Cooper, 2002; Boni, 2002; Salerno, 2005; Elliott and Lemert, 2006). The quality of advice online varies even more than in print media since techni-cally anyone with web access can set themselves up as an advisor, and whilst the inclusion of different voices and opinions can be an effective means of education and empowerment, this also means an increase in sex information that is incorrect, outdated or prejudiced. Unfortunately, it is likely that we will see advice giving linked to commercial ventures increasing.

If we are to ensure the availability of good sex advice in the future, we need to take steps to improve the quality of service currently offered. At present a number of agony aunts and uncles are setting up support groups to improve skills, provide informal training and challenge the use of underqualified 'sexperts' to give advice within mainstream media (Boynton, 2006; Boynton and Callaghan, 2006).

Opportunities are also increasing for improved sex reporting in the media, with organizations like the Kinsey Institute offering training for journalists and sexologists to address their skills and competencies.

We need to challenge the sexualization of advice giving and the outdated and conservative sex information that often passes for expert knowledge in the mainstream media. We also need to challenge the commercialization of sexual culture and the relation of advice giving to products which allow the pharmaceutical industry and sex-product promoters to take advantage of people's lack of sex information and to create sexual insecurities (Tiefer, 2004). We need more research to examine how people use problem pages, assess how these construct sexuality and impact on readers' sex lives, and explore the motivations and skills of those offering advice. Within mainstream media and social science, sexual problems and sex advice have been overlooked, ignored or oversimplified. The time has come to see this as a legitimate area of research and practice.

ACKNOWLEDGEMENTS

With thanks to those who have requested advice and given me feedback as an agony aunt, and to Annie Auerbach, Simon Geller, Will Callaghan, Gillian Baker and Dotun Adebayo for helping me with advice giving.

NOTES

1.   All problems are included with the permission of their authors.

Part 3

STRIPTEASE CULTURE

Chapter 8

TOO MUCH TOO YOUNG?: YOUNG PEOPLE, SEXUAL MEDIA AND LEARNING

SARA BRAGG AND DAVID BUCKINGHAM

The relationship between children, sex and the media is, in some respects, an old issue. The presence of 'sexually explicit' material in the media has routinely generated concern on the part of many commentators, even if what counts as 'explicit' has changed markedly over time. In recent years, however, this debate seems to have taken on a new urgency. The advent of new technologies - video, cable, satellite and the Internet - has made it increasingly difficult to prevent young people from gaining access to such material; and it is of course a premise of this book that Western culture has in general become more 'sexualized'.

The concerns expressed in this debate often appear to reflect much broader anxieties about the changing nature of childhood in contemporary societies: children are seen to be growing up too soon, they are being sexualized and their childhood is being destroyed through, amongst other things, their access to sexual knowledge. As these passive linguistic constructions suggest, blame is laid at the door of external forces, most commonly the media and consumer culture. If they buy their children clothes with suggestive slogans, parents are held to be complicit or powerless to resist the tide of consumer culture that pushes sexuality at their children. Young people, meanwhile, are assumed to be incompetent and unable to negotiate this new sexual culture because they lack the skills of critical media consumption that might enable them to resist it and because they are in any case ideally asexual or sexually innocent.

Research in this field, particularly in the USA, has often sought to provide evidence about the negative effects of the media, for instance, correlating links between media consumption and what are considered 'undesirable' actions such as 'premature' sexual activity. This research implies that the causes of such behaviour lie beyond and outside young people's own desires and choices (Bragg and Buckingham, 2002). Sexuality continues to be seen as an adult concept, which should not be allowed to intrude on the 'sanitized space of natural childhood' (Walkerdine, 1997: 169). Such assumptions mean that questions about adults' own ambivalent feelings towards children can be marginalized, as can those about whether children themselves bring anything to the process of sexualization (Walkerdine, 1997: 169-70). Children are predominantly perceived as in need of protection – although this often involves measures that are also designed to control them (Buckingham, 2000: 12).

The debate about sex education in the UK has been highly politicized for decades, as many writers have pointed out (Thomson, 1993). It condenses many of these concerns about attitudes to children's sexuality and particularly towards teenagers, whose liminal status between child and adult makes them especially problematic. Broadly speaking, the post-1997 New Labour government has adopted a less moralistic stance than the Conservative Party, issuing new guidance on Sex and Relationship Education (DFEE, 2000), supporting new training schemes for teachers and entering into discussions with editors of teenage magazines. In this way the government has tried pragmatically to compromise between local authority and parental control of sex education, and to acknowledge children's sexuality whilst upholding the norm of children as ideally non-sexual (Monk, 2001). Monk, citing Thomson (2000), argues that locating sex and relationship education within the curriculum for Personal, Social and Health Education (PSHE) and Citizenship 'represents a significant shift from the language of morality to that of citizenship and personal development' (Monk, 2001: 277).

Nevertheless, young people's views are generally conspicuous by their absence from these debates. In seeking to redress this situation, this chapter reports on the findings of two projects that aimed to explore young people's own perspectives. One was a research project carried out from 2001 to 2003, entitled *Children, Media and Personal Relationships,* funded by a consortium of British broadcasting and regulatory bodies (see Buckingham and Bragg, 2003, 2004). The aim was to investigate young people's responses to media images of love, sex and relationships. The second, *Media Relate* (2003–5), built on the findings of that research, as well as on media education pedagogies, to develop teaching materials on sex and the media, for use in school sex education classes (Bragg, 2006). Our starting point in both cases was that media are more diverse and contradictory than simply a collection of 'negative' messages: they act as cultural resources or 'tools to think with' for young people, rather than sources of oppression or manipulation. We also began from a belief that the formation of sexual identity is a complex process, which is unstable, insecure, always under construction in ways that cannot be explained by mechanistic psychological notions of role modelling or sexual socialization. And whilst we did not want to romanticize young people's views on these topics, we also did not assume that they would necessarily be coterminous with those of adults.

The first research project involved extensive qualitative work – over 100 pair and focus group interviews with 120 young people aged from nine to 17 (as well as approximately 70 parents) – and a survey of nearly 800 young people. We worked with a range of young people, both working and middle class, in the south east and the north of England. We aimed to allow them to express their views in different forms, so, in addition to pair and group interviews, participants completed a scrapbook or diary on the theme of media images of love, sex and relationships. The scrapbooks enabled young people to talk to us in ways they chose, about what they saw as important; they acted as both a record and reflection, thus bringing their voices into the project in more diverse ways. They also helped us to grasp in a tangible way what young people were talking about when they referred to media texts such as newspaper or magazine articles or advertisements that they included. Our approach was broadly to begin at a more personal or individual level and then to move on to the more social context of the peer group.

In the *Media Relate* project, we worked with various partners to develop a set of teaching materials consisting of worksheets and a DVD targeting teachers and students aged 12–15.[1] The materials were piloted in a range of schools, and teachers and students were interviewed about their experiences and opinions of using them.

YOUNG PEOPLE SPEAKING BACK

In research, young participants – like adults – inevitably adopt particular subject positions, or construct versions of the self and others in relation to widely circulated public discourses on the topic at hand (see Buckingham, 1993). All the young people we talked to showed an acute awareness of the public debate about their relationship to sexual media, and this shaped the narratives and presentations of self they offered in interviews. Since they were aware of their positioning as innocent, vulnerable or media-incompetent, both in the domain of public debate and frequently in the family, their response was often to emphasize their knowingness, be it about sex or the media, and thereby to construct a powerful counter-position to the powerless one marked out for them. Thus young people tended to present themselves as 'media-savvy' (MacKeogh, 2001) and 'sex-savvy'. Even some of our youngest participants engaged with and 'spoke back to' adult views; one ten-year-old, Lysa, cut out a problem page from a girls' magazine to include in her scrapbook and wrote above it, 'I want you to know that the page below does not make me feel uncomfortable in any way, it's excellent!', as if she anticipated disapproving adult responses.

However, on other occasions, young people adopted a moralistic voice about sex in the media that was almost indistinguishable from the views commonly expressed in newspapers. For instance, some echoed the notion that the media offer 'bad role models', accusing texts such as *Bridget Jones's Diary* (2001) of encouraging 'failing, pathetic relationships' (Trevor, aged 17), and condemning celebrities such as Britney Spears for showing 'poor moral fibre' (Jeff, aged 17). However, these concerns were often ironically expressed, voiced in relation to audiences who were always 'other' than them, and generally in relation to texts other than those they enjoyed. In their expression they demonstrated an adult knowingness about the terms of the debate that in itself challenged adult assumptions of youthful ignorance. In addition, young people often expressed a conventional moral agenda – one that confounded popular representations of them as lost in a moral vacuum. They were aware of the ethics of relationships and often explained and understood the behaviour of fictional characters in these terms. They referred to notions of decency and propriety in relation to sexual images in the public domain, although their exact analysis varied according to age. In relation to the display of women's bodies, however, they were resistant to suggestions that this was objectifying or sexist. They were more likely to propose an 'equal opportunities sexism' that would involve the wider publication of semi-naked images of men rather than curtailing institutions such as the tabloid Sun's 'page 3' bare-breasted models.

Our research participants were at pains to demonstrate that they were responsible enough to be trusted to make their own decisions, illustrating their media competence and literacy in a number of ways. For instance, Lysa argued that she understood what she should expect to see if she was illicitly watching Channel 4 programmes late at night (these have a partially deserved reputation for explicit sexual subject matter), and so would not be upset by them. Alma, aged ten, explained how, when concerned about how a soap opera storyline might develop, she comforted herself with the thought that 'they [the producers] wouldn't do that because of all the little people who watch'. A group of older teenagers were scornful about those who complained about the sexual focus of a Friday night chat show, pointing out that the reputation of its presenter, its scheduling and the images in the title sequence already offered enough warning about its likely content. They argued that audiences had the opportunity to switch over or off, mobilizing the kinds of justificatory discourses about 'choice' that media institutions also use – although we might note how limited such choices tend to be.

The voices young people adopted in their scrapbooks were also coded generically in ways that reveal how the media serve them as a resource. For instance, some students treated the scrapbooks as a school project and adopted the kind of tone they thought would be deemed appropriate there – one that was distant and moralistic, involving a language of 'critique' that mobilized media-negative concepts such as 'stereotyping' or the idea that 'sex sells'. This was often at odds with the more pleasurable engagements with the media that they described in interviews, such as passionate fandom for particular films, programmes or pop stars that were often shared with (and therefore helped consolidate) friendship groups. At other times, however, the scrapbooks did enable different voices to emerge. Sometimes this was simply because they allowed children to be more enthusiastic about the media – described as 'heavy phat wicked cool brill!' by Tania (aged ten) on the cover of hers. Others drew on media formats to play with identities, for instance, introducing themselves through the magazine interview format, listing favourite activities, music, ambitions and so on, as if they were a celebrity being quizzed. Krystal (aged 14) drew on the conventions of teenage magazines, constructing a layout of short 'soundbites' (often raising questions rather than providing answers – 'why are girls mainly the softer sex?'), interspersed with icons of hearts and flowers and doodles, using colour to highlight key statements and a conversational, informal tone that also engaged her friends in writing contributions to capture 'how we really talk'. This 'youth magazine' style may have enabled her to explore a range of contradictory feelings and views without enforcing closure. Such media literacies could be seen to give young people rather different speaking positions than the scholastic 'voice of critique' – voices that are noticeably less moralistic and definitive, and more self-conscious, reflective and open.

DEFINING WHAT'S 'APPROPRIATE'

Both in themselves, and by virtue of the ways in which they are distributed, regulated and used, the media provide a powerful set of definitions about what is 'appropriate' for children at particular ages; and while these definitions may be disputed, they are nevertheless widely acknowledged by children and parents. They provide at least some of the terms within which young people think about their relations with the media, and against which they calibrate their own developmental levels. Bea, aged ten, for example, described how her mother allowed her to buy a girls' magazine like *Shout* (aimed at her age range but pitched as though for slightly older readers) because she was '*fast at growing up*'. Growing up, in her account, is not something that happens to her, but something she can achieve – and her media consumption is a measure of her speed and success in doing so. Chloe (aged 17) described her mother's shock the first time she bought a teenage girls' magazine: 'she just didn't realize that I wanted to read more about stuff like that, rather than comics like the *Beano* and stuff'. Young people's active choice of media was caught up in family dynamics, and could serve as a way of communicating needs and a sense of identity. Chloe's co-interviewee, Angela, remarked of Chloe's purchase, 'it's you growing up'; that is, it enabled her to convey not just her reading preferences but her development towards adulthood. Similar stories were told by others, where laughing at innuendo on TV in the presence of parents revealed that they had greater sexual knowledge than they believed their parents attributed to them. Family viewing of sexual material emerged in interview accounts as a source of considerable tension, necessarily entailing assumptions about what was appropriate or necessary and what should be proscribed or forbidden, both for males and females, and for adults and children. It was a site of struggle, in which competing definitions of identity were constructed, challenged, negotiated and defined as young people exhibited resistance or compliance with parental prohibitions or encouragement of appropriate viewing behaviours (Bragg and Buckingham, 2004).

Our interviews with children and parents suggested that what it now means to be a child or a teenager needs to be constantly defined, reasserted and worked over rather than being taken for granted – and that sex becomes another terrain on which that definition has to occur. In some instances, as we have seen, the children actively resisted adult constructions of 'childishness', although in others they sought to reclaim or reinforce these. For example, ten-year-old Will included in his scrapbook an article about an advertisement for Carlsberg lager using the model Helena Christensen, headlined 'Probably the sexiest advert in the world'. He wrote underneath, 'I think I should know about it but not right now because I think I am too young to understand' – the ambiguous use of 'it' conveying and concealing a mixture of confusion and ignorance on his part. In this sense, perhaps, the media are creating new ways of being a child – not corrupting but confronting young people with choices about whether to 'remain' a child or whether and when to enter the 'adult' world of sexual media.

Will's serious, reflective tone captured the ambivalence of many of our participants who simultaneously claimed their rights to information and to self-regulation. They saw themselves as autonomous, calculating and self-regulating entities, in control of their own quest for knowledge in relation to sex and sexual media material. They wanted to make judgements about what they did or did not 'need to know' and resisted or rejected parents' attempts to decide on their behalf, often relating how they had outwitted parental attempts to do so. Yet they were also aware that current definitions of 'good' or responsible parenting almost necessarily entail regulating and restricting children's access to the media. If they did describe their parents as allowing them access to more 'adult' material, they were careful to protect their parents from accusations of being lax and uncaring by arguing that they themselves were uniquely mature and trustworthy. They did not necessarily reject the principle of regulation. Will (aged ten) solemnly reported that his five-year-old sister hadn't seen 'it' (that is, sexual material of one sort or another) but had got 'very close to seeing it'. Fortunately, he reassured us, 'I always manage to get the control off her.' For many children, seeing material 'over their age' was a mark of adulthood, but so too was regulating material on behalf of even younger viewers. For themselves, they claimed a right to choose – and this was one that their parents increasingly recognized, particularly once their children reached the age of ten or 12.

Our findings suggest that young people frequently encounter 'sexual' media material, but that relatively little of this material contains 'explicit' representations of sexual activity. Nonetheless, the emphasis our interviewees placed on their self-governing capacities may help explain the particular dilemmas of regulating sexual material. Sexual media material has been increasingly drawn into the domain of personal ethics, conceived of as an occasion for individuals to scrutinize their own desires, conduct and responses, rather than one of social harm, as is the case still with media images of

violence. For this reason, it may be harder for centralized regulatory bodies to obtain the degree of consensus that is necessary to
win legitimacy when it comes to controlling sexual material. As a
result, debate around media regulation seems to be shifting away
from a state censorship model to an informed consumer model, as
demonstrated by the recently declared commitment of Ofcom, the
UK media 'watchdog', to media literacy. Whilst this seems a liberal,
even audience-empowering move, it also places an additional burden
of choice and responsibility on individual viewers.

REPRESENTING DIVERSITY

As many critics and commentators have observed, the media show
an increasing diversity of sexual representations, often customized
to particular social groups in the audience (Arthurs, 2004). Our
participants certainly perceived the media as offering more diverse
sexual representations than they could find in the school or family.
For instance, many perceived a moral agenda in sex education that
was fundamentally about 'just saying no' and that ruled out pleasure
and fun: as Chantel (aged 14) asserted, 'school puts like a downer on
things ... it should be something that you like!' In contrast, they said,
the media would explain 'anything you wanna know' and were more
likely to discuss the *feelings* involved in relationships.

All our interviewees demonstrated a familiarity and confidence
with the categories of lesbian and gay – whether as sexual popula-
tions represented in the media or as audiences for particular texts.
Responses varied, however: younger boys in particular exhibited
considerable anxiety, insisting on their interest only 'in the girls
not the boy' when looking at sexual scenes on television, prefacing
statements about male images by insisting, 'I'm not gay or anything'
and even expressing concern that merely looking at images of male
models might make them 'turn gay'. Such declarations suggest that
heterosexuality is incredibly fragile if it is so easily overturned by the
simple act of looking. To this extent, we might even conclude that
the media play a greater role in *disturbing* gender and sexual identities
than they do in confirming them.

In contrast, older participants, and girls across the age range, tended to take lesbian and gay issues as an opportunity to rehearse liberal versions of the self. For instance, they were critical of 'compulsory heterosexuality' in the media, vocally asserted support for gay rights, and expressed enthusiasm for the liberal treatments of gay relationships in some drama and comedy. At the same time, they acknowledged that much of this was utopian, an image of how they might like life to be, rather than reflecting their actual experience. Indeed, none of the young people in our research identified as lesbian or gay. As others have argued, there is uneven development rather than a smooth narrative of increasing progressivism around sexuality (Jackson and Scott, 2004). So alongside these professions of tolerating diversity, interview data also revealed much about schools and families as sites for 'producing heterosexualities' (Kehily, 2002), whether through teachers using homophobic language as a tool for classroom control or parents disciplining children into appropriate heterosexual desires.

In a sense, however, the substantive positions the young people took up on these issues are not as significant as the broader discourses about the self that they entailed. None of our young participants presented themselves as dependent for moral guidance on the authority of religion, traditional morality or established experts such as teachers, even where they came from strongly religious family backgrounds. Nikolas Rose (1999a) has argued that this can be seen as part of a broader social shift, in which traditional codes of morality are in decline, giving way to questions of ethics or 'work on the self'. For instance, in our research, lesbian and gay sexuality was rarely discussed in terms of whether it was 'right' or 'wrong', but instead as a question of self-determination, being 'true to oneself' and respecting the identities of others. Tanya (aged ten) exemplified this when she included in her scrapbook a newspaper image showing two women lovers, and remarked approvingly of it that, 'I think these two women who are lovers are OK to be in a newspaper because they are happy and if they're happy they're happy.' Honesty, happiness and personal freedom, rather than following externally imposed moral codes, seemed to be the pre-eminent ethical choices here. Such findings have significant implications for sex education, suggesting that it is likely to alienate students if they perceive it as overly didactic or aiming to instil 'correct' moral values.

LEARNING ABOUT SEX — AND SEX EDUCATION

Our interviewees were often negative about parents and schools as a means for learning about sex. Parents were often represented as ignorant, either of the extent of their children's actual sexual knowledge, or, paradoxically, of their need for greater knowledge than parents were prepared or able to provide. Many described parental 'discussions' about sex as shrouded in mutual embarrassment. When we discussed sex education in our interviews, young people were very disparaging, perhaps ritualistically so, since the anonymous survey results were more positive about it. They echoed what other researchers in this area (Measor et al, 2000; Hilton, 2003) have found, criticizing the focus on girls' issues, the bad behaviour of boys in the class and instances of dismal pedagogy, such as being shown the same video about puberty two or three years running by different teachers. They claimed that sex education in schools taught them little that was new, and that the focus was much too narrowly medical or scientific, on 'the insides and all that' as Glenn (aged 17) put it. They argued that it was set in a preventative and biological framework, trying to alert students to the dangers and difficulties of sex rather than dealing with aspects of relationships.

The media therefore came to fill what young people perceived as a gap: in our survey, the media were rated as highly as mothers as a useful source of sexual information, and considerably higher than fathers. However, if young people do learn about sex and relationships from the media, this is not a straightforward or reliable process. Young people often rejected overt attempts by the media to teach them about sexual matters, for example in more didactic teen dramas like *Dawson's Creek* (1998–2003), and they were often sceptical about the advice they were offered in problem pages or talkshows. They were not uniformly voracious in their desire for information either, as we have seen from Will's comment about being 'too young' for some kinds of material. Similarly, several girls explained that they had stopped reading particular teenage magazines because they contained information they felt they did not yet 'need to know'.

When we asked Will whether he expected to find out about sex from school or from his parents, he replied, 'Neither. I think I've got to work it out myself ... by doing research. And then eventually when

I get older I'll find out.' His curiously academic notion of 'research' seems to encapsulate something of the gradual, even haphazard nature of sexual learning. His insistence on 'working it out himself' was also typical of the independent approach many of the children adopted or sought to adopt: they very much wanted to be in charge of their own learning. Learning about sex and relationships was seen as a matter of actively seeking information from several sources and making judgements for themselves about a range of potentially conflicting messages. Such learning was often a collective process, conducted among the peer group (for instance at sleepovers), rather than a one-way, top-down transmission of knowledge – in marked contrast to formal sex education. Participants emphasized that they were learning to become self-regulating sexual subjects, responsible for their own fulfilment, rather than being passively socialized into a moral code.

AN ALTERNATIVE APPROACH

Part of the challenge of developing the *Media Relate* teaching pack was to address young people as 'their' media texts do, as knowledgeable, mature and 'savvy'. The materials covered four areas: research, drama and soap operas, magazines and health-education advertising. They drew on a range of best practices in media education, which emphasize talk-based, open-ended, hands-on activities involving media production. For instance, students are asked to create soap opera storylines involving teenage pregnancy, or to develop health education campaigns on issues such as condom use or support for lesbian and gay teenagers. Through these processes, they engage actively with how meanings and ideas are represented, the constraints limiting the messages on offer and the opportunities for change (Buckingham, 2003). Media education practice of this kind is collective and social in its conception of learning, rather than individualist, and values informal learning, hence the role of group work and the focus on talk. It is not 'preventative' or prophylactic: it does not seek to inoculate students against pernicious media influence, but to enable them to participate actively in media cultures by making their own meanings and interpretations. Again, this contrasts with models of sex education that see it as a way of preventing teenage pregnancy or only communicating 'facts' about sex.

There are obvious dangers in the originators of an approach also evaluating it, so our comments here are not designed to promote our materials above others. However, our interviews with students who used some of the materials were revealing. Students repeatedly told us how much they enjoyed 'being able to have a real debate', which perhaps tells us more about existing school lessons in this area than about the virtues of our materials. A task involving creating scrapbooks similar to the one we used in our first project elicited comments such as, 'that's really good because we get to write down our thoughts ... we can write about ... practically anything we want that's to do with love, sex and relationships' (girl aged 12). One girl, aged 12, wrote that her scrapbook showed 'how much more we know', referring, presumably, to ignorant previous generations. Another presented her views of horoscopes and of problem pages in a teenage magazine, in each case summarizing what she saw as their 'message' and delivering her verdict as an already critical consumer. This degree of self-awareness is not taken into account by many sex educators, who tend to see young people as manipulated by media they cannot resist.

In feedback, students also often focused on lesbian and gay issues, raised by a role-play exercise in which they debated how well magazines served lesbian and gay teenagers. Once again, this provided an opportunity for girls in particular to articulate progressive positions: 'I thought it was an issue that does need to be discussed and I wanted to give my opinion about why I don't think it's wrong to be gay' (girl aged 13). A teacher reported that a 12-year-old boy had commented in class that a homophobic boy 'must be gay because he's got a real problem with it, he's obviously in denial!' Even where students did not share the liberal consensus of a class, it seemed that they valued an environment in which they would not be judged for their views.

Teachers said that they were 'pleasantly surprised' and even 'amazed' at the work students put into their scrapbooks, relating how diverse and challenging their ideas had been. It seems that many teachers, like adults generally, under-estimate young people's existing critical faculties and their ability to highlight contradictions and inconsistencies in the media's treatment of sex. So whilst teachers saw the scrapbooks as motivating for students, from our point of view it was equally significant that they seemed to have helped teachers to understand more about the world their students inhabit outside school, and thereby to develop different kinds of classroom dialogue about such issues.

Nonetheless, the materials did indicate problems in reaching boys, which have also been noted in previous research into sex education (Kehily, 2002; Hilton, 2003). For instance, there were gender differences in responses to the scrapbooks: girls took to the task more willingly, writing at length in a personal tone and paying a great deal of attention to presentation. They may also have had access to more visual material than boys in the form of magazines. Boys tended to write less, and their textual reference points were different: instead of magazines, they referred more to TV, computer games, music and (tabloid) newspapers, for example. In the context of the school, these media forms may be seen by teachers as more problematic than those preferred by girls. Mary Jane Kehily's work suggests that teenage magazines provide young women with 'a discourse that they can appropriate in creative ways as a form of expertise which links verbal competence with femininity' (2002: 203). However, for boys to do the same risks accusations of not being masculine enough. In our own research, many boys adhered to what Pfeil (1995) has termed 'warrior' or 'heroic' versions of traditional masculinity, which insist on invulnerability, individualism and 'knowing it all'. In discussing a 'guide to kissing' in a girls' magazine, for example, Wesley, aged 12, insisted that such teaching should not be necessary for boys. 'It's a boy!,' he exclaimed. 'He should *already* know how to turn a girl on, and nibble and all!' Such ideals of masculinity may conflict with redefinitions of the self as always incomplete and requiring continuous work that have been encouraged by consumer culture and by a new 'ethics of the self' that stresses self-creation rather than following prescribed moralities (Rose, 1999a). Moreover, a focus on forms of popular culture with which girls are more familiar may flatter their existing skills, whilst potentially leaving boys behind or reinforcing gender divisions in the classroom.

CONTINUING DILEMMAS

Whilst our educational strategies and our research findings reflect a broader emphasis in childhood and cultural studies on the importance of recognizing young people's competence and agency, they also point to some of the limitations of this approach – and in particular to the dangers of reproducing approaches from popular culture rather than offering critical purchase on them. There are dilemmas and tensions that arise for young people in this new environment.

Anita Harris refers to the 'regulation of interiority' to describe the work on the self encouraged by media and celebrity culture, and points out that the confessional mode has become a common way of engaging young women in popular culture (Harris, 2004). As we have argued, the media increasingly constitute their audiences in ethical terms – that is, they invite them to engage actively with the dilemmas and issues they portray and to take responsibility for their responses and views. Our interviewees in both projects were often sceptical about such material, yet this does not necessarily imply that they are immune to it. For example, problem pages, which most claimed not to read anyway, may be less significant for the solutions they offer than for the ways they define certain kinds of behaviour as problematic in the first place, or encourage readers to imagine themselves, for instance, as individuals in control of their sexual identity and conduct. Similarly, many young people spoke of completing the quizzes in youth magazines – which, albeit often in parodic or joking ways, are designed to yield information about the self for the purposes of self-assessment and judgement. Such media practices may help to habituate audiences to the rituals of assessing their own desires, attitudes and conduct in relation to criteria set out by the new secular 'experts' (Rose, 1999a).

Critics such as Nikolas Rose see such heightened reflexivity as a feature of the neo-liberal consumer cultures that have emerged over the past few decades (Rose, 1999a, 1999b). The rise of ideas of 'active citizenship' and of values of choice, autonomy and self-realization have produced individuals who are 'capable of bearing the burdens of liberty' in advanced democracies (Rose, 1999a). Rose argues that such notions also have costs. They generate the 'commitment of selves to the values and forms of life supported by authorities', particularly those of consumption. 'It is through the promotion of "lifestyle" by the mass media, advertising and experts, through the obligation to shape a life through choices in a world of self-referenced objects and images, that the modern subject is governed' (Rose, 1999a: 261). In this new world, broader structures of support and stability have been undermined; individuals have been bound to become self-regulating consumers who are responsible for their own ethical self-development and well being (Rimke, 2000; Rose, 1999a). Yet the discourses of voluntarism, autonomy and individuality that are so dominant today provide little space for other more critical frameworks that might offer different ways of making meaning of our lives and of the structured inequalities we also experience.

On occasions, we wondered if some of this might explain the anger and frustration sometimes vented by young people on the media – for instance, criticizing them for creating pressures around body image, appearance, sexual activity, and so on. In some ways, these echoed adult discourses about the harmful effects of the media and they may have also reflected the expected discourses of the school. But they also suggest a lack of access to other more complicated explanatory discourses with which to explain the pressures they faced. And it could be argued that our own teaching approaches also 'regulate interiority', inviting the display of the self and experiences. They might be seen as part of the same technology through which self-regulating and responsible individuals are created, rather than a critique of such practices.

We have argued that the media should be seen as a diverse set of 'symbolic resources', and that young people are often critical and reflexive readers. As noted above, whilst our research participants frequently encountered 'sexual' media material, relatively little of it seemed to be highly explicit, and it was heterogeneous and often contradictory in terms of the 'messages' it was seen to contain. The young people in our research clearly valued the media as information sources, arguing that they were often more informative, less embarrassing to access and more in touch with their needs and concerns than parents or school sex education. Yet they were not the naive or incompetent consumers children are frequently assumed to be. They used a range of critical skills and perspectives when interpreting sexual content, which developed both with age and with their media experience. They were sensitive to issues of 'morality' and right and wrong in their debates about characters' motivations and the consequences of their behaviour. To this extent, familiar adult concerns about the harmful effects of the media on children's sexual development might be seen to be misplaced or at least overstated.

Nevertheless, these concerns about the prominence of sexual content in the media – while they are often exaggerated – provide powerful indications of the changing meanings of modern childhood. Children today may or may not know more about sex than previous generations, but in their dealings with the media they are increasingly called upon to make choices about who they are, and in particular whether they want to remain 'a child'. The young people in our research showed an acute awareness of the public debates about their relationship to sexual media and this shaped the stories and presentations of self they offered in interviews. The growing visibility of sexual material makes 'childhood' problematic for children themselves and not merely for the adults who so frequently seek to comment on their behalf.

Sex educators face considerable dilemmas on the ground, such as conflicts of interest between parents and local authorities, pressures to achieve good exam results that often squeeze out the pastoral curriculum and issues over teachers' lack of time, training and support. However, we also need to bear in mind the wider contexts here. As Thorogood (2000) has argued, the contemporary 'explosion of discourse' around sex education indicates its centrality as a site for surveillance, or indeed as a technique of governance that seeks to produce sexually responsible citizens and 'normal' (hetero)masculinity and femininity. To this extent, we would challenge the idea that more open, student-centred approaches to sex education – or indeed the greater visibility of sexual material in the media – are likely to be straightforwardly liberating or empowering. Our findings do not support unduly alarmist positions about the 'death of childhood', but nor do they sanction an uncritical celebration of young people's agency and empowerment as consumers in the new media landscape. Our research, the materials we produced and the responses to them, illustrate the continuing necessity of frameworks for sex education and for media education that are reflective, critical and dialogic.

NOTES

1. The partners in the *Media Relate* project were, in the UK, the Institute of Education and the media education specialists, the English and Media Centre in London. The project was funded mainly by the European Community, so it also had partners in Spain and the Netherlands. Some of the materials can be downloaded for free from www.mediarelate.org.

Chapter 9

SOME TEXTS DO IT BETTER: WOMEN, SEXUALLY EXPLICIT TEXTS AND THE EVERYDAY

DANA WILSON-KOVACS

The consumption of sexual resources – both material and symbolic – is central to the processes of creating a sexual self and organizing a sex life in contemporary society. However, with few exceptions (Storr, 2003; Wilson-Kovacs, 2007), academic literature has paid little attention to the relation between consumption, intimacy and sex and the creation of a sexual realm in everyday life. The interconnections between consumption, lifestyle, relationships and social conditions are important for an understanding of the politics of the private in late modernity (Plummer, 1995; Weeks, 1998; Richardson, 2000) and we need to examine these much more closely. Little is known about the ways in which sex is related to texts and images, and even less about how women make use of sexually explicit texts. In order to develop our understanding of women's sexual consumption, sexual agency and intimacy, we need to document how women use and make sense of the various resources available to them – from top-shelf magazines to Ann Summers merchandise and erotic fiction.

This chapter examines the ways in which 34 women of mainly heterosexual orientation use sexually explicit media texts in their sexually intimate encounters. Work in this area is scarce, but what does exist shows that these kinds of texts can cause problems for women in a number of ways, both within heterosexual relationships and in female peer groups. Women face particularly complicated problems in relating femininity, feminism and pornography (Ciclitira, 2002, 2004). Some women report that although they dislike their partners' use of pornography within heterosexual relationships, they feel unable to object to its use because of a concern with 'freedom of choice' and of seeming 'anti-sex' (Shaw, 1999). For others, the problems are around the difficulty of speaking openly about their enjoyment of pornography, because this might mark them as unfeminine and/or unfeminist (Ciclitira, 2002, 2004). Some say that public debates about porn have made them 're-evaluate whether or not they want to be a part of the feminist movement' (Ciclitira, 2004: 296). Most have a complicated relationship with pornography, which includes 'contradictions between their beliefs, feelings and actions' (Ciclitira, 2004: 293).

Although most discussions of porn tend to focus on its 'harmfulness', some research suggests that women may have other concerns about sexually explicit media; issues of body image and sexual attractiveness may be more pressing than the links that are often made between pornography and sexual violence (Boynton, 1999). The importance of aesthetics in various genres of sexually explicit media has also become a focus of interest for researchers. The acceptability and accessibility of texts structure the way they are perceived and the way women negotiate them (Juffer, 1998). What is particularly evident here is the relation of particular genres to appropriate forms of gender representation and consumption (Boynton, 1999; Eck, 2003). Erotica is associated with women while porn is associated with men. The consumption of sexually explicit media therefore depends on a wide range of social and cultural factors, such as social relationships, class, discourses of sex and gender and aesthetic hierarchies.

My chapter considers women's reactions to what they identify as 'pornography' and how they distinguish this from what they label as 'erotica'. It examines how the interpretation and manipulation of representations takes place in sexual encounters and discusses the pleasures and restrictions associated with their consumption. It explores how intimate practices are circumscribed, routines legitimized and boundaries drawn between acceptable and non-acceptable, desirable and undesirable, through the participants' categorization and use of sexually explicit resources.

My aim is to document the role played by such materials – traditionally perceived as beyond the reach and interest of women consumers – in the participants' intimate routines. In doing so, I hope to contribute to recent discussions about the commercialization of sexual desire (Attwood, 2002; Arthurs, 2003), the de-traditionalization of gender relationships (Beck-Gernsheim, 2002; Evans, 2003) and new forms of sexual citizenship (Plummer, 1995; Weeks, 1998; Richardson, 2000). I also seek to open up to debate the politics and economics of everyday practice by providing some tentative answers to the following questions: How do women distinguish between erotica and pornography? How do they explain their preferences? How are erotica and pornography used in constructing and maintaining sexual intimacy? How do women reflect on their consumption?

The participants' accounts were collected between 2000 and 2002 as part of a project on sexual intimacy. Participants were recruited through local women's initiatives, antenatal classes and mother-and-toddler groups. The self-selected group of women, between 18 and 67 years of age, mostly white and heterosexual, and all describing themselves as middle class, shared an interest in well-being issues. They were asked to describe how they had achieved sexual closeness with different partners at various stages in their lives, and to reflect on self-pleasure and the resources that they had encountered and used in accomplishing it. The participants described a range of practices and resources. Creating and maintaining proper spaces for intimacy to take place was important to many of them; this generally centred on producing the bedroom as a sexual space through the choice and arrangement of furniture, accessories and lighting. The bedroom became a space of further consumption, for example, of films, books and lingerie, and also of production – some couples would photograph or record themselves in the bedroom. The creation of a sexy body was also important; the careful choice of lingerie figured heavily in women's preparation for sex, allowing them to articulate a sexual repertoire – 'slut one night and virginal the next', as Gabrielle, a 36-year-old podiatrist put it. It also worked to bolster self-esteem by helping to produce an appropriately sexual version of the self – 'the sexy me' (Denise, a 55-year-old paediatrician). Media texts were important resources in the women's sex lives too. Participants were encouraged to use their own understandings of sexual genres by articulating the categories of pornography and erotica for themselves, and the majority introduced distinctions between these categories in relation to their personal practice.

Among the media resources mentioned by participants were top-shelf magazines such as *Men Only, Club International, Penthouse* and *Playboy*; erotic books, including D.H. Lawrence's *Lady Chatterley's Lover* (1928), Erica Jong's *Fear of Flying* (1973) and Nancy Friday's *Women on Top* (1991); photography – especially Victorian erotic pictures; mainstream films including *9½ Weeks* (1986) and *Last Tango in Paris* (1972); and more sexually explicit films and magazines that participants could not remember by name but referred to as 'hard-core'. Most of the more mainstream materials had been familiar to the women since their adolescence. Some women employed them regularly in sexual episodes; for instance, one participant regularly used *Women on Top* for masturbation while others would read the same text with a partner as a preamble to sex.

Some texts were classified in quite different ways; the same text might be 'pornography' or 'erotica' for different participants, and this indicates both the considerable confusion surrounding the classification of explicit materials (Kendrick, 1987; Attwood, 2002) and the ways that people impose their own meanings on them. However, a significant factor in articulating the difference between pornography and erotica was the circumstances in which materials were presented, purchased and consumed, and more generally the routines and practices through which the participants became accustomed to them.

WOMEN'S PERSPECTIVES ON PORNOGRAPHY

Throughout the sample there was a widespread view of pornography as a genre that caters to men's needs and that can be seen as demeaning to women. Most participants talked about pornography as objectionable and sought to distance themselves from it. For instance, Clara, a heterosexual 36-year-old homeopath, stated:

> Pornography does nothing for women apart from just showing them as men would like to imagine them, always gagging for it,

always ready always with sex on their mind and ready to please, and this is not how it is in real life now, is it? Well at least not in my experience and I haven't to this day met anyone like that anyway, so eager, and so far away from how life really is.

A related belief was that pornography was marginal to women's use and had little in common with their views of sexual passion. Participants described how they incorporated pornography into everyday life in order to please their male partners. This consisted mainly of agreeing to engage in sexual intercourse while watching porn brought in by their partners, or to replicate suggested scenarios and positions inspired by porn. Chantelle, a heterosexual 18-year-old hair stylist, commented:

I don't like it or dislike it, it's kind of hard to explain because it's like this, sometimes I like it but sometimes it does not suit my mood but then I still go on with it, otherwise it's disappointing for him, so I would indulge him, because he likes it. But having said this, it's like take it or leave it for me, if I wasn't to watch it again, you know, I don't know, I wouldn't miss it.

Women reported becoming acquainted with pornography long before it came to play a part in their sex lives, for instance through the discovery of their fathers' or brothers' porn magazines or videos, but their use of it generally only began when male partners introduced it into the couple's sexual routines. As Chantelle noted, there is considerable emotional work involved in engaging with pornography in this setting – she puts up with it 'because he likes it'. This kind of emotional work was evident elsewhere in women's intimate relationships with their partners. For example, they might accept and wear gifts of lingerie from their partners that they would never have chosen for themselves, usually because they perceived them as 'tarty'. However, as Chantelle's remark shows, the recognition of emotional labour may be complicated by other factors – in this instance, by her awkward confession of enjoying porn herself on occasion. Similarly, the inappropriate underwear that men sometimes bought acquired more pleasurable meanings, partly because the men enjoyed seeing their partners wearing it and partly because of the history it acquired within the relationship. Kimberley, a 38-year-old therapist, noted of a red suspender belt that her partner gave her as a Valentine's Day present that, 'it's not any red Valentine underwear, it's the one we've had some of our best moments in'.

For some women, pornography and erotica were 'fun' things that could be shared with a partner:

> We used to pick sex top-shelf magazines, and have fun. And also, it was a little book, I think it was called *Experience*, just a little book it was only stories, no pictures, we would go out on a Saturday afternoon, buy it and read it out loud to each other, and be at it, all afternoon, just the two of us. I don't mind pictures, but I loved the stories, because they would stir my imagination, I have no problem with that ... it was tremendous fun (Ellie, 38-year-old shopkeeper).

However, women's enjoyment of porn is rarely straightforward, as Di, a heterosexual 42-year-old market researcher, observed:

> It would be hypocritical to say that I never got turned on by it, but it's always with this guilt: that I'm not doing what I'm supposed to do. I don't go searching for it and I think that it is, you know, bad, and I had times when I felt dirty, not really being comfortable with the idea that my mother or my friends might find out. I don't think I am supposed to like it.

Shaw's (1999) research on women's reactions to pornography and its impact on their lives found that they resisted porn in a muted way, rarely voicing their opinions or standing up to their partners. Some participants also felt that they did not have the right to speak out or restrict their partners' consumption of pornography. No instances of being coerced into the use of pornography or silently resisting it were presented. Di's admission is illustrative of a more general unease surrounding pornography: participants felt that they had little peer support to share their experiences of using porn, or their thoughts on either resisting or enjoying it. Although they discussed some aspects of sex with female friends and colleagues – for example, articles of lingerie bought for 'special' occasions – they did not talk about pornography. Porn did not fall within the scope of 'suitable' sexual consumption for women. Discussing the enjoyment of pornography with a partner can be equally problematic; reputations and relationships can suffer if women show they know too much about sex (Gavey et al, 1999; Holland et al, 1998). The participants were apprehensive about showing themselves as equally or more knowledgeable than their partners. Some felt that this would present them as 'cheap' and having 'a reckless sexual appetite' and this would affect the opinion their partners held of their suitability as mothers and partners outside the bedroom. Others felt that it would undermine their partners' sexual confidence. Another fear was that expressing enjoyment might lead to their partners asking them to engage in unwanted, 'more extreme' sexual practices – bondage and swinging being the two instances given by the participants.

Within this general unease about the place of pornography in their sex lives, women specifically objected to the ways men introduced porn into their relationships and their expectations about women's responses to this, as Jenna, a 21-year-old student, explained:

> He can't just go, 'here you go, bit of porn' and imagine me go, 'oh I'm SO horny, do it to me, big boy', then, bang, 'thank you ma'am', at least not all the time. It is insulting, even if you like it. I'm not an inflatable doll. I need some TLC, some attention, some persuasion or I won't play, it's as simple as that.

These concerns were widespread throughout the sample. Women expected and wanted empathy and understanding as part of their intimate routines, but more often than not they found that their partners lacked the 'knack' for when and how to introduce pornography, as Maggie, a 44-year-old community worker, remarked of her partner:

> He wouldn't know how to make me do it, he just doesn't have the 'knack' for that, it's more like 'fancy some porn?' and if I say 'yes', so be it, if I say 'no' well, tough, we'll do something else instead.

Maggie's suggestion that a partner might have the 'knack' to make her 'do it' suggests that women expect men to organize the use of porn in their sex lives and 'sell' it successfully, showing in the process that they have some understanding of the sensitivities of their partners. Denise, a 55-year-old paediatrician, explained this view in more detail:

> While in principle I am open to trying out new things, I think it
> is important to know when to do it, a bit like getting a 'vibe' that
> it is OK to do it, that your girlfriend is relaxed and confident,
> and for all I know it might need some work. How many sensitive
> men are out there? Or let me rephrase this, how many sensitive
> men who want their girlfriends to use porn are out there? Well
> I don't think that many, this must surely be a contradiction in
> terms because if anything, pornography tells you that all women
> need to open their legs is a wink, which means that you can just
> barge in, and it is not surprising then that women find this off-
> putting.

We can see here how disenchantment with pornography may spring
partly from the ways in which it is used to initiate passionate routines
and partly from the representations themselves. Context and circum-
stance are important in introducing pornography into sexual routines,
and men are seen as rarely paying enough attention to creating the
right mood and engaging with their partners' reactions to porn. But
this may be irrelevant in any case because the ways in which women
are represented in porn discourage this kind of attentiveness in the
first place.

In his research on men's use of top-shelf magazines, Simon Hardy
(1998) describes the trajectory of their discovery and subsequent use
of porn and the difficulty of integrating the unproblematic satisfaction they experience in their solitary porn use with the more complex
negotiation of real-life sex. The introduction of pornography into
shared everyday scenarios rarely proved successful and female partners had little patience with it. Hardy's observation that men usually
find themselves isolated in their use of pornography within a relationship is borne out in Denise's comments. Other participants also
highlighted the need to prepare the introduction of pornography
more carefully in order to 'get it right' and to create a mutually enjoyable mood where each partner's needs are recognized and actively
pursued. Such observations emphasize the importance of procedure:
the 'style' of introduction is as important to the success of an intimate episode as the generic characteristics of pornography.

Even so, pornography was perceived as devoid of any acknowledgment of women's desires and of real-life sex:

It's how everything is portrayed that I find disturbing. It's too black and white. Women are always eager and all they can think of is sex ... It's not that sex for sex's sake is bad, but getting off like this I think is moronic, and I for one prefer stuff that leaves it open to the imagination (Lauren, bisexual, 26-year-old community worker).

Here the formulaic character of pornography comes under scrutiny and its simple message and lack of nuance are seen as undermining sexual pleasure. Lauren's remark introduces a set of aesthetic concerns. Porn leaves nothing to the imagination and this reduces the possibility of exploration and experimentation. Pornography is seen as mechanical, a genre where female characters are roughly and unsympathetically drawn. Its simple aim, 'to get you off, just' (Clara), may provide some diversion, but not enough to sustain an inspiring repertoire of sexual routines.

Women were also critical of porn's operative speed, as Anne Marie, a heterosexual 41-year-old therapist, noted:

With porn everything is over in a flash. It's quick and it leaves this bitter-sweet taste like, I'm not sure if I liked that and I don't think I'm supposed to like it but on second thoughts I might've liked it, so it's not just that you did something you shouldn't have, but worse you liked it, which I think is one tremendous guilt trip and very confusing as you don't know any more what you are.

The complexity of this response is striking. Anne Marie expresses a range of responses to porn: she is not sure if she likes it, she might've liked it, she liked it. That porn is marked as unsuitable for women is also quite clear here: she's not supposed to like it. Women's engagements with porn are therefore tremendously difficult, provoking feelings of self-doubt, guilt, confusion and loss of identity: 'you don't know any more what you are'. What was interesting throughout the participants' comments was this very strong sense of ambivalence about porn, generated on the one hand by its power to arouse them, and on the other by a complex set of factors. Women encounter difficulties in approaching the subject of porn with their peers and partners as well as consuming pornography as part of their sexual routine. They are resentful about their partners' lack of insight and understanding of their sexual needs and this makes the negotiation of porn use and the pursuit of personal pleasure even more problematic. Porn is lacking aesthetically, leaving nothing to the imagination and giving little room for exploration, self-discovery and reflection. It is not only that pornography is simply what the male partner invariably chooses, but rather that there are too many specific problems with it and too few ways of resolving them. Moreover, while some needs are met by pornography, there is also a widespread feeling that something other than porn would 'do it' better. One such contender is what the participants identified as erotica.

EROTICA: A WOMAN'S ALTERNATIVE TO PORNOGRAPHY?

Although participants differed in their categorization of specific texts as pornography or erotica, they all distinguished clearly between pornography and erotica as categories. They understood 'pornography' and 'erotica' as a pair of opposites, with erotica characterized by what porn lacks: suggestiveness and a quality of leaving room for the imagination. Participants also perceived fundamental stylistic distinctions between porn and erotica, as this discussion with Susie, a heterosexual 40-year-old classroom assistant, shows:

> A: There were several things that influenced me, and probably porn is one of them, I mean by porn anything with sex in it and little else, I think, anything that is like, for men, I mean you can see that this stuff is for men, it's mostly men who buy it and get turned on by it, it's what they like, but then, then you also have erotica, which I like more.
>
> Q: What do you mean by erotica? What do you like about it?
>
> A: I quite like the Erotic Print Society catalogues. They are nice, they have drawings and stories and little vignettes, and oh, I had a Victorian photograph album, very, very good photos. I mean they gave you a feel of what it must've been like, the women are

not beautiful ... most of the time you can't really see their bodies, they don't tease you, it's more like concentrating on what they are doing ... They had for instance couples, threesomes, foursomes, women masturbating ...

Q: Is there anything in particular that makes you prefer this?

A: Come to think of it, what I like most about it is the lack of detail, you know, there is no sharp focus or zoom in on the blow-job, but just the suggestion of it, if that makes sense ... It's there, but not right in your face ... you can think about it, and create your scene and the colour of the photos and everything in them gives you a feeling of 'old' and I suppose 'exotic'.

Susie's distinction between erotica and pornography is framed within aesthetic parameters, which she uses to explain her preference for erotica. Her predilection for written texts and Victorian photography is justified by the belief that the conventions of these genres are superior to those of mainstream pornography – a belief that prevents her from commenting on their association with a female audience in the same way that she associates porn with men. Susie's position also suggests that the difference between erotica and pornography is one of style. In this, erotica is similar to other sexual products aimed at women, such as Victoria's Secrets lingerie merchandising, which addresses a discerning client with a penchant for risqué items (Workman, 1996). In the same way, the Erotic Print Society reprints are seen by Susie and many others in the sample as elegant and tasteful.

The high-quality prints of the Erotic Print Society represent one instance of commercial erotica which is readily available through advertisements in broadsheets. But more generally the erotica business is burgeoning. Jane Juffer (1998) has described contemporary sexual resources for women as a network of publicly produced texts, representations and artefacts, marketed for domestic use with a set of commercial definitions and a form of branding that allows them to be accessed by specific audiences, despite similarities in content. Simon Hardy (2001, 2004) also notes that pornographic clichés are perceived by women as limited in scope, full of reductive meanings and predictable action, while erotica is seen as catering to women in a more 'approachable' and 'understanding' manner. Descriptions of erotica emphasize its 'more lavish' character, with more attention devoted to describing settings and characters in greater detail.

For my participants, the attention paid to detail, rather than the degree of sexual explicitness, was what distinguished erotica from pornography. Moreover, they favoured the written word over the image, describing it as 'more powerful than any visuals', which they referred to as a 'male turn-on'. Participants talked about erotica as liberating. They described it as 'essential reading', said it 'opened my eyes', 'made me realize what it's all about', 'put me in touch with myself'. For them, erotica was also 'formative', 'informative' and 'inspiring' in relation to their individual sexual routines. It helped them to articulate personal preferences and everyday practices, as Gina, a heterosexual 47-year-old midwife, explained:

> The closest I could get [to using erotica] is reading a novel, a personal thing, and I think 'oh, yes, that would be quite nice'. So it's the fictional aspect of it that I like. I've also enjoyed a book on women's erotic writing, *Slow Hand* was it? A mixture of autobiographical and fictional stories, which I found fascinating. Thinking that some of these things really happened – it opened me up more, made me more aware of what I'm doing. This is the thing, the more I read, the more I think about how I would like it all to pan out. Sometimes I buy little things, candles, incense, making more of an effort, if you know what I mean ... Is it all worth it? In the end I think it is. It makes me feel better, not because I tried but because I discover new things about myself.

We can see here the role played by erotica in inspiring everyday routines and pursuits. The act of reading opens a fantasy world where Gina can speculate on the potential of the fictional situation and imagine 'oh, yes, that would be quite nice'. The mixture of autobiographical and fictional stories allows her to consider her own personal preferences and reflect on her own practices, while at the same time encouraging her to 'make more of an effort' to create intimate moods and to think about herself as a sexual being. For Gina this is a process of self-discovery. When participants talked about erotica, they focused on the sexual self and the process through which this is articulated. What is remarkable about Gina's account is not only how she incorporates the act of reading into the pursuit of personal pleasure, but also the tentative way in which she alludes to how she puts her sexual self together.

Women's comments on different erotic texts demonstrated their engagement with the genre and their confidence in using it:

> I like a lot of books and the more I read the more I discover. I started by reading the *Black Lace* stories, they've been around for a while, I remember something called the *Amulet*, which I really liked because, it was one of the first I read and was really impressed by the quality of its writing. I've come to realize that erotica ... has more weight to it. To start with it's written by women and you can see that in the way in which it's done: more time to write the story, more care with the story itself and each character. You can see this in how they are presented, it makes a difference to me if I have someone I can identify to. It's so much more than simply saying 'let's do it', it gives you a real story to steal you away (Maggie, 44-year-old social worker).

This appreciation of well-defined characters and set-ups and the care with which erotic stories are written was typical of the sample. Women saw erotica as playing a role in their sexual self-awareness and contributing to their sexual knowledge, fantasies and practices. Erotica creates a slower, more leisurely type of arousal than porn, using conventions and stylistic turns that make it safe to explore and indulge in. This requires the patience of reading and the skill of imagination rather than the 'uncontrollable titillation' of pornography. Most participants readily accepted the idea that men are 'more visual' that women. Reinforced by popular public discourses, this view has been profitably capitalized upon by various sections of the erotica industry that cater solely to women readers (Faust, 1980) – readers who feel more comfortable purchasing sexually explicit literature through a safe outlet (Juffer, 1998). Yet, rather than simply pointing to taken-for-granted biological differences in sexual arousal, women's use of erotic texts indicates a different context of consumption, one that is not necessarily configured by a pressure to perform. Fiona, a bisexual 54-year-old sculptor, expressed this point:

I like reading more because it's just me. I can fantasize, and no one pushes me. I like taking my time. I don't have to do anything unless I want to, and do you know, if I want to skip a page, or put the book down there's no one huffing and puffing. I do things to myself for my own pleasure. You could say it's selfish, but I enjoy it ... I like doing it by myself. I've never done it with someone else, can't really imagine how that would be, reading to each other.

Here, we can see the difference between the role of media resources in a sexual relationship with the self and within a relationship. Finding a comfortable and confident sexual voice and language to express pleasure has been acknowledged as problematic for women (Holland et al, 1998) and can be seen in the participants' use of 'it' as a term to describe both intercourse and self-sexual exploration and the pleasures they may derive from both of these. What is more, women may find it difficult to incorporate erotica into their relationships. As Denise, a 55-year-old paediatrician, observes, it is as if:

Men have the upper hand when it comes to decide. I can say 'no', or I can say 'yes', but if I say 'how about this instead' he never seems happy. Don't get me wrong, he IS happy ... for me, and ... pleased, but he has to give in and does not like that, but we don't really impose upon each other, so to speak. This way I can get on with reading wet, trashy novels, and he can buy himself a Penthouse as long as I don't have to suffer it. The trouble is that I find myself looking at it, whereas he would never read mine.

Despite these problems, women's discussion of erotica gives us an insight into how they pursue pleasure and the context within which they do this. Using erotica appears to give women room for intimate manoeuvre without the emotional labour involved in consuming pornography. Reading time is time for oneself (Radway, 1987; Snitow, 1978), and reading erotica allows women to dedicate time to develop personal fantasies around masturbation and to plan intimate encounters, sometimes in step-by-step sequences which move from foreplay to various sexual positions and types of sexual contact. Women's preference for erotic reading materials depends on the way it allows them to secure a private environment where they can escape domestic, sexual and emotional duties and focus on the self. Their

choice reveals a desire to try to find a voice for expressing a sexual
self with and without a partner, and to explore fantasy for their own
enjoyment. Erotica is also more easily accessible, as Tanya, a heterosexual 30-year-old teacher, remarked:

> I was early for an appointment, so I went in a bookstore, was
> it Waterstone's maybe? and started looking through the shelves,
> and I saw the women's section, or some such, and looked at the
> titles. I picked a book and looked through and started reading
> about someone's fantasy. Was it about a builder or an electrician
> coming to the house and peeping through the bathroom window
> while the woman was taking a shower? The catch was that he did
> not know that she knew he was watching her, so the story was
> about her manipulating this guy into having it off with her. I was
> completely immersed in it, and then I realized where I was, and
> looked around, and no one seemed to bother that I was there
> reading this steamy stuff. I don't think they could even see me. I
> couldn't believe it. I was so turned on. In the middle of the book-
> shop. It was just so strange.

This vignette captures Tanya's uneasy negotiation of public and
private sites, and about ideas of appropriateness and pleasure. She
feels exposed, visible in her act of reading an erotic book as she real-
izes how her action challenges cultural norms. Yet, the familiarity
and assurance of the location counterbalances the perceived illicit-
ness of the act and Tanya's uncertainties. Her experience illustrates
how wider structures of distribution are instrumental in organizing
women's choices of sexual resources. As Juffer (1998, 2005) argues,
understanding women's access to sexually explicit materials helps us
to understand why women prefer some discourses and develop reservations about others. Although the growth of print erotica and porn
are related as part of a growing commodification of sex, in marketing terms erotica is presented as an alternative to porn, published
by respectable mainstream houses and easily available in bookshops
(Juffer, 1998: 6). Thus the issue of access is also one of agency, identity
and empowerment. The sexual self is formulated through the circulation and management of available resources. Women's choices are
also circumscribed by a judgement of taste: pornography is regarded

by participants as a less tasteful medium, with representations that follow few, if any, traditional aesthetic conventions and focus entirely on the sexual arousal of the user.

Women's understanding of sexual agency goes beyond the textual circumscription offered or denied by each genre. The participants' accounts identify different strategies of managing desire that in turn point to the contexts in which erotica and pornography are used. Although what is erotic and what is pornographic is regarded as a matter of private choice, this choice is clearly arbitrated through the success of previous experiences and understandings of what is culturally and socially understood as tasteful and acceptable. Participants' views engage less with the highly contentious issue of gender power relations at a representational level; instead they emphasize how materials are 'domesticated' (Juffer, 1998), that is, adopted for personal use according to their style, visibility and moral transparency. They are used to create spaces, bodies and states of mind which mark some occasions as sexual and to structure those occasions. It is the social and economic contexts in which porn and erotica are circulated that ultimately affect how they are perceived and distinguished. All the same, women play an active role in choosing sexual texts and using them to produce their sexual identities and relationships.

Recent writing on the dynamics of sexuality in contemporary society highlights an increasing sexualization of culture (Attwood, 2006), an escalating commodification of sex and sexual consumerism (McNair, 1996) and a preoccupation with self-disclosure (Plummer, 1995). These trends open up the possibility of more visible ways of 'doing' intimacy and set up a normative framework for the dos and don'ts of intimate routines. Yet, to date we know very little about such routines and the ways in which material and symbolic resources are increasingly used in these interactions. I have tried to redress this here by looking at the role that sexually explicit representations play in the articulation of intimate routines. The approach I have adopted highlights the situated character of sexual episodes. It allows us to see how people classify sexual resources and how sexual practices and relationships are connected to norms of sex and gender and of taste and consumption. This allows us to situate existing theoretical work on sexuality, identity and consumption in specific contexts. If we are to make sense of the increasing sexualization of our culture, we will need much more work of this kind.

ACKNOWLEDGMENTS

I would like to thank all those who participated in this research and agreed to share their thoughts about their intimate past and present. Many thanks also to those who commented on previous drafts of this chapter, and to Feona Attwood for all her help with bringing this to print.

Chapter 10

KEEPING FIT IN SIX INCH HEELS: THE MAINSTREAMING OF POLE DANCING

SAMANTHA HOLLAND AND FEONA ATTWOOD

'Pole dancing is irrefutably linked with sex, which is why it has become a feature in exotic-dance clubs worldwide. And now it has infiltrated everyday life as an excellent form of exercise. Of course, the disapproving voices can still be heard, but we can silence them – by learning a great dance style, getting fit and having a real laugh!' (Rebecca Drury, *Pole Dancing: The Naughty Girl's Guide*, 2006).

Pole dancing is a form of erotic performance composed of a series of spins, climbs and other moves around a vertical pole which is attached to floor and ceiling. It originated, according to many accounts, in Canadian strip clubs in the 1980s, but may have its roots in older cultural forms such as Maypole dancing, Mallakhamb – a type of yoga practised on a wooden pole (Moody, 2005), the circus and music hall. It is generally associated with sex work, particularly with strip clubs where a range of erotic performances such as striptease, table dancing and lap dancing are also performed, usually by women for men. However, it is increasingly visible in other settings such as cabaret and is beginning to be widely practised as a form of exercise for women. In the UK, pole exercise classes run in most large towns and cities. Music CDs for lap dancing, pole dancing and striptease routines are widely available. Rebecca Drury's guide, *Pole Dancing: The Naughty Girl's Guide* (2006), is typical of the way in which pole dancing is represented in this kind of merchandising, as 'a raunchy way to both thrill your man and improve your fitness'. A 'peekaboo' pole-dancing kit is available through mainstream catalogues such as Littlewoods and there is a multitude of specialist pole websites advertising classes and selling items such as shoes and instructional DVDs. Here pole dancing is reclaimed as a means of staying in shape with 'hidden benefits such as feeling sexy, building confidence and self-esteem and creating a supportive female-only environment' (www. polestars.net). This chapter examines the current vogue for pole dancing as a popular mainstream exercise activity for women. Using data collected from participant observation at pole-dancing classes and interviews with teachers and students, it explores what the mainstreaming of this type of sexually explicit dance means for the women who practise it and how it fits into contemporary discourses around sexualization and femininity.

MAINSTREAMING SEX WORK?

Pole dancing can be understood as part of the wider sexualization of the high street, and indeed it is often used as an emblem of sexualization along with sex toys such as the Rampant Rabbit vibrator and other items such as 'Porn Star' and 'Playboy' fashion logos. The strip clubs with which it is traditionally associated are characterized by a seedy image and backstreet location, but contemporary erotic dancing clubs are now being re-marketed as sophisticated settings for 'gentlemen' and they are one of the fastest growing elements in the UK's leisure services industry (Jones et al, 2003: 215). Stripping is also more visible in mainstream media than it has been before. Brian McNair has documented a late twentieth-century cinematic trend for films focused on erotic performances, such as *Showgirls* (1995), *Striptease* (1996) and *The Full Monty* (1997), marking a shift in the representation of strippers from 'exploited victims' to 'feisty independent souls' (2002: 90). A vogue for celebrity stripping has also been evident throughout this period – part of an increasing fascination with celebrities' sex lives. In a culture where media and celebrity are so central, and taste and fame are so prized, these new representations of striptease have interesting implications for the way sexual display is perceived. As Ruth Barcan argues, the status of the female celebrity, whose nudity is understood as a highly desirable image rather than a form of cheap labour (2004: 243), means that some forms of striptease have become able to signify sexual liberation, economic freedom and even a 'victory for feminism' (2004: 242).

Naked and otherwise sexualized images of celebrities have appeared widely in mainstream media since the early 1990s, Demi Moore's *Vanity Fair* cover in 1991 and Madonna's *Sex* book in 1992 being the most famous examples. More recently, Keira Knightley and Scarlett Johansson – both popular and highly acclaimed actresses – have appeared naked on the cover of *Vanity Fair* (March 2006). Stolen or fabricated images of naked stars excite huge interest: there is a magazine, *Celebrity Skin*, devoted to images of naked and semi-naked celebrities, and scandals over the circulation of sex tapes of celebrities including Pamela Anderson, Paris Hilton and Britney Spears have become a regular occurrence. The knowing performance of female raunchiness, exemplified by Madonna's onstage smooching with Britney Spears and Christina Aguilera at the MTV Music Awards in 2003, showed how firmly celebrity sexual spectacle is now integrated into the most mainstream of media events.

Representations of feisty strippers and raunchy celebrities have worked to strengthen a view of body display and erotic performance as a sign of power. For some, sexualized images can now connote strength, independence and the expression of a confident self, as has been claimed of Madonna's various personae over the years and of more specific images such as the advert for Yves St Laurent's Opium perfume in 2000 featuring Sophie Dahl (Attwood, 2004). The association of celebrity with sexual display appears to override the connotations of an undervalued object which anonymous naked performers carry because the women on display are 'somebodies' rather than 'nobodies'.

Celebrity stripping is part of the development of a broader cultural sexualization which is connected to what Brian McNair has described as the emergence of a 'striptease culture' in contemporary Western societies. Elements of 'striptease' are evident in the media in 'various forms of sexual self-revelation and bodily exposure' (McNair, 2002: 81), for example, in confessional talkshows and docu-soaps. It is rooted in the same set of processes which have led to the expansion of pornography and the development of 'porn chic', the appropriation of porn style and content in mainstream forms of media, but is distinct from them in that it is 'often the outcome of media activity by people who are, at least when they start out, amateurs and non-celebrities – "ordinary people"' (McNair, 2002: 88).

Forms of sexual self-exposure and porn chic make up what Ariel Levy has called a 'raunch culture' (2005) in which the kinds of sexual 'image work' previously undertaken only by media performers become available to ordinary people. The development of boudoir photography, for example, enables women to commission self-portraits which draw on the codes and conventions of glamour photography. Ruth Barcan argues that this is a way in which ordinary people prove their potential fitness to belong in a celebrity culture, but it is also a form of identity work which is often undertaken 'at symbolic moments like anniversaries or after key moments of identity transformation, such as post-divorce or post-childbirth' when 'identity and/or body image have become self-conscious or precarious in some way' (Barcan, 2004: 249). Here, forms of sexualization work to fix and dignify shaky or poor self-image.

The new fashionability of erotic performance and the establishment of raunch culture are now visible in a range of sites. Sex shops targeting their merchandise at women offer classes in striptease and lap dancing. These kinds of pursuits, along with the employment of male strippers, have become associated with young women's leisure practices, particularly at events such as hen parties. A neo-burlesque scene has emerged with a diverse audience made up of 'refugees from the swing revival, tattooed rockabilly chicks, strippers bored with the same old pole dance, dancers and artists looking for a more risqué outlet, and ordinary folks' (Baldwin, 2004: 19). Alongside a newly revived fetish scene, burlesque has become visible in the mainstream through high-profile solo performers such as Dita von Teese, the burlesque-influenced pop act the Pussycat Dolls and the burlesque tours of 'alternative porn' performers, the Suicide Girls. The UK TV show *Faking It*, a programme which documents the attempts of an 'ordinary person' to learn a new skill and pass themselves off as expert in it, chose burlesque as its theme at the end of 2006, following Sharon, a cleaner from Wales, as she learnt to perform a burlesque number, struggling with shyness and poor body image along the way. *Faking It* is representative of striptease culture in two senses – an exploration of erotic performance and an enactment of the breaking of boundaries between ordinary people and celebrities, everyday life and media performance. Sharon's self-revelation takes the form of a literal and emotional stripping, and by embracing sexual display she remakes herself as a more confident, happier, sexier woman. Sexualization becomes a means of transformation.

Burlesque, 'the funnier, glitterier, over-the-top sister of perform- ance art, cabaret, legitimate theatre, modern dance, comedy and circus' (Baldwin, 2004: 32), is regularly claimed by its performers and historians as a source of empowerment for contemporary women who don't see 'glamour and feminism as mutually exclusive' (Baldwin, 2004: 47), particularly when it can be disentangled from sex work. Laura Herbert makes the distinction like this: commercial strip- ping or 'humping' is a sexual transaction while burlesque is a form of self-expression (in Baldwin, 2004: 50). Because of this, burlesque may represent for women 'the female fantasy of the stripper who has command of the audience by doing what she wants onstage, rather than what she thinks she has to do to retain the male gaze' (Beretta in Baldwin, 2004: 133). This kind of claim – that women gain power from sexual display – has become a familiar one in relation to various forms of contemporary sexualization. But stripping and other forms of erotic performance continue to be an issue of concern in public debate and practice. For example, Glasgow City Council has objected to all lap-dancing club applications on the grounds that lap dancing is 'a form of commercial sexual exploitation that demeans and exploits women and encourages the perception by some men, of women as sex objects' (Jones et al, 2003: 217). The children's charity Kidscape has described pole exercise as inappropriate for children because of its association with sex work. The BBC announced, then scrapped, plans for a pole-dancing show featuring celebrities such as Zoe Ball as part of its fundraising event *Sport Relief* in 2006, for similar reasons. Despite the use of celebrities and popular media forms to normalize and domesticate it, pole dancing continues to teeter on the edge of respectability.

In May 2006, a Pole Idol competition, taking its name from the internationally successful *Pop Idol* television show, was held in a city-centre nightclub in Leeds, West Yorkshire. Competitions like these are the most obvious way in which pole dancing is being 'mainstreamed', re-branded as exercise or 'vertical dance'. The World Pole Sport Federation now hosts an annual Miss Pole Dance World event in which there is no stripping and the focus is on the athletic and artistic elements of pole dancing. The UK hosted its first Pole Princess competition in March 2006. It was open to male and female amateur competitors (though no men entered) and the rules prohibited nudity, stripping, thongs, négligés and fetish wear. Of the five judges, three were men and two were women – both with their own pole-dancing schools. The pole-dancing teachers we met saw this as a positive move towards the acceptance of pole dancing as 'artistic' and 'a sport' rather than being 'all about getting your kit off'.

The re-branding of erotic performance is not new. In the late 1950s, Roland Barthes described how, at the Moulin Rouge, stripping was being redefined as a sport. He wrote, 'there is a Striptease Club, which organizes healthy contests whose winners come out crowned and rewarded with edifying prizes ... striptease is identified with a *career* ... competitors are socially situated: one is a salesgirl, another a secretary ... Striptease ... is made to rejoin the world of the public, is made familiar and bourgeois' (1993: 86–7). The significance of pole dancing is altered when it becomes a form of exercise. The focus is on the enjoyment of the performers rather than the audience; indeed the performers and audience are one and the same. The female participants perform for each other rather than servicing men for money and in this context pole dancing ceases to be sex work and becomes something new.

However, writers such as Sheila Jeffreys argue that this kind of shift, in which commercial erotic performance is normalized as 'art', perpetuates 'a culture of prostitution' (in Head, 2006). Ariel Levy claims that the new raunch culture, far from being sexually liberating for women, encourages them to collude in their own objectification (2005). The contradictions and tensions around the rise of raunch are also evident in the way pole dancing and pole equipment are typically marketed. For example, despite assertions that pole dancing is a form of exercise requiring skill and strength, images of young, slim, scantily clad women hanging, apparently effortlessly, from a pole or moving seductively with the pole between their legs are almost always used. Muscular endurance and coordination are much less likely to be represented. Poles sold for home use are often accompanied by accessories which allow them to be taken down and the ceiling attachment disguised with a fake smoke alarm. Pole dancing is therefore placed in a paradoxical position: as a form of exercise which is simultaneously associated with sexual performance and which may therefore need to be hidden from friends and family.

LEARNING TO DANCE

In May 2006 we both attended a seven-week pole-dancing course in Leeds, and Sam attended a second course several months later. From participant observation of these classes and a further set of interviews which Sam carried out with pole-dance teachers and students between the ages of 20 and 44, we hoped to explore women's motivations for choosing pole exercise and the appeal and benefits of the classes. Participants were asked about their leisure and exercise histories, their choice of pole dance as a form of exercise and their feelings about erotic female display, body image and enjoyment. Pseudonyms are used for all participants except Rachel who requested the use of her real name.

The classes we attended were held in the back room of a large modern pub in Leeds city centre, with curtains partially screening us from the drinkers in the front of the pub. The experience was, therefore, quite different to attending a class in a sports centre or gym. The space was only temporarily a sports environment: pole teachers brought the poles with them and these were erected and dismantled at the beginning and end of each class. Our first experience of exercising in this kind of space was nerve-wracking to say the least; we felt out of place and on display and we were initially very uncomfortable with changing into our relatively skimpy outfits in a pub toilet. However, none of the women interviewed seemed to have a problem with the venue or suggested they would have been more comfortable in a fitness club, and in fact we very quickly got over our own anxieties about the venue.

Our classes began with a warm-up on exercise mats, followed by a series of teacher demonstrations and student practices, with students generally working in pairs. The individual moves, whether these were the swings and climbs on the pole, or the floor work that takes place around and away from the pole, built into a dance sequence which students were encouraged to learn and perform. During the classes the students copied what the teacher did, asked for advice, discussed amongst themselves how to perform the moves and sometimes talked about other things. The warm-up and warm-down sessions at either end of the classes produced some grumbling because of the difficulty of the exercises, and it was clear from this that the students were there for the pole dancing rather than for exercise per se. The classes were physically demanding because of the difficulty of the moves and the high levels of fitness and strength required to perform many of them. Despite this, classes did not deliver a sustained work-out, mainly because of lack of space – up to 12 students shared one pole and much of the class time was consequently spent waiting in turn for the opportunity to practise. However, the quite serious muscle soreness and bruising that we suffered in the first few weeks demonstrated that we had indeed been exercising.

Keeping fit is an ongoing project with no finite result (Turner, 1996; Grogan, 1999; Holland, 2004) and people are constantly seeking new ways to maintain their interest – many of the students said that they had turned to pole dancing because they had become bored with other forms of exercise such as pilates or aerobics. Generally speaking, though, they had a history of limited or sporadic physical activity. They were typically sedentary or even complete exercisephobes. Carrie and Lisa's responses were typical: 'I hate exercise, to be honest', 'I hated P.E. at school, I hate gyms, I hate it all, it's mindnumbing, I can't be arsed'. However, both women enjoyed going to nightclubs to dance. Some students had come to pole classes because they had enjoyed another sort of dance, most commonly Arabic dance or salsa, and several students had first encountered poles in nightclubs or bars or at hen parties which had included a pole-dancing session. Most chose pole dancing as a form of exercise because they expected it to be enjoyable; they thought it 'looked sexy and fun' (Nicky), 'a good laugh, something different' (Kate). However, the main reason for students' choice of pole exercise was its high media profile and its association with female celebrities – Darryl Hannah, Kate Moss, Pamela Anderson and Madonna all reportedly include pole dance in their exercise regimes. Every student had read something about pole dancing in women's magazines, and Rachel, one of the teachers, claimed that many women think 'Kate Moss does it, so I am going to go and give it a go'. According to Rachel, some women even pretend to have attended pole-dancing classes because it is 'a good conversation piece ... It says "I am not boring".' In this sense, pole dancing is taking on a new significance as an indicator of women's engagement with raunch culture.

Like the students, the teachers Sam spoke to tended not to have a dance or fitness background; one described herself as 'very lazy', while another claimed she was 'not a keep-fit type'. The sexual connotations of pole dancing were something that the teachers had to negotiate, but as Rachel commented, 'No one is breaking any laws, no one is taking any clothes off, no one is offending anybody – there is nothing ... I do feel irreproachable, I do.' One of the teachers, Silke, used her pole-exercise teaching as a 'front' for her other work as a professional pole dancer. This allowed her to work on a level where 'my boyfriend can't say anything, my parents know about it, you don't need to hide it from anybody'. For Silke, pole exercise's mainstream image enabled the continuation of her much more lucrative, and to her much more enjoyable, pole-dancing career. This was necessary given pole dancing's rather tenuous grip on respectability. She said that her friends thought her pole dancing was 'great fun, a great idea'. All the same, she worried about some people knowing that she did it for a living. She talked about a particular girl she wanted to avoid who had been a pole dancer much longer than she had and who her friends had said quite negative things about: 'they forget that I did it and they call her ... things ... and I know that when they think about me doing it, they don't think of it the same way. They don't like her and they never liked her, so that is why it is a negative thing ... when I talk about it we have a laugh about it or they think it is great fun. But that is what I am talking about, you know, that it can be portrayed quite differently.' Clearly, despite the new fashionability of pole dancing, the status of women who perform it for money remains precarious.

Much of the discussion about whether pole dancing can be classed as a genuine form of exercise centres on women's appearance, and especially whether what women wear for pole dancing indicates sex or exercise. The website Polestars tells potential attendees that they will 'need to be able to complete the warm-up session, grip the pole effectively, have freedom of movement and feel comfortable', and that therefore 'The ideal outfit is a pair of fairly short shorts or hot-pants, and something comfortable but not restrictive on your top half ... some trainers for the warm-up session and ideally high heels (shoes or boots) for the rest of the class' (www.polestars.net). The teacher of our classes wore a very skimpy outfit of hotpants, high heels and a vest as required by the company that employed her. The students wore shorts and t-shirts or vests. Most brought high heels or intended to buy them. These are recommended to give you the 'strut' that pole dancers use and also because they act as hooks on to the pole and make it possible to grip the pole at a higher point. Only Rachel thought it was unnecessary for dancers to go 'tottering around' in shoes like these. From our own experience, we felt it was better and easier to accomplish many of the moves in heels. Very high-heeled shoes, which have six-inch heels and a thin strap across the top of the foot and are generally sold as fetish shoes, are now promoted for pole exercise and these are available through most pole-dancing websites. Students liked the fetish shoes because they thought them beautiful to look at, and our experience was that our shoes excited curiosity and admiration. However, they were also associated with men's sexual pleasure and with restriction and pain. Grace described how her boyfriend couldn't stop looking at her gold platform shoes which were 'like skyscrapers'. Carole said that her shoes 'really hurt!' while Kate reported that her feet were 'in agony ... covered in blisters!' However, all the students who initially found them uncomfortable and difficult to walk in saw the point of wearing them for pole exercise and got used to them relatively quickly.

FEELING SEXY

As the weeks went by, there was a distinct shift in the way students dressed. Some of them bought fetish shoes to wear to class. Shorts got shorter and tops got tighter. The interviews revealed that this was a response to the realization that women in the classes had a range of body shapes and sizes, but that 'we all looked good when we were on the pole'. More revealing clothing was linked to a feeling of camaraderie in the class and to women's growing confidence. As Lizzie said, 'I started to feel better about my body, oh, quite quickly, week two or something. Partly cos the pole, well its hard work and that, but also cos of the other girls, the other women, in the class. We had a good laugh and we egged each other on.' All the participants were very clear that the camaraderie had been an integral part of their enjoyment and had been dependent on the classes being women-only.

Our own experiences bore this out: learning to perform very difficult dance moves in very high heels was scary and we felt self-conscious, but doing it with a group of supportive women made it exciting and exhilarating. There is a particular pleasure in knowing that you have performed a sequence of moves in a way that feels good, that you experience as physically enjoyable and that meets with the approval of your 'audience'. Sam and Silke discussed this at length in Silke's interview. Silke noted how scary the pole was at first for the women she taught. Yet this was always combined with excitement: 'you see it and it looks so exciting and exotic and sexy on the TV or wherever you see it – and you want to have a go, and the fact that you can have a go I think is really ... they find it quite exciting'.

This movement in which women cross the boundary that marks the pole out as something which is *not for them* because of its exoticism and its otherness is a very powerful one. The chance to 'have a go' combines with what Silke described as the pole's 'addictive' power which left women leaving the classes on 'a real high'. For Sam, the enjoyment of pole dancing was reminiscent of the physical pleasures of children's play – being on a bike, running around, playing on bars in the playground, all the ways to 'just go "whoo"' which become less and less frequent as women grow up. But this is also combined with the very adult feminine pleasure of 'feeling sexy', a pleasure that most women in the classes commented on. In addition to feeling sexy, women also associated pole dancing with achievement and confidence. Silke said that it made her feel good about herself and in control, to the extent that pole dancing was probably 'the thing that made me survive going through the breakup with my last boyfriend'.

One theme that was particularly strong in all the interviews was the admiration that teachers and students felt for pole dancers. They saw pole dancing as a difficult and athletic skill, and as an art form. They were particularly aware of the strength required to pole dance well and this increased their admiration of its beauty. One of the teachers, Chrissy, had this to say:

> Pole [exercise] is so athletic and balletic. It takes power to do it, you need balance and control and strength and grace, and you need confidence as well, swinging, climbing, you are upside down, you are hanging off there and no one but you is doing it, you are using your own power.

Silke expressed her concern that for most people, this strength and skill was invisible:

> I think it is amazing to look at, really amazing, when you think that someone is holding herself up there like that, and she can do all those things, just by using her muscles and a vertical pole. It's very sad really that, you know, that people can't get past it being about stripping and supposedly being a spectacle for men's eyes only. It really should be seen as more than that.

Rachel also described men's inability to see pole dancing as anything other than a 'titillating thing', which she contrasted with her own experience of watching other women pole dance. For her, this evoked a whole series of powerful and pleasurable feelings: '"I could do that – I could make myself feel good, I could feel powerful up there"... It is a thing of beauty ... it is pure enjoyment.' The students made similar points. They found pole dancing 'brilliant to look at' (Lizzie) and 'beautiful to watch' (Jane), and described themselves as 'awed' by skilful pole dancers (Kate). A tension between the strength and beauty of pole dancing was apparent in many of their comments. Jane compared pole dancers to 'swans with all the beauty on top, on show, and all the paddling, the strength, going on underneath'. The comparison of pole dancers to swans, and Chrissy's description of pole dancing as 'balletic', draws on a tradition of women's strength being concealed or controlled rather than displayed – a feature of performances associated with women, whether in the form of dance or sports such as gymnastics. Indeed, a knowledge of just how much strength and skill is being concealed may make pole dancing particularly awe-inspiring for women who both perform and watch.

These women's descriptions of themselves as strong and powerful, filled with admiration for pole dancers, contradicts the popular image of pole dancing as *only* titillating for heterosexual men. Nevertheless, the sexual connotations of pole dancing remain problematic for women. In particular, women at pole-dancing classes resisted the idea of objectification, even while they pursued their desire to identify with and become a 'thing of beauty'. This contradiction is found elsewhere in women's relationships with the images and performances of femininity. Even where women are resistant to conventional notions of femininity, as in the performance of subcultural or alternative identities, they may have complicated relationships with conventional feminine characteristics. For example, in Sam's study of alternative women, the very conventional figure of the fairy princess was particularly important in women's accounts of their developing self-images. They liked how she looked, though they were less keen on the way she symbolized 'complicity and passivity' (Holland, 2004: 58). Some women described the 'princess play' they had engaged in as children in terms of its 'physicality and pleasure' rather than weakness (Holland, 2004: 57). It seems that women understand femininity as far more complex than media representations suggest, and that they draw on particular elements of traditional femininity and rework and combine them with other signs, whether these are clothes, musical tastes or leisure practices, in order to connote new and more positive ways of being women. A similar process is evident in women's enjoyment of pole dancing, where very traditional indicators of femininity such as gracefulness and sexual objectification are reworked into experiences of sexual agency and power. To be a 'thing of beauty' is to embody femininity in an extremely complex way which involves strength, grace, accomplishment and exhilaration, as well as sexual allure and display.

EMBRACING THE POLE

Merl Storr has noted that the Ann Summers party, which, like pole exercise, has become emblematic of sexualization, takes a particularly postfeminist form. This is evident in the way it celebrates 'the primacy of pleasure and the centrality of an active (hetero)sexuality to women's selves and lives' (Storr, 2003: 31). Women are encouraged to be open about sex and to pursue individual pleasure and empowerment through the consumption of consumer goods such as sex toys and lingerie. But sexual pleasure takes on a 'strangely literal form' at the parties. While the penis figures as men's sexual 'equipment', the goods women buy – their Ann Summers collection – is understood as the feminine equivalent. Women buy 'sexy' consumer goods to turn men on (Storr, 2003: 176). In a climate where women are encouraged to be actively sexual, yet have inherited a tradition which provides them with little idea of how to manifest this, the pole, like lingerie and sex toys, may also 'stand in' for women's sexuality and give them a means of articulating it.

The particular pleasure sold to women at Ann Summers parties is that of 'feeling sexy', a state which Storr characterizes as being 'about desiring and being desirable ... being a subject and being an object' (Storr, 2003: 92). Being sexually active and visible in this way is a way of gaining power over men *and* a site of gender identification. It allows women to show an interest in sex while remaining 'one of the girls'; they can perform a sexual identity which is 'both feminine and fun' (Storr, 2003: 96). As Storr notes, this kind of identification often depends on the mockery of men – at Ann Summers parties, men's bodies and behaviours are a source of comedy and they are routinely presented as 'useless'. Hilary Radner has also argued that the narcissistic reproduction of femininity through contemporary beauty and fitness regimes works to marginalize men and their demands by encouraging women to focus on developing an independence which is achieved through consumption and self-construction. Rather than performing for a male gaze, self-fashioning of this kind may provide women with a culturally approved way of producing themselves *for themselves*, though clearly this production is also expected to prove attractive to men. Radner suggests that self-fashioning produces 'a moment of gloriousness' (Radner, 1995: xii). Here, in this moment of pleasure and achievement, women may experience a sense of their own self-possession. At the same time, these moments and the settings in which they are produced work as spaces where women 'acquire the "know-how" to be feminine' (Storr, 2003: 221).

Pole-dancing classes can be understood as a similar kind of post-feminist homosocial space because of their focus on constructing the self as sexy and pleasure-seeking, and because they are women-only spaces which foreground identification with other women through the pursuit of femininity and fun. In this instance, the enjoyment also incorporates particularly physical pleasures – effort and control, exhilaration and accomplishment. Both Ann Summers parties and pole-dancing classes operate in line with other 'sexy practices' which are currently marketed to women, all of which draw on a contemporary porn chic in which the sleazy style of sexually explicit practices is rearticulated as tasteful and sometimes ironic. Aestheticizing and domesticating the sexual is crucial to the marketing of sex to women, enabling its rearticulation as a new set of things – art, dance, sport, 'thing of beauty'.

The presentation of contemporary pole dancing draws on a range of signifiers which are already understood as acceptably feminine: dancing, display, an interest in shoes, a concern with health, exercise and self-development. Its visibility in women's media and in its association with female celebrities who represent an acceptably raunchy version of femininity in the public eye also works to position it as an acceptable feminine practice. Its redeployment for 'ordinary' women, like boudoir photography and the Ann Summers party, means that it combines characteristics of porn chic and striptease culture at the same time. Not only does it become an instance of contemporary raunch within the media, used to demonstrate the acceptability of women's sexual agency, it becomes a practice in women's everyday lives which enables them to engage with, articulate and embody a particular set of characteristics which are currently prized in our culture: sexual hedonism, feistiness, confidence, independence, taste, style, heterosexual desire and solidarity with other women. But this set of characteristics is not simply 'given' to them. Rather they are forged through women's engagement and embodiment.

Pole dancing offers women a safe space in which they can engage with issues of sexual display, body image and body management in ways which make them feel powerful. Like the burlesque performer, women who practise pole dancing may access a fantasy of a woman who is able to be sexy and take command 'by doing what she wants ... rather than what she thinks she has to do'. While there is often a disjuncture between women's experiences of their sexuality and the images and discourses which describe and proscribe what it is to be sexy, an activity like pole dancing makes it possible for women to embody sexiness in a way that is physically exhilarating and enjoyable. Being both performer and audience enables women to 'see', 'be' and 'do' sexiness, and doing this while other women cheer on and applaud may be as close as we currently get to a positive experience of sexualization in contemporary culture. That success in this arena is not linked directly to appearance, as it is in most women's media from chick-lit to magazine sex advice, may be crucial in explaining why women experience pole exercise as particularly pleasurable. According to Rachel, pole dancing is 'a big leveller' in this respect. She had this to say about the importance of appearance in pole classes:

> I see people's faces when you get the sort of wannabe lap danc-
> ers coming along, and they see someone who has been sitting
> at the back in a scruffy loose T-shirt and baggy old shorts, and
> they see them get up on the pole – and all of a sudden they are
> transformed into someone doing something beautiful. And they
> are thinking 'oh shit, it is not all about what you look like – oh
> God, I am going to have to reassess it'. And I am not being mean
> to those girls, but I think it is good for them to realize that it is
> not all about what you look like. For the people who have got it
> and for the people who haven't got it – it is good for those who
> haven't to know that it can all be compensated for by attitude and
> by sexiness, rather than just having your bone structure right.

Successful pole dancing in this context is no longer dependent on conventional attractiveness, sexual availability and financial pressure, but on all kinds of other things – grace, charisma, talent and attitude.

Women who use pole dancing as a form of exercise experience it as extremely positive. All of the teachers and most of the students we met bought their own pole and had it fitted at home. They described real progress in their fitness and body confidence, both during and after the classes. Every woman used the term 'power' or 'empowerment' to describe their experiences and had only good things to say about the classes. Pole exercise is not easy; it requires strength, stamina, coordination and confidence – things that many women may not experience in their everyday lives. Doing pole exercise helped the women we met to acquire these qualities. They were affronted by the idea that doing and enjoying pole exercise demeaned them.

Of course we cannot see pole exercise in isolation from its associations with sex work, but, as Joke Hermes suggests, popular culture is open to exciting new definitions and identities which add new representations rather than replacing the old ones (2006: 93). As Merl Storr has argued, 'feeling sexy' and 'feeling powerful' are no substitutes for *being* sexy and powerful, but at the same time it is hard to see why we should unquestioningly reject those feelings. While it is important to remain critical of the way new sexualized practices for women are developing, it is equally important not to dismiss them out of hand if we are genuinely interested in working out what an active and empowered female sexuality might look and feel and really be like.

Chapter 11

BUST-ING THE THIRD WAVE: BARBIES, BLOWJOBS AND GIRLIE FEMINISM

REBECCA MUNFORD

'Call us do-me feminists, call us prosex feminists, just don't call us late for the sale at Good Vibrations. In our quest for total sexual satisfaction we shall leave no sex toy unturned and no sexual avenue unexplored. Women are trying their hands (and other body parts) at everything from phone sex to cybersex, solo sex to group sex, heterosex to homosex. Lusty feminists of the third wave, we're more than ready to drag-race down sexual roads less traveled. Ladies, start your engines' (Debbie Stoller, *The BUST Guide to the New Girl Order*, 1999).

'Women were the major beneficiary of the sexual revolution. It permitted them to be natural sexual beings, as men are. That's where feminism should have been all along. Unfortunately, within feminism, there has been a puritan, prohibitionist element that is antisexual. *Playboy* is the antidote to puritanism' (Hugh Hefner, *Esquire*, 2002).

Sexual politics and the politics of sexual representation have for a long time provided a site of vigorous debate within Western feminist discourse, crystallizing around the sex wars of the 1970s and 1980s.[1] Lynne Segal recounts her 'own entrapment in a maddeningly deadlocked debate' owing to the impossibility, since the close of the 1970s, of writing 'about sexuality or sexual politics (as a feminist) without being hi-jacked by, and forced to take a stand upon, the issue of pornography' (Segal, 2004: 59). The maddening deadlock Segal describes has been reinforced by a tendency to narrativize feminist debates about sexual politics along the dichotomous axes of anti- and pro-sex feminisms. Since the mid-1990s the public lambasting of second-wave 'victim feminism' undertaken by writers such as Naomi Wolf, Rene Denfeld and Camille Paglia has been concomitant with a demand for a more powerful, chic and sexual version of feminism.[2] For example, in *Fire with Fire*, Wolf positions 'power feminism' as an antidote to the supposed lack of agency in second-wave feminism: in contrast to 'victim feminism', 'power feminism' is 'unapologetically sexual' and 'understands that good pleasures make good politics' (Wolf, 1993: 147). This victim/power binary, Wolf suggests, emerges from two distinct traditions of feminism: 'One tradition is severe, morally superior and self-denying; the other is free-thinking, plea-sure-loving and self-assertive' (1993: 181). If the former tradition is epitomized by second-wave anti-pornography campaigns and their straightforward alignment with an 'anti-sex' (and, implicitly, anti-*plea-sure*) feminism, then the latter tradition is exemplified by the current appeal for a more sexual, if not *sexualized*, feminism, especially as it manifests in the pro-sex writings and sexual confessions of third-wave feminism.

In a cultural moment characterized by the widespread rise of raunch and the popularization of pornographic codes and conven-tions – what Brian McNair has described as the 'pornographication' of the mainstream[3] – in Western culture, the politics of any plea for an 'unapologetically sexual' feminism remain an ongoing area for consideration and concern. As Pamela Church Gibson warns in her introduction to *More Dirty Looks: Gender, Pornography and Power*, 'in the increasingly sexualized atmosphere of Western society, where ... sexually explicit images are to be found everywhere ... the relevant debates, within feminism and elsewhere, have certainly not been resolved' (Church Gibson, 2004: vii).

When university sports centres run pole-dancing classes and pre-pubescent girls buy their Playboy pencil cases from high-street stationers, and when 'power feminists' use the same vocabulary as Hugh Hefner to critique the 'puritan, prohibitionist element' in second-wave feminism, we need to explore exactly what is at stake in popular conceptualizations and representations of the sexualized forms of contemporary feminism.

My concern in this chapter is not, however, to replay the pornography debates, although their contours inexorably provide a backdrop for this discussion. Nor is it to chronicle the various manifestations of 'raunch' in contemporary culture – an endeavour recently undertaken by Ariel Levy in her provocative exposition of the commercialization of raunch images and practices in *Female Chauvinist Pigs* (2005). Rather, this chapter will examine some of the ways in which sexual politics continue to incite and excite discussion for a 'new' generation of pro-sex feminists who, to quote Marcelle Karp and Debbie Stoller, the editors of the third-wave feminist zine *BUST*, are not 'afraid of any f-words – from feminism to fucking to fashion' (1999: xiii). Drawing on a range of third-wave texts, I will focus in particular on *The BUST Guide to the New Girl Order*, a collection of essays from the first six years of the zine *BUST*, published by Penguin in 1999. Claiming to be 'busting stereotypes about women' and 'telling the truth about women's lives', *BUST* shares the broader concerns of third-wave zines such as *Bitch*, *Hues* and *Maxi* in its critical engagement with popular culture.[4] However, as I will illustrate, *BUST* is distinct from these because of the emphasis it places on a call to 'sex-up' feminism – both in terms of putting sex and, specifically, sexual pleasure back on the feminist agenda, and offering a sexier 'brand' of feminism. While contextualizing its discussion in relation to a broader current in contemporary feminism, this chapter will examine the ways in which *BUST* promotes 'Girlie feminism' as a 'shared set of female experiences that includes Barbies and blowjobs, sexism and shoplifting, *Vogue* and vaginas' (1999: xiv–xv). In so doing, it will investigate the political implications of a shift in feminist concern to the realms of the strictly sexual – especially in an era characterized by the rise of raunch in mainstream culture.

FEMINIST BATTLEGROUNDS: GIRLS ON TOP

In contemporary discussions of feminist sexual politics, there has been a tendency to draw the terms of debate along the lines of generational difference, with the circulation of monolithic accounts of second-wave feminism rendering it a stable and discrete object for attack.[5] In *The New Victorians: A Young Woman's Challenge to the Old Feminist Order*, Rene Denfeld who, like Wolf, identifies herself as a feminist, proposes that second-wave debates surrounding sexuality, sexual violence and pornography have produced a neo-Victorian discourse of sexual repression and political powerlessness. Focusing on such prominent figures as Catherine MacKinnon, Mary Daly, Andrea Dworkin and Robin Morgan, as well as Women's Studies professors on American campuses, Denfeld argues that, since the 1970s, second-wave feminists have become 'the new Victorians' in their promotion of 'nineteenth-century values of sexual morality, spiritual purity, and political helplessness' (1995: 10). According to Denfeld, 'new Victorian' feminism promotes a vision of female sexuality as chaste and sexless, one that mirrors late nineteenth-century feminist leaders' protests against 'sexual freedoms, birth control, promiscuity, sexual literature, and the evils of male sexuality' (1995: 20). Moreover, she continues, this language of martyrdom and victimhood has alienated a new generation of women who can no longer identify with the vocabulary of the women's movement and are now turning away from feminism.

Redeploying a seminal image of second-wave feminist activism – that of the 'Freedom Trash Can', into which was hurled the paraphernalia of traditional sexualized femininity – Denfeld proposes that we must 'toss New Victorianism in the rubbish can and return to a movement that addresses women's concerns while respecting their personal lives and empowering their choices' (1995: 20–1). Although Denfeld is referring here to concerns such as child care, abortion and economic opportunity, her allusion to the New York Radical Women's demonstration against the Miss America pageant in Atlantic City in 1968 is revealing. While functioning as another univocal moment in her reductive history of feminist (anti)sexual politics, the reference to the Freedom Trash Can and the more prevalent image of 'bra-burning' it conjures up also works to expose a more ambivalent convergence of discourses. As Imelda Whelehan has highlighted, the idea of the bra-less woman was quickly taken up by the mainstream media as simultaneously an image of 'sexiness' and 'unattractiveness'.

'Breasts and bras,' she continues, 'whether we like it or not, have dogged the women's movement since the sixties just as breast imagery has invaded the mass media and advertising' (Whelehan, 2000: 1–2). Betraying its dangerous proximity to mainstream representations of the women's movement, Denfeld's discussion of 'new Victorianism' relies on and perpetuates an understanding of second-wave feminism where radical feminist anti-pornography campaigners such as Dworkin, MacKinnon and Morgan stand in for all second-wave feminist activity. In this respect, it is complicit with a broader erasure of the multifarious feminist approaches to pornography, sex and sexuality in the 1970s and 1980s – ranging from the diverse writings of Angela Carter and Nancy Friday to the contributions of feminist sex workers such as Annie Sprinkle.[6]

Contemporary debates surrounding female empowerment in mainstream and feminist discourse have replicated this dualistic approach to feminist sexual politics, transposing the anti-sex/pro-sex binary on to a new dichotomy of the good girl/bad girl. Since the 1990s, the figure of the 'girl' – in her various incarnations – has become a ubiquitous subject of popular culture, emerging as 'an unstoppable superhero, a savvy supermodel, a combative action chick, a media goddess, a popstar who wants to rule the world' (Hopkins, 2002: 1). Sassy, sexy and strong, the girl embraces the trappings of traditional femininity – her 'girliness' – as the enactment of her empowerment. Popular culture, Susan Hopkins proposes, 'has never been so pervasively girl-powered' (2002: 1). From Paris Hilton and Britney Spears to Lara Croft and *Buffy the Vampire Slayer*, the figure of the girl continues to reign supreme as an icon of postfeminist consciousness in mainstream popular culture. Nevertheless, this understanding of girl power as synonymous with a postfeminist position – one that suggests that feminism is passé, its aims met or unnecessary to the lives of everyday women – conflates mass-mediated representations with the recuperations of 'girl' that have been central to the pro-sex, pro-pleasure stance of third-wave feminist identities since the 1990s.[7]

Although third-wave feminism remains an ongoing topic of discussion and definition, in the broadest sense it refers to a generation of women who, according to self-identified third wavers, Jennifer Baumgardner and Amy Richards, 'were reared in the wake of the women's liberation movement of the seventies' (2000: 15).[8] As they argue in *Manifesta: Young Women, Feminism, and the Future* (2000), although the third wave 'doesn't have an easily identifiable presence', its various manifestations are concerned with 'expanding feminism, and reclaiming the word *girl*, but in very different ways' (2000: 79–80). This recuperation of 'girl' is central to third-wave feminism's broader project of cultural re-appropriation and re-evaluation. For example, while acknowledging its debt to 'the struggles of the second wave', Melanie Klein claims that third-wave feminism is defined by

> a postmodern emphasis on contradiction and duality, as well as a conviction that S-M, pornography, the words *cunt* and *queer* and *pussy* and *girl* – are all things to be re-examined or reclaimed … We want not to get rid of the trappings of traditional feminin-ity or sexuality so much as to pair them with demonstrations of strength or power. We are much less likely to burn our bras communally than to run down the street together clad in noth-ing but our bras, yelling 'Fuck you!'[9]

But to whom is this defiant 'fuck you!' directed? Although wide rang-ing in the positions they adopt in relation to questions of feminist theory and praxis, many third-wave texts share a common ground in their eagerness to signal a break from an earlier feminist genera-tion. This break is embedded in a celebration of 'girl' identity and its implicit framing of feminist histories through the mother–daughter relationship.

As Lynn Spigel puts it in her essay on the bachelorette, the wave narrative inevitably works to 'place old feminists on the beach – washed up like fish on the shore. Meanwhile … the "new" feminist (regardless of her age) is somehow taken to be an immersive body, fully refreshed by the sea change and outfitted in new feminist swim-suit styles' (2004: 212). As this sartorial analogy suggests, for third-wave feminists the paraphernalia of 'femininity' is no longer at odds with 'feminism', but re-located at the very centre of a 're-fashioned' politics of sexual agency and confidence – one that can be located within the tradition of pleasure-loving and self-assertive feminism identified by Wolf. It is a reclaiming of traditional femininity – as recuperation and ironic play – that underlies Girlie feminism.

While Girlie replicates the multiple character of third-wave feminism, it is largely understood as referring to predominantly, though not exclusively, white, middle-class women in their late 20s and early 30s who embrace the disparaged artefacts of girlhood such as fashion, make-up and knitting. As Baumgardner and Richards describe in their 'glossary':

> A Girlie-girl can be a stereotypically feminine one – into manicures and hairstyles and cooking and indoorsy activities. Girlie is also a feminist philosophy put forth most assertively by the folks at BUST. Girlies are adult women, usually in their mid-twenties to late thirties, whose feminist principles are based on a reclaiming of girl culture (of feminine accoutrements that were tossed out with sexism during the Second Wave), be it Barbie, housekeeping, or girl talk (2000: 400).

Girlie feminism is positioned here not only as a recuperation of 'girl' as a marginalized subjectivity within mainstream, patriarchal culture, but also as a recovery of a version of traditional femininity 'rubbished' by an earlier generation of feminists.

Thus in an interview for *Grrly Show* (2000), a short documentary on girl-centric zines, Debbie Stoller proposes that young women must return to the Freedom Trash Can and take another look at the 'woman garbage' disposed inside of it – 'because one thing that got overlooked is that there is pleasure in some of that stuff'.[10] Vital to the reinstatement of pleasure at the centre of Girlie's 'feminist philosophy', then, is a boldly voiced response to what is perceived as the anti-sex and anti-pleasure legacy of second-wave feminism. Accordingly, Stoller demands a 'Sexual Revolution Grrl-Style Now' with the following call to arms:

> In the '90s, the women of the New Girl Order are ready to go out and get what's cumming to us. Our mission is to seek out pleasure wherever we can find it. In other words, if it feels good, screw it. Vibrators in hand, we're ready to fight the good fight ... as sexual freedom fighters, we've crossed enemy lines and are getting ready to release women from the shackles of the evil double standard. From fucking around to cursing like sailors to watching porn to shaking our booties at the local strip joint, we are sexual adven-

turesses who, unlike our foremothers, don't dare to assume that we know what 'female sexuality' is all about (Stoller, 1999: 84).

Explicitly redeploying the vocabulary of the sex wars, Stoller locates pleasure squarely at the centre of Girlie's feminist agenda. Indeed, filled with ads for feminist sex shops such as Good Vibrations and essays on masturbation and sex toys, as well as 'buxom images from vintage soft-core porn, images now in the control of women' (Baumgardner and Richards, 2000: 133), the pages of BUST represent a vociferous distancing from the purportedly anti-sex/anti-pleasure frameworks of second-wave feminism and promise a new and improved, sexed-up feminism centred around pleasure and play. Focused on topics ranging from the virtues of blowjobs, Hitachi wands and canine cunnilingus, to expositions of the racial homogeny of pornographic representation, the articles in BUST do, indubitably, begin to close what Stoller describes as the 'orgasm gap' (Stoller, 1999: 76) that continues to exist between men and women. Moreover, the articulation of these erotic fantasies and practices shapes a valuable forum for young women to share and explore their diverse sexual experiences and expressions. Still, what remains less clear is whether these 'true confessions of feminist desire' – to cite the subtitle of Merri Lisa Johnson's collection of third-wave writings, Jane Sexes it Up – offer a sufficiently robust bedrock upon which to construct a feminist politics. While recognizing the vital historical role of personal stories and memoirs in shaping and driving the collective aims and actions of the women's movement, we need to interrogate whether the third wave's preference for the confessional model can provide 'the foundation of the personal ethics upon which a political women's movement will be built' (Baumgardner and Richards, 2000: 20).

'IF IT FEELS GOOD, SCREW IT': GUILTY PLEASURES AND FEMINIST CONFESSIONS

The notion that 'testimony is where feminism starts', and that, historically, women's personal stories have been the evidence of where the movement needs to go politically' (Baumgardner and Richards, 2000: 20), provide the ethos for numerous third-wave publications. From Rebecca Walker's To Be Real: Telling the Truth and Changing the Face of

Feminism (1995) and Barbara Findlen's Listen Up: Voices From the Next Feminist Generation (1995) to Johnson's Jane Sexes it Up and Jessica Berens and Kerri Sharp's Inappropriate Behaviour: Prada Sucks and Other Demented Descants (2002), third-wave feminist publications have tended towards an experiential and anecdotal narrative mode. The emphasis in third-wave writing on providing 'true', 'real' and 'authentic' stories about women's experience can be located in relation to the broader tradition of consciousness-raising so central to the shared discursive environments of second-wave feminism. Founded on the principle that 'the personal is political', consciousness-raising groups provided a space for women to articulate and analyse personal and shared experiences as a starting point for collective political action. This tenet thus encapsulates the ways in which women's private lives, including their sexual lives, are structured by broader social relations, and provides the basis for a political analysis of personal life, including sexual meanings and practices.

Debates surrounding the political potential of the autobiographical impetus of third-wave writing have tended to focus on the (ab)use of this axiom. For some, second-wave feminism's proposal that 'the personal is political' has been equated with a prescriptive and restrictive set of behavioural codes and with the inflexibility of identity politics. Natasha Walter, for example, suggests in The New Feminism that feminism has 'overpersonalised the political and overpoliticised the personal, and in the processs has lost sight of its two great, long-standing goals: political equality and personal freedom' (1999: 62). Submitting to a similar logic, Rebecca Walker avers that for 'many of us it seems that to be a feminist in the way that we have seen or understood feminism is to conform to an identity and way of living that doesn't allow for individuality, complexity, or less than perfect personal histories' (1995: xxxiii). Underlying third-wave feminist understandings of sexual identity, then, is not only a demystification of patriarchal definitions of proper feminine behaviours, but also second-wave definitions of proper feminist behaviours. Nevertheless, the notion that 'the personal is political' is too frequently misappropriated in order to rationalize the personal account as a straightforward political action. In other words, it functions to valorize the confessional mode of third-wave feminist writing and its claims for

a re-examination of the relationship between (hetero)sexual pleasures and practices as part of a kind of 'sexual laissez-faire' (Coward,
1984b: xiv) – the idea that 'feminism is all about how the individual
feels right here, right now, rather than the bigger picture' (Viner in
Walter, 1999: 22).

It is this misappropriation of the relationship between the
personal and the political that too often appears in the pages of *The
BUST Guide to the New Girl Order*. Offering articles such as 'How to
be as horny as a guy,' 'Me and my cunt' and 'Watching him fuck her',
an interview with 'feminist' porn star Nina Hartley and an essay by
Courtney Love on 'bad girls', *The BUST Guide to the New Girl Order*
privileges the confessional as its modus operandi. In 'More than a
blow job: it's a career', for example, Dixie LaRue provides a detailed
account of her 'predilection for cock-suckage':

> I suck cocks. I am a woman who likes to put penises in her
> mouth, and then suck said penises for all they're worth ... Imag-
> ine the impression you can make on a fourteen-year-old boy when
> you pulled fellatio out of your bag of tricks ... Naturally, in college
> the field was more crowded. A virgin in tramp's clothing, I honed
> my craft to include a special, shall we say melodramatically hearty
> rendition of the swallow ... It was one of the few times a girl could
> feel as if she were making an impression. Usually my friends and
> I just felt, well, used. Sucking cock, you felt important (1999:
> 100–1).

Although the opening confession, self-consciously styled in the
manner of a sex addict, gestures towards a parodic debunking of
female sexuality as pathology, the wry tone of this essay quickly adopts
the tenor of self-satisfied declaration. Moreover, although it operates
as a recuperation of 'sucking cock' as a position of feminist agency
– the essay makes explicit reference to Germaine Greer's description
of the experience of giving a blowjob as 'like being attacked by a giant
snail' – it offers no critique of the ideological structures which render
the act of fellatio a space in which a girl can 'feel important'. Indeed,
the confession is firmly situated within a patriarchal field of reference centred on female competition ('in college the field was more
crowded') and traditional mappings of female sexual identity across

the Madonna/whore dichotomy ('a virgin in tramp's clothing'). Here, then, personal experience claims its 'political' dimension only by virtue of the act of narration; the relationship between the personal and the political is treated as synonymous rather than dialectical.

As Johnson recognizes in her introduction to *Jane Sexes it Up*, another collection of 'confessions and kinks' (2002: 1), it is vital that the personal freedoms claimed by third-wave writers are not divorced from their relevant social and cultural contexts, or the political factors that shape and define them. Alluding to Carole S. Vance's landmark *Pleasure and Danger* (1984), she proposes: 'Our writing *is* play, but it is play *despite* and *in resistance to* a context of danger and prohibition, *not* a result of imagining there is none' (2002: 2). If the maddening deadlock of the feminist sex wars of the 1970s and 1980s hinged on its insistence of either fighting *for* sexual pleasure or *against* sexual violence, then the *Jane* generation is focused on continuing feminism's critiques of sexual politics, while reinstating sexual pleasure as the 'great guilty secret among feminists' (2002: 4). In other words, it is intent on reconnecting 'the critique' with 'the clit' (2002: 6). Nevertheless, in spite of historicizing third-wave feminism's sex-positive position in relation to previous feminist debates about female sexuality, Johnson's celebration of the erotic autobiography in her collection – which includes pieces on 'spanking chic', strap-ons and masturbation fantasies – fails to acknowledge its location in relation to the sexualization of *contemporary* mainstream culture.

The introduction to the collection opens with the following statement: 'The world polices women – even now in this so-called post-feminist era – into silence about sex, socially constructed modesty, and self-regulating repression of behaviour and fantasy' (2002: 1). However, far from advocating socially constructed modesty, the rise of raunch culture marks a proliferation of invitations for young women to exhibit their Brazilian-waxed, thong-clad bodies, to attend pole-dancing classes and to don 'Playboy' and 'Porn Star' tees. Raunch culture polices female sexuality through its hyper-sexualization rather than its repression. They might have travelled some way from the pages of *Cosmo*, but essays such as 'Spanking and the single girl' and 'More than a blow job: it's a career' bear a startling resemblance to the 'true' confessions of 'real' girls and girlfriends that fill the pages of lad mags such as *Nuts*, *Zoo* and *Loaded*.[11] Thus the act of feminist confession – exemplified by the sexual kinks in Johnson's collection, as well as the pages of Girlie zines – needs to be more rigorously located in relation to the currency of sexual revelation and disclosure in mainstream popular culture – what McNair describes as 'striptease culture' [12] – as well as the confession as a structuring device of pornographic narrative.[13]

Indeed, it is in its positioning in relation to the widespread dissemination of pornographic representations and paraphernalia that Girlie feminism abandons its political engagement. Stoller, for example, locates Girlie feminism's redeployment of pornographic codes and pro-sex stance firmly in relation to the pornographication of mainstream culture:

> With X-rated movies available to rent at every local video store and Hooters considered a family restaurant, we realize that American porn culture is here to stay. So, rather than trying to rid the world of sexual images we think are negative, as some of our sisters have done, we're far more interested in encouraging women to explore porn, to find out whether it gets them hot or merely bothered (1999: 82–3).

While acknowledging that most porn is 'ruthlessly sexist' and 'might need to change if women are going to derive the kind of pleasure from it that men have enjoyed all these years', Stoller's discussion moves dangerously close to a reactionary politics forged as a response to the popular legacy of second-wave feminism, rather than as a critique of raunch culture itself. Although *The BUST Guide to the New Girl Order* makes explicit claims to be 'doing' the sex wars, it suggests 'precisely the opposite: that the debate has already happened, and that a pro-porn, pro-sex stance has been adopted as third-wave feminism's default position' (Waters, 2007: 258). Levelling its attack at second-wave feminism, rather than American porn culture, means that Girlie feminism constrains serious and productive debates about sexual representation within a generational framework that enables internal conflict rather than external critique.

One of the key problems with Girlie is that its frequent recourse to dualistic thinking – in the form of victim/power, good girl/bad girl, rebellious daughter/abstemious mother dichotomies – implicates it in the binary logic of a masculinist pornographic fantasy. In this respect, the sexualization of feminism and its deployment of 'the media of sexual confession and self-revelation' (McNair, 2002: 88) are inextricable from its commodification. In a discussion of the 'pink pound', McNair highlights the extent to which the promise of pleasure in mainstream culture has been transformed into various types of commodity, from pornographic materials and sex aids to fashion and accessories. Always on time for 'the sale at Good Vibrations' and decked out in her lipgloss and high heels, the Girlie feminist embodies a sexed-up 'brand' of feminism centred precisely around such materials; she also looks misleadingly like the lad mags' pin-up. Sex sells and it is in the realm of the marketplace, then, that Girlie feminism risks becoming a bedfellow of 'consumer feminism'; the extent to which it focuses its 'sexual revolution' on the *pleasures* and paraphernalia of popular culture, rather than the *politics* of popular culture (not to mention the politics of pleasure) betrays its susceptibility to the uniformity of the 'raunch culture' industry.

Stoller laments how, during the pornography debates, feminism's 'focus turned to issues of power and of politics, and turned away from what was really at stake all along: our pleasure' (1999: 78). It is precisely this disconnection of pleasure and desire from the structures and operations of power that may stall Girlie feminism's formulation of a new feminist sexual politics. There is a radical difference between embracing 'Barbies and blowjobs, sexism and shoplifting, *Vogue* and vaginas' as lifestyle choices and lobbying for changes in legislation and public policy. In *BITCHfest: Ten Years of Cultural Criticism from the Pages of Bitch Magazine*, Lisa Jervis acknowledges the precarious line that young women need to walk when offering 'forthright assertions' of their desires, given both their potential misinterpretation by mainstream culture and their vulnerability to popular culture's desire to channel the promise of pleasure into profitable avenues:

> Anything we say risks reaffirming one of the many stereotypes out there: Feminism leads to [fill in the blank with promiscuity, frigidity, lesbianism, abortion]. Women's sexuality [doesn't exist, is out of control, depends on emotion, is about being looked at, is the polar opposite of some stereotypical visually driven male

sexuality]' (Jervis, 2006: 165).

This is not to advocate the self-policing of female sexuality, nor is it to deny the important and powerful function of pleasure and play in configuring feminist subjectivities. Rather, it is to recommend vigilant and strategic interventions in popular culture. In contrast to the more flamboyant and decontextualized redeployments of traditional images of sexualized femininity which characterize some of the essays in The BUST Guide to the New Girl Order, BITCHfest includes a 'feminist advocacy guide' on 'how to reclaim, reframe, and reform the media'. Outlining various possible strategies (legal, educational, professional) for agitating for positive media coverage of women and feminism as well as structural reform, this guide brings an activist slant to Bitch's agenda and thus provides a more useful model for a feminist politics that takes account of the shifting terrain of mainstream culture. Certainly, Girlie culture has 'created a joyful culture that makes being an adult woman who calls herself a feminist seem thrilling, sexy, and creative' (Baumgardner and Richards, 2000: xx), and this joyful culture should be embraced. But it needs to be embraced in conjunction with a relentless critique of and intervention in the still pervasive forms of – frequently girl-powered – 'ruthless sexism' in mainstream culture.

NOTES

1. For an account of the sex wars see Duggan and Hunter, 1995.
2. This is not to suggest that these writers occupy an identical position in relation to issues of sex and sexuality, but, rather, that their arguments share some commonality in their consensus that 'the gains forged by previous generations of women have so completely pervaded all tiers of our social existence that those still "harping" about women's victim status are embarrassingly out of touch'. See Siegel, 1997: 75.
3. This is 'the *representation* of porn in non-pornographic art and culture; the pastiche and parody of, the homage to and investigation of porn into mainstream cultural artefact for a variety of purposes including ... advertising, art, comedy and education.' McNair, 2004: 6.

4. Founded in 1996 by Lisa Jervis and Andi Zeisler, *Bitch* magazine, the subtitle of which is 'feminist responses to popular culture', has the mission of 'formulating replies to the sexist and narrow-minded media diet that we all – intentionally or not – consume. 'About *Bitch*', http://www.bitchmagazine.com/about.shtml (accessed 12.7.06). For more on zines and third-wave feminism, see Bates and Carter McHugh, 2005.

5. For a critical introduction to second-wave feminism, see Whelehan, 1997.

6. For more on the diversity of pornographic forms and feminist approaches to them see Cornell (ed), 2000; for more on sex radicals and sex workers see Doyle and Lacombe, 1996.

7. For more on the distinctions between postfeminism and third-wave feminism see Gillis and Munford, 2004.

8. For more on third-wave feminism, see Heywood and Drake (eds), 1997, and Gillis et al (eds), 2007.

9. Klein's reference is to punk and, more generally, to the alternative music community. However, the ambivalent view of second-wave feminism articulated here is resonant with the broader attitudes of third-wave feminism. Klein, 1997.

10. Herold, *Grrly Show* (2000).

11. See Turner, 2005.

12. According to McNair, striptease culture 'frequently involves ordinary people talking about sex and their own sexualities, revealing intimate details of their feelings and their bodies in the public sphere' (2002: 88).

13. For more on pornography and confession see Waters, 2007.

Film and TV Guide

8mm (Joel Schumacher, 1998)
9 Songs (Michael Winterbottom, 2003)
9½ Weeks (Adrian Lyne, 1986)
1001 Ways to Eat My Jizz (August Arkham, 2002)
A Ma Soeur (Catherine Breillat, 2001)
Amateur Porn (David Clews, 2005)
American Beauty (Sam Mendes, 1999)
American Porn (Michael Kirk, 2002)
Anatomy of Hell (Catherine Breillat, 2004)
Annie Hall (Woody Allen, 1977)
Ass 2 Mouth 2 (John Strong, 2005)
Ass Clowns 3 (Thomas Zupko, 2001)
Ass Worship 9 (Jules Jordan, 2006)
Autofocus (Paul Schrader, 2002)
Back 2 Evil 2 (Nacho Vidal, 2006)
Baise Moi (Virginie Despentes and Coralie Trinh Thi, 2000)
Barely Legal Schoolgirls (Will Rider, 2006)
Basic Instinct (Paul Verhoeven, 1992)
The Best of Louis Theroux's Weird Weekends: Porn (Louis Theroux, 2001)
Bewitched (Nora Ephron, 2005)
Blow Job (Andy Warhol, 1966)
Boogie Nights (Paul Thomas Anderson, 1997)
Bridget Jones's Diary (Sharon Maguire, 2001)
Buttman's Rio Carnival Hardcore (John Stagliano, 2002)
The Cell (Tarsem Singh, 1999)
Cocktails 2 (Lizzie Borden, 2001)
Crash (David Cronenberg, 1996)
Dawson's Creek (1998-2003)
Debbie Does Dallas: The Musical (Susan L. Schwartz, 2001)
Deep Throat (Gerard Damiano, 1972)
Desperate Housewives (2004-)

Dirty Pictures (Frank Pierson, 2000)
Extreme Teen 24 (Stanley Ferrara, 2002)
Eye of the Beholder (Stefan Elliott, 1999)
Faking It: Burlesque Special (Ruth Newman, 2006)
Forced Entry (Lizzie Borden, 2002)
Gag the Fag (Mark Savage, 2004)
The Girl Next Door (Luke Greenfield, 2004)
Grrly Show (Kara Herold, 2000)
Hard Core (Paul Schrader, 1979)
Hardcore (Stephen Walker, 2001)
Haute Tension – Switchblade Romance (Alexandra Aja, 2003)
Henry and June (Philip Kaufman, 1990)
Hogan's Heroes (1965–71)
A Hole In My Heart (Lucas Moodyson, 2004)
Intimacy (Patrice Chereaux, 2001)
Jackass (2000–2)
Jesse Jane: Sexual Freak (Robby D, 2006)
Last Tango In Paris (Bernardo Bertolucci, 1972)
Men Behaving Badly (1992–98)
The Merchants of Cool (Barak Goodman, 2001)
The Moguls (Michael Traeger, 2005)
Mulholland Drive (David Lynch, 2001)
The People Versus Larry Flynt (Milos Forman, 1996)
Porn: A Family Business (Jay Blumenfield and Anthony Marsh, 2003)
Pornography: The Musical (Brian Hill, 2003)
Pornucopia: Going Down in the Valley (Dan Chaykin, 2004)
The Postman Always Rings Twice (Bob Rafelson, 1981)
Psycho (Gus Van Sant, 1998)
Quills (Phillip Kaufman, 2000)
Rated X (Emilio Estevez, 2000)
Rocco Animal Trainer (Rocco Siffredi, 2000)
Rocco Meats Trinity (Rocco Siffredi, 2004)
Romance (Catherine Breillat, 1999)
Scary Movie (Kennan Ivory Wayans, 2000)
Scream (Wes Craven, 1996)
Sex and the City (1998–2004)
Sex is Comedy (Catherine Breillat, 2002)
Sex: The Annabel Chong Story (Gough Lewis, 1998)
Shortbus (John Cameron Mitchell, 2006)
Silence of the Lambs (Jonathan Demme, 1991)

Skin (Jim Leonard, 2003)
Super Size Me (Morgan Spurlock, 2004)
Taken (Brad Armstrong, 2006)
There's Something About Mary (Bobby and Peter Farrelly, 1998)
Trophy Whores (Jonni Darkko, 2005)
Wonderland (James Cox, 2003)

BIBLIOGRAPHY

Allen, Peter Lewis (2000), *The Wages of Sin: Sex and Disease, Past and Present*. Chicago: University of Chicago Press

Altman, Rick (1999), *Film/Genre*. London: British Film Institute

American Psychological Association (2007), *Report of the APA Task Force on the Sexualization of Girls*. Washington, DC: American Psychological Association, www.apa.org/pi/wpo/sexualization.html

Amis, Martin (2001), 'A rough trade', *Guardian*, 17 March

Amy-Chinn, Dee (2006), 'This is just for me(n): How the regulation of post-feminist lingerie advertising perpetuates woman as object', *Journal of Consumer Culture* 6 (2): 155–75

Ang, Ien (1985), *Watching Dallas: Soap Opera and the Melodramatic Imagination*. London: Methuen

Anonymous (1723), *Onania, or the Heinous Sin of Self-Pollution, and all its Frightful Consequences, in Both Sexes, Considered*. 8th edition. London: Thomas Crouch Booksellers

Araki, Nobuyoshi (2005), *Self, Life, Death*. London: Phaidon

Arthurs, Jane (2003), 'Sex and the City and consumer culture: remediating post feminist drama', *Feminist Media Studies* 3 (1): 83–98

Arthurs, Jane (2004), *Television and Sexuality: Regulation and the Politics of Taste*. Maidenhead: Open University Press

Attwood, Feona (2002), 'Reading Porn: The Paradigm Shift in Pornography Research', *Sexualities* 5 (1): 91–105

Attwood, Feona (2004), 'Pornography and Objectification: Re-reading "the picture that divided Britain"', *Feminist Media Studies* 4 (1): 7–19

Attwood, Feona (2005a), 'Fashion and Passion: Marketing Sex to Women', *Sexualities* 8 (4): 392–406

Attwood, Feona (2005b), '"Tits and ass and porn and fighting": Male heterosexuality in magazines for men', *International Journal of Cultural Studies* 8 (1): 83–100

Attwood, Feona (2006), 'Sexed up: Theorizing the Sexualization of Culture', *Sexualities* 9 (1): 99–116

Baker, Gillian and Boynton, Petra (2005), 'A different picture of Africa', *British Medical Journal* 331: 782

Baldwin, Michelle (2004), *Burlesque and the New Bump-n-Grind*. Denver: Speck Press

Barcan, Ruth (2002), 'In the Raw: "Home-Made" Porn and Reality Genres', *Journal of Mundane Behavior* 3 (1), http://www.mundanebehavior.org/issues/v3n1/barcan.htm

Barcan, Ruth (2004), *Nudity: A Cultural Anatomy*. Oxford and New York: Berg

Barker, Martin (1989), *Comics: Ideology, Power and the Critics*. Manchester: Manchester University Press

Barker, Martin et al (2001), *The Crash Controversy: Censorship Campaigns and Film Reception*. London: Wallflower Press

Barker, Martin (2005), 'The Lord of the Rings and "Identification": A Critical Encounter', *European Journal of Communication* 20 (3): 353–78

Barker, Martin, and Brooks, Kate (1998), *Knowing Audiences: Judge Dredd: Its Friends, Fans and Foes*. Luton: University of Luton Press

Barthes, Roland (1981), *Camera Lucida*. New York: NoonDay Press

Barthes, Roland (1993), 'Striptease', in *Mythologies*. London: Vintage: 84–7

Bartky, Sandra (1990), 'Feminine Masochism and the Politics of Personal Transformation', *Hypatia* 2 (special issue of *Women's Studies International Forum*) 7 (5): 323–34

Bates, Dawn and Carter McHugh, Maureen (2005), 'Zines: voices of third wave feminists', in Jo Reger (ed), *Different Wavelengths: Studies of the Contemporary Women's Movement*. New York: Routledge: 179–94

Bauman, Zygmunt (2003), *Liquid Love: On the Frailty of Human Bonds*. Cambridge: Polity Press

Baumgardner, Jennifer and Richards, Amy (2000), *Manifesta: Young Women, Feminism, and the Future*. New York: Farrar, Straus, Giroux

Beato, Greg (2004), 'Xtreme Measures: Washington's New Crackdown on Pornography', http://www.reason.com/0405/fe.gb.xtreme.shtml

Beautiful Agony, http://www.beautifulagony.com/public/main.php

Beck-Gernsheim, Elisabeth (2002), *Reinventing the Family: In Search of New Life-Styles*. Cambridge: Polity

Beckman, Andrea (2001), 'Deconstructing Myths: the Social Construction of "Sadomasochism" versus "Subjugated Knowledges" of Practitioners of Consensual SM', *Journal of Criminal Justice and Popular Culture* 8 (2): 66–95

Bell, Rachel (2007), 'University challenge', *Guardian*, 9 February

Belle du Jour: Diary of a London Call Girl, http://belledujour-uk.blogspot. com

Bennett, Paula and Rosario, Vernon A. (eds) (1995), *Solitary Pleasures: The Historical, Literary, and Artistic Discourses of Autoeroticism*. London: Routledge

Berens, Jessica and Sharp, Kerri (2002), *Inappropriate Behaviour: Prada Sucks! and other Demented Descants*. London: Serpent's Tail

Bitch, http://www.bitchmagazine.com

Boni, Federico (2002), 'Framing Media Masculinities: Men's Lifestyle Magazines and the Biopolitics of the Male Body', *European Journal of Communication* 17 (4): 465–78

Bourdieu, Pierre (1984), *Distinction: A Social Critique of the Judgment of Taste*. Cambridge: Polity Press

Boynton, Petra (1999), '"Is That Supposed to be Sexy?" Women Discuss Women in "Top Shelf" Magazines', *Journal of Community and Applied Social Psychology* 9: 449–61

Boynton, Petra (2003), '"Much, Much, Much Better Sex'" – Was That Ever True? Revisiting an Evaluation of Sex Information in Women's Magazines', unpublished paper

Boynton, Petra (2004), 'Better dicks through drugs? The penis as a pharmaceutical target', *SCAN Journal of Media Arts Culture* 1 (3), http://scan.net.au/scan/journal/display.php?journal_id=37

Boynton, Petra (2006), '"Enough with tips and advice and thangs": The experience of a critically reflexive, evidence-based Agony Aunt', *Feminist Media Studies* 6 (4): 541–6

Boynton, Petra (2007), 'Advice for sex advisors: A guide for "agony aunts", relationship therapists, and sex educators who want to work with the media', *Sex Education* (forthcoming)

Boynton, Petra and Callaghan, Will (2006), 'Understanding media coverage of sex: A practical discussion paper for sexologists and journalists', *Sexual and Relationship Therapy* 21 (3): 333–46

Bragg, Sara (2006), '"Having a real debate": using media as a resource in sex education', *Sex Education* 6 (4): 317–31

Bragg, Sara and Buckingham, David (2002), *Young People and Sexual Content on Television*. London: Broadcasting Standards Commission

Bragg, Sara and Buckingham, David (2004), 'Embarrassment, Education and Erotics: The Sexual Politics of Family Viewing', *European Journal of Cultural Studies* 7 (4): 441–59

Brooks, Xan (2005), 'Dirty Business', *Guardian*, 4 January

Buckingham, David (1993), *Children Talking Television: The Making of Television Literacy*. London and Bristol, PA: Falmer Press

Buckingham, David (2000), *After the Death of Childhood: Growing Up in the Age of Electronic Media*. Cambridge: Polity Press

Buckingham, David (2003), *Media Education: Literacy, Learning and Contemporary Culture*. Cambridge: Polity Press

Buckingham, David and Bragg, Sara (2003), *Children, Media and Personal Relationships*. London: Advertising Standards Authority, British Board of Film Classification, BBC, Broadcasting Standards Commission, Independent Television Commission, www.mediarelate. org

Buckingham, David and Bragg, Sara (2004), *Young People, Sex and the Media: The Facts of Life?* Basingstoke: Palgrave Macmillan

Califia, Pat (1997), 'Identity Sedition and Pornography', in Carol Queen and Lawrence Schimel (eds), *PoMoSexuals: Challenging Assumptions about Gender and Sexuality*. San Francisco: Cleis Press: 87–106

Carter, Cynthia and Weaver, Kay (2003), *Violence and the Media*. Buckingham: Open University Press

Christensen, Clark (1995), 'Prescribed Masturbation in Sex Therapy: A Critique', *Journal of Sex and Marital Therapy* 21 (2): 87–99

Christian, M. (2006), 'Answers', in Russ Kick (ed), *Everything You Know about Sex is Wrong*. New York: The Disinformation Company: 9–12

Church Gibson, Pamela (1993), *Dirty Looks: Women, Pornography, Power*. London: BFI

Church Gibson, Pamela (ed) (2004), *More Dirty Looks: Gender, Pornography and Power*. London: BFI

Church Gibson, Pamela (2004), 'Preface: Porn Again? Or Why the Editor Might have Misgivings', in Pamela Church Gibson (ed), *More Dirty Looks: Gender, Pornography and Power*. London: BFI: vii–xii

Ciclitira, Karen (2002), 'Researching pornography and sexual bodies', *The Psychologist* 15 (4): 191–4

Ciclitira, Karen (2004), 'Pornography, Women and Feminism: Between Pleasure and Politics', *Sexualities* 7 (3): 281–301

Cooper, Al (ed) (2000), *Cybersex: The Dark Side of the Force – A special issue of the journal Sexual Addiction and Compulsion*. Philadelphia: Brunner-Routledge

Cooper, Al (2002), *Sex and the Internet: A Guide for Clinicians*. New York and London: Brunner Routledge

Cornell, Drucilla (ed) (2000), *Feminism and Pornography*. Oxford: Oxford University Press

Coward, Rosalind (1984a), *Female Desire*. London: Paladin

Coward, Rosalind (1984b), 'Preface to the British edition', in Ann Snitow et al (eds), *Desire: The Politics of Sexuality*. London: Virago: xi–xvii

Davidson, Andrew (2006), 'Top shelf tycoon bares all', *Sunday*, 7 May

Denfeld, Rene (1995), *The New Victorians: A Young Woman's Challenge to the Old Feminist Order*. London: Warner

DFEE (2000), *Sex and Relationship Education Guidance*. Nottingham: Department for Education and Employment

Dodson, Betty (1974), *Liberating Masturbation: A Meditation on Self Love*. New York: Bodysex Designs

Doyle, Kegan and Lacombe, Dany (1996), 'Porn Power: Sex, Violence, and the Meaning of Images in 1980s Feminism', in Nan Bauer Maglin and Donna Perry (eds), *'Bad Girls/Good Girls': Women, Sex, and Power in the Nineties*. New Brunswick: Rutgers University Press: 188–204

Drury, Rebecca (2006), *Pole Dancing: The Naughty Girl's Guide*. London: Connections Book Publishing

Duggan, Lisa and Hunter, Nan (1995), *Sex Wars: Sexual Dissent and Political Culture*. London: Routledge

Dworkin, Andrea (1981), *Pornography: Men Possessing Women*. London: The Women's Press

Dyer, Gillian (1982), *Advertising as Communication*. London: Methuen, Routledge

Dyer, Richard (1992), 'Coming to Terms; Gay Pornography', in *Only Entertainment*. London and New York: Routledge: 121–34

Eck, Beth A. (2003), 'Men Are Much Harder: Gendered Viewing of Nude Images', *Gender and Society* 17 (5): 691–710

Ehrenreich, Barbara and English, Deidre (1979), *For Her Own Good: 150 Years of Advice to Women*. London: Pluto Press

Elliott, Anthony and Lemert, Charles (2006), *The New Individualism: The Emotional Costs of Globalisation*. London and New York: Routledge

Ellis, John (1992), 'On pornography', in *The Sexual Subject: A Screen Reader in Sexuality*. London: Routledge: 146–70

Evans, Mary (2003), *Love: An Unromantic Discussion*. Cambridge: Polity

Faludi, Susan (1991), *Backlash*. London: Verso

Faust, Beatrice (1980), *Women, Sex and Pornography*. London: Melbourne House Ltd

Findlay, Heather (1999), '"Freud's Fetishism" and the Lesbian Dildo Debates', in Janet Price and Margrit Shildrick (eds), *Feminist Theory and the Body: A Reader*. New York: Routledge: 466–76

Findlen, Barbara (1995), *Listen Up: Voices from the Next Feminist Generation*. Seattle, Washington: Seal Press

Fleming, Jacky (1996), *Hello Boys*. London: Penguin

Fleshbot, http://www.fleshbot.com

Forum: The International Journal of Human Relations 34, nos. 1–12 (2000)

Foucault, Michel (1981), *The History of Sexuality: An Introduction*. Harmondsworth: Pelican

Frank, Lisa and Smith, Paul (eds) (1993), *Madonnarama: Essays on Sex and Popular Culture*. Pittsburgh: Cleis Press

Freud, Sigmund (1905/1977), *On Sexuality*. Penguin Freud Library, 7. Translated by James Strachey. London: Pelican

Freud, Sigmund (1961), 'The Economic Problem of Masochism', in *The Standard Edition of the Complete Psychological Works of Sigmund Freud*. Translated by James Strachey, vol. 19. London: Hogarth: 159–70

Friday, Nancy (1991), *Women on Top: How Real Life Has Changed Women's Sexual Fantasies*. New York: Simon and Schuster

Friday, Nancy (2001), *My Secret Garden: Women's Sexual Fantasies*. London: Quartet Books

Furnham, Adrian and Bitar, Nadine (1993), 'The stereotyped portrayal of men and women in British television advertisements', *Sex Roles* 29 (3/4): 297–310

Gaines, Jane (2004), 'Machines That Make the Body Do Things', in Pamela Church Gibson (ed), *More Dirty Looks: Gender, Pornography and Power*. London: BFI: 31–44

Gallagher, Bob and Wilson, Alexander (1984), 'Michel Foucault, An Interview: Sex, Power and the Politics of Identity', *The Advocate* 400 (7 August)

Gallagher, Catherine and Lacquer, Thomas (eds) (1987), *The Making of the Modern Body*. Berkeley: University of California Press

Gavey, Nicola et al (1999), 'Interruptus Coitus: Heterosexuals Accounting for Intercourse', *Sexualities* 2 (1): 35–68

Giddens, Anthony (1992), *The Transformation of Intimacy: Sexuality, Love and Eroticism in Modern Societies*. Cambridge: Polity Press

Gill, Rosalind (2003), 'From Sexual Objectification to Sexual Subjectification: The Resexualisation of Women's Bodies in the Media', *Feminist Media Studies* 3 (1): 100–6

Gill, Rosalind (2007a), *Gender and the Media*. Cambridge: Polity Press

Gill, Rosalind (2007b), 'Postfeminist Media Culture: Elements of a Sensibility', *European Journal of Cultural Studies* 10 (2): 147–66

Gill, Rosalind (2007c), 'Critical Respect: Dilemmas of Choice and

Agency in Feminism (A response to Duits and Van Zoonen)', *European Journal of Women's Studies* 14 (1): 69–80

Gill, Rosalind (2008), '"Beyond Sexualization": Sexual Representations in Advertising', *Sexualities* (forthcoming)

Gillis, Stacy and Munford, Rebecca (2004), 'Genealogies and Generations: The Politics and Praxis of Third Wave Feminism', *Women's History Review* 13 (2): 165–82

Gillis, Stacy et al (eds) (2007), *Third Wave Feminism: A Critical Exploration*. 2nd edition. Basingstoke: Palgrave

Girl with a One-Track Mind, http://girlwithaonetrackmind.blogspot.com

Goffman, Erving (1979), *Gender Advertisements*. London: Macmillan

Goldman, Robert (1992), *Reading Ads Socially*. London and New York: Routledge

Gossett, Sherrie, 'Bogus GI rape photos used as Arab propaganda', http://www.worldnetdaily.com/new/article.aspARTICLE_ID=38335

Gossett, Sherrie, 'Fake rape photos infuriate Arab World', http://www.worldnetdaily.com/new/article.aspARTICLE_ID=38408

Grayling, A.C. (2002), 'Sex and sensibility', *Guardian*, 9 February

Grimshaw, Jean (1993), 'Ethics, Fantasy and Self-Transformation', in A. Phillips Griffiths (ed), *Ethics* (Royal Institute of Philosophy Supplement 35). New York: Cambridge University Press: 145–58

Grogan, Sarah (1999), *Body Image: Understanding Body Dissatisfaction in Men, Women and Children*. London: Routledge

Grosz, Elizabeth (1995), *Space, Time and Perversion*. London: Routledge

Gunter, Barrie (1994), *Television and Gender Representation*. London: John Libbey

Hardy, Simon (1998), *The Reader, the Author, His Woman and Her Lover: Soft-Core Pornography and Heterosexual Men*. London: Cassell

Hardy, Simon (2001), 'More Black Lace: Women, Eroticism and Subjecthood', *Sexualities* 4 (4): 435–53

Hardy, Simon (2004), 'Reading pornography', *Sex Education: Sexuality, Society and Learning* 4 (1): 3–18

Harlow, John (2006), 'Booming porn faces backlash', *Sunday Times*, 29 October

Harris, Anita (2004), *Future Girl: Young Women in the Twenty-First Century*. London and New York: Routledge

Head, Jacqui (2006), 'Dirty Dancing', http://news.bbc.co.uk/go/pr/fr/-/1/hi/magazine/4939752.stm

Hefner, Hugh (2002), 'What I've learned', *Esquire*, June

Hermes, Joke (2006), 'Ally McBeal, Sex and the City and the Tragic Success of Feminism', in Joanne Hollows and Rachel Moseley (eds), *Feminism in Popular Culture*. Oxford and New York: Berg: 79-96

Hersh, Seymour, 'Torture at Abu Ghraib', http://www.newyorker.com/archive/2004/05/10/040510fa_fact

Heywood, Leslie and Drake, Jennifer (eds) (1997), *Third Wave Agenda: Being Feminist, Doing Feminism*. Minneapolis: University of Minnesota Press

Higgins, Charlotte (2004), 'Why I made that film', *Guardian*, 20 May

Hill, Annette (1997), *Shocking Entertainment: Viewer Response to Violent Movies*. Luton: University of Luton Press

Hillyer, Minette (2004), 'Sex in the Suburban: Porn, Home Movies, and the Live Action Performance of Love in "Pam and Tommy Lee: Hardcore and Uncensored"', in Linda Williams (ed), *Porn Studies*. London: Duke University Press: 50-76

Hilton, Gillian (2003), 'Listening to the Boys: English boys' views on the desirable characteristics of teachers of sex education', *Sex Education* 3 (1): 33-45

Hite, Shere (1993), *Women as Revolutionary Agents of Change: The Hite Reports, 1972-1993*. London: Bloomsbury

Holland, Janet et al (1998), *The Male in the Head: Young People, Heterosexuality and Power*. London: Tufnell Press

Holland, Samantha (2004), *Alternative Femininities: Body, Age and Identity*. Oxford and New York: Berg

Hopkins, Susan (2002), *Girl Heroes: The New Force in Popular Culture*. Annadale: Pluto Press

Hunt, Lynne (ed) (1996), *The Invention of Pornography: Obscenity and the Origins of Modernity, 1500-1800*. New York: Zone Books

I Feel Myself, http://www.ifeelmyself.com/public/main.php

I Shot Myself, http://www.ishotmyself.com/public/main.php

Illouz, Eva (1999), 'The Lost Innocence of Love: Romance as a Postmodern Condition', in Mike Featherstone (ed), *Love and Eroticism*. London: Thousand Oaks; New Delhi: Theory, Culture and Society/Sage: 161-86

Institute of Contemporary Art (eds) (1993), *Bad Girls*. London: Institute of Contemporary Art

Irigaray, Luce (1985), *This Sex Which is Not One*. New York: Cornell University Press

Itzin, Catherine (ed) (1992), *Pornography: Women, Violence and Civil Liberties*. Oxford: Oxford University Press

Jackson, Peter et al (2001), *Making Sense of Men's Magazines*. Cambridge: Polity

Jackson, Stevi and Scott, Sue (2004), 'Sexual Antinomies in Late Modernity', *Sexualities* 7 (2): 233–48

Jackson, Sue (2005a), '"I'm 15 and desperate for sex": "Doing" and "undoing" desire in letters to a teenage magazine', *Feminism and Psychology* 15 (3): 295-313

Jackson, Sue (2005b), 'Dear Girlfriend: Constructions of sexual health problems and sexual identities in letters to a teenage magazine', *Sexualities* 8 (3): 282-305

Jacobs, Katrien (2004), 'The New Media Schooling of the Amateur Pornographer: Negotiating Contracts and Singing Orgasm', http://www.libidot.org/katrien/tester/articles/negotiating-print.html

Jeffries, Stuart (2006), 'Are women human', *Guardian*, 12 April

Jervis, Lisa (2006), *BITCHfest: Ten Years of Cultural Criticism from the Pages of Bitch Magazine*. New York: Farrar, Straus and Giroux

Johnson, Merri Lisa (ed) (2002), *Jane Sexes it Up: True Confessions of Feminist Desire*. New York: Thunder's Mouth Press

Johnson, Merri Lisa (2002), 'Jane hocus, Jane focus: an introduction', in Merri Lisa Johnson (ed), *Jane Sexes it Up: True Confessions of Feminist Desire*. New York: Thunder's Mouth Press: 1-11

Jones, Peter et al (2003), 'Retailing and the regulatory state: a case study of lap dancing clubs in the UK', *International Journal of Retail and Distribution Management* 31 (4): 214-21

Jong, Erica (1973), *Fear of Flying*. New York: Holt, Rinehart and Winston

Juffer, Jane (1998), *At Home with Pornography: Women, Sex and Everyday Life*. New York: New York University Press

Juffer, Jane (2005), 'Excessive Practices: Aesthetics, Erotica and Cultural Studies', in Michael Bérubé (ed), *The Aesthetics of Cultural Studies*. Malden: Blackwell Publishing: 58-79

Kant, Immanuel (1785/1996), *The Metaphysics of Morals*. Mary Gregor (ed), *Cambridge Texts in the History of Philiosophy*. Cambridge: Cambridge University Press

Karp, Marcelle and Stoller, Debbie (1999), 'The Birth of BUST', in Marcelle Karp and Debbie Stoller (eds), *The BUST Guide to the New Girl Order* New York: Penguin: xii-xv

Kehily, Mary Jane (2002), *Sexuality, Gender and Schooling: Shifting Agendas in Social Learning*. London: Routledge Falmer

Kendrick, Walter (1987), *The Secret Museum: Pornography in Modern Culture*. New York: Viking

Kilbourne, Jean (1999), *Can't Buy My Love: How Advertising Changes the Way We Think and Feel.* New York and London: Touchstone

Kinsey, Alfred C. (1948/1998), *Sexual Behaviour in the Human Male.* Bloomington: Indiana University Press

Kinsey, Alfred C. (1953/1998), *Sexual Behaviour in the Human Female.* Bloomington: Indiana University Press

Kipnis, Laura (1996), *Bound and Gagged: Pornography and the Politics of Fantasy in America.* New York: Grove Press

Klein, Melanie (1997), 'Duality and Redefinition: Young Feminism and the Alternative Music Community', in Leslie Heywood and Jennifer Drake (eds), *Third Wave Agenda: Being Feminist, Doing Feminism.* Minneapolis: University of Minnesota Press: 207-25

Krum, Sharon (2006), 'No more faking', *Guardian*, 13 March

Lacan, Jacques (1973/1999), *Encore: The Seminar of Jacques Lacan, Book XX (1972-1973).* Translated by Bruce Fink. New York and London: W.W. Norton and Co.

Langdridge, Darren and Butt, Trevor (2004), 'A Hermeneutic Phenomenological Investigation of the Construction of Sadomasochistic Identities, *Sexualities* 7 (1): 31-53

Laqueur, Thomas (1990), *Making Sex: Body and Gender from the Greeks to Freud.* Cambridge: Harvard University Press

Laqueur, Thomas (1995), 'The Social Evil, the Solitary Vice and Pouring Tea', in Paula Bennett and Vernon A. Rosario (eds), *Solitary Pleasures: The Historical, Literary and Artistic Discourses of Autoeroticism.* London: Routledge: 155-62

Laqueur, Thomas (2000), 'Amor Veneris, vel Dulcedo Appeletur', in Londa Schiebinger (ed), *Feminism and the Body.* Oxford: Oxford University Press

Laqueur, Thomas (2003), *Solitary Sex: A Cultural History of Masturbation.* New York: Zone Books

LaRue, Dixie (1999), 'More than a blow job: it's a career', in Marcelle Karp and Debbie Stoller (eds), *The BUST Guide to the New Girl Order* London: Penguin: 99-102

Lawrence, D.H. (1928/1960), *Lady Chatterley's Lover.* London: Penguin

Lazar, Michelle (2006), '"Discover the Power of Femininity!": Analysing Global "Power Femininity" in Local Advertising', *Feminist Media Studies* 6 (4): 505-17

Lazier-Smith, Linda (1989), 'Advertising: Women's Place and Image - A New "Generation" of Images to Women', in Pamela J. Creedon (ed), *Women in Mass Communication: Challenging Gender Values.* London:

Sage: 247-62

Lee, Abby (2006), *Girl with a One-Track Mind*. London: Ebury Press

Leiss, William et al (1986), *Social Communication in Advertising: Persons, Products and Images of Well-Being*. Toronto and London: Methuen

Levy, Ariel (2005), *Female Chauvinist Pigs: Women and the Rise of Raunch Culture*. London: Simon and Schuster

Lin, Carolyn A. (1998), 'Uses of Sex Appeals in Prime-Time Television Commercials', *Sex Roles: A Journal of Research* 38 (5-6): 461-75

Livingstone, Sonia and Green, Gloria (1986), 'Television Advertisements and the Portrayal of Gender', *British Journal of Social Psychology* 25: 149-54

Lovdal, Lynn (1989), 'Sex Role Messages in Television Commercials: An Update', *Sex Roles* 21: 715-24

Lumby, Catherine (1997), *Bad Girls: The Media, Sex and Feminism in the 90s*. St Leonards: Allen and Unwin

MacKeogh, Carol (2001), 'Taking Account of the Macro in the Micro-Politics of Family Viewing - Generational Strategies', *Sociological Research Online* 6 (1): 109-26

MacKinnon, Catherine (2006), *Are Women Human?* Harvard: Harvard University Press

McNair, Brian (1996), *Mediated Sex: Pornography and Postmodern Culture*. London: Arnold

McNair, Brian (2002), *Striptease Culture: Sex, Media and the Democratisation of Desire*. London and New York: Routledge

McRobbie, Angela (1991), *Feminism and Youth Culture: From Jackie to Just Seventeen*. Basingstoke and London: Macmillan

McRobbie, Angela (1996), 'More! New Sexualities in Girls' and Women's Magazines', in James Curran et al (eds), *Cultural Studies and Communications*. London: Arnold: 172-94

McRobbie, Angela (2004), 'Notes on "What Not to Wear" and Post-Feminist Symbolic Violence', in Lisa Adkins and Beverley Skeggs (eds), *Feminism after Bourdieu*. Oxford: Blackwell/The Sociological Review: 97-109

Maddison, Stephen (2004), 'From Porno-topia to Total Information Awareness, or, What Forces Really Govern Access to Porn?', *New Formations* 52: 35-57

Madonna (1992), *Sex*. London: Martin Secker and Warburg

Marcus, Stephen (2003), 'Pornotopia', from *The Other Victorians*, 1966, reprinted in Jeffrey Escoffier (ed), *The Sexual Revolution*. New York: Thunder's Mouth Press: 380-98

Marshall, Barbara L. (2002), '"Hard science": gendered constructions of sexual dysfunction in the "Viagra Age"', *Sexualities* 5 (2): 131-58

Measor, Lynda et al (2000), *Young People's Views on Sex Education: Education, Attitudes, Behaviour*. London: Routledge

Mercer, John (2003), 'Homosexual Prototypes: Repetition and the Construction of the Generic in the Iconography of Gay Pornography', *Paragraph* 26 (1-2): 280-90

Messina, Sergio (2006), 'Realcore: The Digital Porno Revolution', http://realcore.radiogladio.it

Michael, Robert T. et al (1994), *Sex in America: A Definitive Survey*. Boston: Little, Brown and Company

Millet, Catherine (2002), *The Sexual Life of Catherine M*. London: Serpent's Tail

Monk, Daniel (2001), 'New Guidance/Old Problems: Recent Developments in Sex Education', *The Journal of Social Welfare and Family Law* 23 (3): 271-91

Moody, Genevieve (2005), 'Pole Dancing ... a Brief History', http://www.strictlypoledancing.co.uk/History.html

Mudge, Bradford K. (2000), *The Whore's Story: Women, Pornography and the British Novel, 1684-1830*. Oxford: Oxford University Press

Naish, John M. (2005), *Put What Where? Over 2000 Years of Bizarre Sex Advice*. London: Harper Element

O'Toole, Laurence (1998), *Pornocopia: Porn, Sex, Technology and Desire*. London: Serpent's Tail

P, Melissa (2004), *One Hundred Strokes of the Brush before Bed*. London: Serpent's Tail

Paglia, Camille (1990), *Sexual Personae*. London: Penguin

Paglia, Camille (1993), *Sex, Art and American Culture*. London: Penguin

Patterson, Zabet (2004), 'Going On-Line: Consuming Pornography in the Digital Era', in Linda Williams (ed), *Porn Studies*. London: Duke University Press: 104-23

Paul, Pamela (2005), *Pornified: How Pornography is Transforming our Lives, our Relationships and our Families*. New York: Times Books

Pease, Alison (2000), *Modernism, Mass Culture and the Aesthetics of Obscenity*. Cambridge: Cambridge University Press

Pfeil, Fred (1995), *White Guys: Studies in Postmodern Domination and Difference*. London: Verso

Phillips, Anita (1998), *A Defence of Masochism*. London: Faber and Faber

Plummer, Ken (1995), *Telling Sexual Stories: Power, Change and Social Worlds*. London: Routledge

Plummer, Kenneth (2003), *Intimate Citizenship: Private Decisions and Public Dialogues*. Seattle and London: University of Washington Press

Polestars, www.polestars.net

Porter, Roy (1997), *The Greatest Benefit to Mankind: A Medical History of Humanity from Antiquity to the Present*. London: Harper Collins

Positive Porn, http://www.positive-porn.com

Quart, Alissa (2003), *Branded: The Buying and Selling of Teenagers*. London: Arrow Books

Radner, Hilary (1995), *Shopping Around: Feminine Culture and the Pursuit of Pleasure*. London and New York: Routledge

Radway, Janice (1987), *Reading the Romance: Women, Patriarchy and Popular Literature*. London: Verso

Rich, Frank (2001), 'Naked Capitalists: There's No Business Like Porn Business', *New York Times Magazine*, 18 May

Richardson, Diane (2000), *Rethinking Sexuality*. London: Sage

Rimke, Heidi Marie (2000), 'Governing Citizens through Self-Help Literature', *Cultural Studies* 14 (1): 61–78

Rose, Nikolas (1999a), *Governing the Soul: The Shaping of the Private Self*. 2nd edition. London and New York: Free Association Books

Rose, Nikolas (1999b), *Powers of Freedom: Reframing Political Thought*. Cambridge: Cambridge University Press

Rutter, Jared (2005), 'Extreme Associates Case Dismissed', *Adult Video News*, http://www.avn.com/index.php?Primary_Navigation=Articl es&Action=View_Article&Content_ID=214089

Salerno, Steve (2005), *SHAM: Self-Help and Actualisation Movement: How the Gurus of the Self-Help Movement Make Us Helpless*. London, Boston: Nicholas Brealey Publishing

Scott, Linda M. (2005), *Fresh Lipstick: Redressing Fashion and Feminism*. New York: Palgrave

Screen (1992), *The Sexual Subject: A Screen Reader in Sexuality*. London: Routledge

Segal, Lynne (1987), *Is the Future Female? Troubled Thoughts on Contemporary Feminism*. London: Virago

Segal, Lynne (1992), 'Sweet Sorrows, Painful Pleasures: Pornography and the Perils of Heterosexual Desire', in Lynne Segal and Mary McIntosh (eds), *Sex Exposed: Sexuality and the Pornography Debate*. London: Virago: 65–91

Segal, Lynne (1993), 'Does Pornography Cause Violence? The Search for Evidence', in Pamela Church Gibson and Roma Gibson (eds), *Dirty Looks: Women, Pornography, Power*. London: BFI: 5–21

Segal, Lynne (2004), 'Only the Literal: The Contradictions of Anti-Pornography Feminism', in Pamela Church Gibson (ed), *More Dirty Looks: Gender, Pornography and Power*. London: BFI: 59–70

Shamoon, Deborah (2004), 'Office Sluts and Rebel Flowers: The Pleasures of Japanese Pornographic Comics for Women', in Linda Williams (ed), *Porn Studies*. Durham and London: Duke University Press: 77–103

Shaw, Sue (1999), 'Men's Impact on Women's Lives: The Impact of Pornography on Women', *Leisure Studies* 18: 197–212

Siegel, Deborah L. (1997), 'Reading between the Waves: Feminist Historiography in a "Postfeminist" Moment', in Leslie Heywood and Jennifer Drake (eds), *Third Wave Agenda: Being Feminist, Doing Feminism*. Minneapolis: University of Minnesota Press: 55–82

Singleton, Andrew (2003), '"Men's Bodies, Men's Selves": Men's Health, Self-Help Books and the Promotion of Health Care', *International Journal of Men's Health* 2 (1): 57–72

Skordarki, Eleni (1991), 'The Production of Men's Magazines: Three Case Studies and a Sociological Analysis'. PhD dissertation. London University

Smith, Adam (1759/2002), *The Theory of Moral Sentiments*. Cambridge: Cambridge University Press

Smith, Clarissa (2005), 'A Perfectly British Business: Stagnation, Continuities and Change on the Top Shelf', in Lisa Z. Sigel (ed), *International Exposure: Perspectives on Modern European Pornography 1800–2000*. New York: Rutgers University Press: 146–72

Smith, Clarissa (2007), *One for the Girls! The Pleasures and Practices of Reading Women's Porn*. Bristol: Intellect

Snitow, Ann (1978), 'Mass Market Romance: Pornography for Women is Different', *Radical History Review* 29: 245–63

Sonnet, Esther (1999), '"Erotic Fiction by Women for Women": The Pleasures of Post-Feminist Heterosexuality', *Sexualities* 2 (2): 167–87

Sontag, Susan (1969/2003), 'The Pornographic Imagination', in Jeffrey Escoffier (ed), *The Sexual Revolution*. New York: Thunder's Mouth Press: 400–14

Spigel, Lynn (2004), 'Theorizing the bachelorette: "waves" of feminist media studies', *Signs: Journal of Women in Culture and Society* 30 (1): 209–21

Stengers, Jean and Van Neck, Anne (2001), *Masturbation: The History of a Great Terror*. New York: Palgrave

Stoller, Debbie (1999), 'Sex and the Thinking Girl', in Marcelle Karp and Debbie Stoller (eds), *The BUST Guide to the New Girl Order*. New York: Penguin: 75-84

Storr, Merl (2003), *Latex and Lingerie: Shopping for Pleasure at Ann Summers Parties*. Oxford and New York: Berg

SuicideGirls, http://suicidegirls.com

Tapper, Jake, 'Court Deals Blow to USA Anti-Porn Campaign', ABC News, http://abcnews.go.co/Nightline/print?id=433956

Taylor, Gary W. and Ussher, Jane M. (2001), 'Making Sense of S & M: A Discourse Analytic Account', *Sexualities* 4 (3): 293-314

Taylor, Kate (2006), 'Today's ultimate feminists are the chicks in crop tops', *Guardian*, 23 March

Thomson, Rachel (1993), 'Unholy Alliances: The Recent Politics of Sex Education', in Joseph Bristow and Angelia R. Wilson (eds), *Activating Theory: Lesbian, Gay, Bisexual Politics*. London: Lawrence and Wishart: 219-45

Thomson, Rachel (2000), 'Legal, protected and timely: Young people's perspectives on the heterosexual age of consent', in Jo Bridgeman and Daniel Monk (eds), *Feminist Perspectives on Child Law*. London: Cavendish: 169-86

Thorogood, Nicki (2000), 'Learning What Comes Naturally: Sex Education as Disciplinary Technique', *Sexualities* 3 (4): 425-38

Tiefer, Leonore (2004), *Sex is Not a Natural Act and Other Essays*. 2nd edition. Boulder, CO: Westview Press

Tom, E. (2001), 'Maybe once in a blue moon', *The Australian*, September: 29-30

Tuck, Greg (2003), 'Mainstreaming the Money Shot: Representations of Ejaculation in Mainstream American Cinema', *Paragraph* 26 (2): 263-79

Tuck, Greg (2005), *Masturbation, Sexual Logic and Capitalism: The Auto-erotic in Contemporary American Cinema and Beyond*. PhD dissertation. Brunel University

Turner, Bryan S. (1996), *The Body and Society*. London: Sage

Turner, Janice (2005), 'Dirty young men', *Guardian Weekend*, 22 October: 28-37

Tyler, Melissa (2004), 'Managing between the Sheets: Lifestyle Magazines and the Management of Sexuality in Everyday Life', *Sexualities* 7 (1): 81-106

Veitch, Sarah (2004), 'Industry Profile: Elizabeth Coldwell', *Submission* 7, Weston-super-Mare: Palmprint: 6-9

Viner, Katharine (1999), 'The Personal is Still Political', in Natasha

Walter (ed), *On the Move: Feminism for a New Generation*. London: Virago: 10–26

Volosinov, Valentin (1973), *Marxism and the Philosophy of Language*. New York: Seminar Press

Vuttanont, Uraiwan et al (2006), '"Smart boys" and "sweet girls" – sex education needs in Thai teenagers: a mixed-method study', *The Lancet* 368 (9552): 2068–80

Walby, Sylvia and Allen, Jonathan (2004), *Domestic Violence, Sexual Assault and Stalking: Findings from the British Crime Survey*: Home Office Research Study 276. London: Home Office

Walker, Rebecca (ed) (1995), *To Be Real: Telling the Truth and Changing the Face of Feminism*. New York: Bantam Doubleday

Walkerdine, Valerie (1997), *Daddy's Girl: Young Girls and Popular Culture*. Basingstoke and London: Macmillan Press

Walter, Natasha (1999), *The New Feminism*. London: Virago

Walters, Ronald G. (ed) (2000), *Primers for Prudery: Sexual Advice to Victorian America*. Baltimore and London: Johns Hopkins University Press

Waters, Melanie (2007), 'Sexing it up? Women, Pornography and Third Wave Feminism', in Stacy Gillis et al (eds), *Third Wave Feminism: A Critical Exploration*. 2nd edition. Basingstoke: Palgrave: 250–65

Watney, Simon (1987), *Policing Desire: Pornography, AIDS and the Media*. London: Comedia

Waugh, Thomas (1996), *Hard to Imagine*. New York: Columbia University Press

Weeks, Jeffrey (1998), 'The Sexual Citizen', *Theory, Culture and Society* 15 (3–4): 35–52

Whelehan, Imelda (1997), *Modern Feminist Thought: From the Second Wave to 'Post-Feminism'*. Edinburgh: Edinburgh University Press

Whelehan, Imelda (2000), *Overloaded: Popular Culture and the Future of Feminism*. London: Women's Press

Willemen, Paul (2004), 'For a Pornoscape', in Pamela Church Gibson (ed), *More Dirty Looks: Gender, Pornography and Power*. London: BFI: 9–27

Williams, Linda (1989), *Hardcore: Power, Pleasure and the 'Frenzy of the Visible'*. Los Angeles: University of California Press

Williams, Linda (ed) (2004), *Porn Studies*, Durham and London: Duke University Press

Williams, Linda (2004), 'Porn Studies: Proliferating Pornographies On/Scene: An Introduction', in Linda Williams (ed), *Porn Studies*.

Durham and London: Duke University Press: 1–23

Williams, Linda Ruth (2004), 'No sex please, we're American', *Sight and Sound*, January

Williamson, Judith (1978), *Decoding Advertisements: Ideology and Meaning in Advertisements*. London: Marion Boyars

Wilson, Elizabeth (1983), *What is to Be Done about Violence against Women?* Harmondsworth: Penguin

Wilson-Kovacs, Dana (2007), 'Agency, Consumption and Sexual Intimacy: Understanding the Importance of Material Culture in Everyday Life', in Lydia Martens and Emma Casey (eds), *Gender and Consumption: Material Culture and the Commercialisation of Everyday Life*. Aldershot: Ashgate: 181–95

Winston, Eric (2006), 'United States of America v. Extreme Associates: The Internet Misunderstood', http://www.ynot.com/modules.php ?op=modload&name=News&file=ea_article&sid=10354&mode=t hread&order=0&thold=0

Wolf, Naomi (1993), *Fire with Fire: The New Female Power and How to Use It*. London: Chatto and Windus

Wolf, Naomi (2003), 'The more you see, the less you want', *Sunday Times*, 19 October

Workman, Nancy (1996), 'From Victorian to Victoria's Secret: The Foundations of Modern Erotic Wear', *Journal of Popular Culture* 30 (2): 61–73

INDEX